The Ruling Dynasty of Benares State

Rise and Development (1740 to 1950)

पितरौ वन्दे

Pitrau Vandé

The Ruling Dynasty of Benares State

Rise and Development (1740 to 1950)

Shreya Pathak

ANAMIKA PUBLISHERS & DISTRIBUTORS (P) LTD.
4697/3, 21A, Ansari Road, Daryaganj, New Delhi 110002
Phone: 23281655, 23270239; Fax. : 011-27868035
E-mail : anamikapublishers@yahoo.co.in

First Published 2014

ISBN 978-81-7975-477-1

PRINTED IN INDIA

Published by Anamika Publishers & Distributors (P) Ltd., 4697/3, 21A, Ansari Road, Daryaganj, New Delhi 110002. Typset by Aadil Printographics, Delhi 110092 and Printed at Vikas Computer & Printers, Tronica City, Ghaziabad

तस्मै श्री गुरवे नमः
Tasmai Srī Guravé Namah

Contents

Preface

The present work is my thesis submitted for the award of Doctorate degree in the Department of Medieval and Modern Indian History, University of Lucknow under the title the "Royal Dynasty of Benares: Rise and Development with Special Reference to its contribution to the Freedom Struggle of India: A Historical Study (1740 A.D. to 1950 A.D.)"

During my graduation and post-graduation studies in Banaras, as a history student, I was very inquisitive to know about the history of the Ruling Dynasty of Banaras. When I commenced my search, I found prolific writings on the religious, commercial, cultural, educational history of Banaras, but not much material was available on the history of the Ruling Dynasty. As a P.G. student I had two questions in my mind: What role did the Ruling Dynasty of Banaras played in the Indian History particularly Raja Chait Singh and how Banaras came under the administration of British. To quench my thirst, I decided to take up this topic for research.

My work has been categorized into seven chapters. Here I want to make clear one point regarding my chapterization that where on one hand, I have discussed one Raja of the Dynasty, Raja Chait Singh in three chapters, on the other hand I have discussed the reign of total six Rajas and Maharajas in the last chapter. After the death of Raja Balwant Singh, his son Raja Chait Singh succeeded him, but it was a bit controversial leading to interference into the matter of coronation by the English in spite of the fact that Benares was under the authority of Nawab *Vizier* Shuja-ud-daula. It was extremely apropos to the English as to who would be placed on the *gaddi* of Benares because *zamindary* was mere 60 miles beyond their boundary and a center of trade, commerce and a holy capital of Hindus. It was time when Indian political conditions were in a state of complete flux, which definitely affected the Benares *zamindary* and these political developments of Benares greatly affected the politics of that time. Moreover, there was a rising in Benares in 1781, which was first of its type and a matter of great concern for the English as the Governor General was in a danger of his life. So, to elucidate the political conditions and developments of Benares, its transfer from Nawab *Vizier* to East India Company in 1775, high-handed interference of the English and eventually, the rising of 1781, I thought it prudent to give it enough space in my work.

After 1781, the Rajas and Maharajas political rights and privileges were in the clutches of the English. In 1794-95, they were limited to Family Domains and later in 1828, the English even entered in the administration of Family Domains. The rights and privileges of the Maharaja were only of name and after 1828 his decisions were made subject to the approbation of the Superintendent of Family Domains. So the Rajas and Maharajas during later years focused more in the cultural, religious, social and educational field.

In my book, I have focused on three points. Firstly, how this Hindu Dynasty emerged on the political scene and why only Mansaram, a Hindu, was chosen as a founder of the Dynasty at a time when there was a Muslim ruler both in Oudh Suba and on Imperial throne. Secondly, the role of Raja Balwant Singh during and after the battle of Buxar has been belittled so far. I have profoundly studied the importance of Benares *zamindary* for the East India Company during that time, which impelled them to give the Raja a place even in the treaty of Allahabad of 1765 and adopt an amiable policy towards the Raja of Benares. Thirdly, I have profoundly discussed the events prior to the rising of 1781 and showed that how the arrest of Raja Chait Singh, one of the most popular episode during the time of Governor General Warren Hastings, was not the result of Raja's conduct or circumstances, but was a premeditated step of the Governor General actuated by his personal resentment against the Raja that eventually led to the rising.

In first chapter, I have mentioned the antiquity and history of Benares in ancient, medieval and modern times, starting from *Dwapar Yuga* till the third decade of the 18th century just before the foundation of the present Dynasty. This chapter reveals the circumstances that led to an emergence of a Hindu Dynasty at that time with the full approbation of Nawab *Vizier* and Mughal Emperor.

The second chapter discusses the early political activities of Mansaram, his prominence and increasing sway in the region and eventually becoming the founder of the Dynasty. It is an analytical study of the political and economic developments of the time that made the circumstances propitious for him, giving him acceptance by the Oudh Nawab, Mughal Emperor and the people of Benares in 1738 as the Raja of Benares.

Third chapter deals with the political activities of Raja Balwant Singh since his succession in 1740 and his emergence as a real architect of the Dynasty. Description of the expansion of the Raja's sway, consolidation of power, the Raja's relations with the Nawab and the English Company before and after the battle of Buxar, his role in the battle of 1764 has been given in detail. It also mentions the increasing prominence of Benares and its Raja for the English and the ulterior motive behind the adoption of amiable policy by the East India Company towards Benares instantly after the battle on October 23, 1764. The articles of the Treaty of Allahabad of 1765 have been studied as far as it was concerned to Benares and its Raja.

Fourth chapter discusses the conditions in which Raja Chait Singh succeeded after his father's death in 1770. It discusses in detail the relations of Raja Chait Singh with the Nawab *Vizier* and the English Company and the Governor General's conference with the *Vizier* in 1773. Analytical study of the political, strategical, economical and religious factors on why and how the Benares was transferred from the Nawab *Vizier* to the English Company by the treaty of 1775, the revenue settlement of the Benares *zamindary* has been conducted with the English Company after the transfer, and the status and privileges of the Raja after the transfer of the *zamindary*. The deliberations of the Bengal Council, members opinion and differences regarding the transfer of Benares and its process of revenue collection and the establishment of the office of Resident have been mentioned in detail.

The fifth chapter is about the change of the policy of the Bengal Council instantly after the transfer of Benares and their high-handed interference into the administration of Raja Chait Singh through the office of the Resident of Benares. It discusses the Council's demand of subsidy and force from the Raja as his burden of the Anglo-French war, the use of the Office of Resident of Benares as an instrument for compelling the Raja to do the needful, and the Raja's reaction to these demands. The relations between Raja and Hastings and how the Raja was subjected to great humiliation that affected the political developments in ensuing years have been studied in detail.

The sixth chapter is totally devoted to the rising in the Benares *zamindary* in 1781. The arrest of the Raja on the orders of the Governor General, reaction of the Raja's men and the inhabitants of Benares, spread of rising in Oudh and Bihar, difficulties that the English army and the Governor General had to face during their stay at Benares city, peoples support to their Raja and finally capture of all the forts of the *zamindary* by the English army are important facts in this chapter. Till now in history it is known that it was Raja Chait Singh who revolted against the English with full support of the people of Benares, but I have tried to explain that how Hastings actuated by his personal resentment against the Raja, instigated him to stand against the Company. Hatings wanted to disinherit that was possible only under to pay the revenue regularly. The facts and events have been mentioned which makes it evident that Hastings had premeditated plans for the arrest of the Raja and eventually his disinheritance.

The last chapter starts with the effect of the rising and the succession by Raja Maheep Narain Singh. Its about how the English silently entered into the administration of the Raja of Benares in spite of restoring him the *zamindary* by the *sunnud* of 1781. First the treaty of 1794 made the Raja limited to his Family Domains and the administration of other regions were now in the hands of the Company. Later on by the Regulation VII of 1828 they entered into the administration of the Family Domains also by the establishment of the office of Superintendent of Family Domains. Though the Raja still enjoys some rights and privileges, but obviously with the establishment of the Office of Superintendent, many of his decisions and actions were subject to the Superintendent's approbation. I have also mentioned the Instrument of Transfer of 1911 by which Benares State was created including Bhadohi, Kara Mangroor and Ramnagar and its Raja was regarded as Maharaja and Ruling Chief of the State. After independence, the State merged into the Dominion of India as part of United Provinces by the treaty with the Government of India in September 5, 1949.

Finally the conclusion carries the views of the researcher and her analysis.

One important source for the history of the dynasty is Khairuddin's *Tuhfa-I-Taza* alias *Balwantnama* in Persian. F. Curwen translated it in English in 1875, but even after making great endeavours I was unable to concern this source due to unavailability of the translated copy till the submission of my thesis. After the awad of Doctorate degree this important source was translated in English by I.H. Ansari and H.A. Qureshi in 2009 from Lucknow under title *Tohfa-i-Taza of Fakhir Khairuddin* and Minutes of Charges of Warren Hastings that has been consulted. My sincere thanks to both the translators. I have consulted the material from National Archives of India, New Delhi, Library of Indian Council of Historical Research, New Delhi; Library of National Museum of India, New Delhi; U.P. State Archives, Lucknow; Regional Archives, Varanasi; Regional

Archives, Allahabad; Kashi Raj Nyas Trust, Ramnagar Fort; Shayaji Gaekwad Central Library, Banaras Hindu University; Bharat Kala Bhawan, Banaras Hindu University; Library of Advance Center of History, Aligarh Muslim University; Central Library, Aligarh Muslim University, Central Library, Allahabad University and Saraswati Bhavan Central library of Sampooranand Sanskrit Vishwavidhyalay.

In presenting my work, first of all I am highly grateful to the Almighty without whose blessed hands I would have never succeeded in accomplishing my work. I am greatly indebted to my father Mr. Shridhar Pathak, Indian Police Service and my mother Mrs. Shashi Pathak, who gave their unstinting support and strengthen my motives whenever, I felt blue. The support and courage given by them cannot be put into words. I am thankful to my sister Dr. Shalini Pathak for encouragement, valuable suggestions and help that she gave me from time to time.

I owe my deep gratitude and obligation to my supervisor, Prof. A.K. Misra, for giving his precious time and for discussing the topic with me in detail. I am highly thankful to Dr. Kunwar Anant Narain Singh Bahadur, Maharaja of Banaras and Kashi Raj Nyas Trust for allowing me to enter the museum and access the library of the fort of Ramnagar and take of notes of material provided. I am also grateful to the staff of President House, India for providing me information regarding the army of Raja Chait Singh, which later became the nucleus of President's Body Guard. I owe my deep gratitude and pay my sincere thanks to the Indian Council of Historical Research for sanctioning me the Junior Research Fellowship for my research work. I owe my special thanks to the Managers and Staff of different institutes and libraries that I have consulted during my research

My sincere thanks to Mr. Pankaj Sharma, Anamika Publishers and Distributors (P) Ltd. and his staff for publishing this work.

Lucknow **Dr. Shreya Pathak**

List of Abbreviations

FPD	Foreign and Political Department
PD	Public Department
GAD	General Administrative Department
SC	Secret Committee
SC Pr.	Secret Committee Proceedings
HPC	Home Public Consultations
DR	Duncan Records
BCO	Benares Commissioners Office
FDMB	Family Domains of Maharaja Benares
CPC	Calendar of Persian Correspondence
BM	British Museum
Add.Mss	Additional Manuscript
NAI	National Archives of India
UPSA	Uttar Pradesh State Archives
RAA	Regional Archives of Allahabad
RAV	Regional Archives of Varanasi
SBE	Sacred Books of East

Chapter 1

Historical Background

The Internationally Celebrated

Benares—more famous as *Kashi* in ancient times, is a city of great reverence and antiquity not only in India but also in the whole world and is recognized as the religious capital of India. *Kashi* has a very glorious and sheen past not only in religious and spiritual context but also in the political and commercial sphere of Indian history. Broadly speaking, it has an incessant history of more than 3,000 years. Referring to *Kashikhand* of *Skandapurana* the term *Kasi* is derived from the root *Kas* meaning 'to shine'.[1]

Benares—situated at the left bank of the river *Ganges*—is bounded by the rivers *Varuna* and *Assi* in the north and south respectively. Benares is an *apbhransh* of *Sanskrit* term Varanasi that has been derived from the rivers *Varuna* and *Assi*, mentioned in the *Vamana Purana,*[2] *Padma Purana*[3] and *Skand Purana.*[4] The city is situated between the parallels of 25 8' and 25 35' north latitude and 78 56' and 79 52' east longitude[5] while Fisher and Hewett mentions that the city lies between 25 8'and 25 35' north latitude and 82 42' and 83 36' east longitude. It is surrounded in the north by Jaunpur district, in the northeast and east by the Gazipur district, in the southwest by Shahabad district of Bihar, wherefrom it is separated by the *Karamnasa* and in the south by

Mirzapur district. The length of the boundary line is about 200 miles (320 Kms). The total area, in conformity with the last official statement of the Department of Agriculture and Commerce dated August 31, 1881 is 998 sq miles, and the density of population, in terms of the census of 1,881 is 894.4 persons per sq mile. The density of the population was greater than any other district under the Government of North Western Provinces and Oudh.[6]

There is no iota of doubt on the antiquity of Benares, which was one of the *Saptpuri* of India. The origin of this holy city has been mentioned in *Kashi Rahasya*, which states that on solicitation of *Saptrishi* to show the road to salvation, Lord Vishnu created a *Lingam* and this was installed in Kashi.[7] The pre-Buddhist history of Benares is mainly mentioned in the ancient Indian literature like *Vedas, Puranas, Mahabharata, Bhagwat gita* etc. There are incidental references and allusions of *Kashi* in *Rigveda,*[8] *Piplad Shakha of Atharvaveda,*[9] *Shaunakiya Shakha of Atharvaveda,*[10] *Shatpath Brahamana,*[11] *Gopath Brahmana,*[12] *Sankhayan Shrautsutra,*[13] *Baudhayana Shrautsutra,*[14] *Brihadaranyaka Upnishad,*[15] *Ashtadhayayi.*[16] Manu Vaivasvata, the originator of human race, who framed rules and laws of the government, was the father of nine valiant sons with the eldest one having dual personality as male Il and as female Ila. Ila's son Pururava, the founder of *Aila* Dynasty, ruled over seven islands with his seat of government at Pratisthan.[17] Pururava's grandson (from his son Ayu) Nahus remained at Pratisthan while his second grandson Kshatravridha established a new state at *Kashi* in the east.[18] The seventh King in line was Kashya or Kash (son of Suhotra and grandson of Kshatravridha), in whose memory the city and the kingdom came to be known as Kashi. Dhanwantri, the originator of *Ayurveda*, and the formulator of Ayurvedic pharamacopea, was the King of same pedigree.[19]

During the pious reign of Deodas, Dhanwantri's great grandson, righteousness prevailed all over and remained supreme, and all the Gods were banished from his capital.[20] None other than Lord Vishnu himself came to Kashi in the form of a *Brahmana* to praise King Deodas and euogise the King's strict adherence to the principle of *dharma*. Induced by a *Brahmana*, Deodas left Kasi after establishing a *Linga* there. During his reign there was a serious battle between Kashi rulers and *Haihayas* of *Chedis Mahismati*, in which *Haihaya* ruler Bhadrasena was killed along with his hundred sons except Durdama, who was spared, considering his tender age.[21] Subsequently, when Durdama ascended the throne, he defeated and killed Kashi King Haryasva and his son Sudaiva, and established an outpost in Kaushambhi. Eventually, Sudaiva's son Deodas II abandoned Varanasi and founded new Varanasi at the confluence of *Ganges* and *Gomti*, but was again attacked by *Haihayas*, who completely expelled the forces. The incessant battle between these two hostile powers finally came to an end during the reign of the successor of Deodas II, King Pratardana, who defeated *Haihayas* King Vitahanya and killed his hundred sons. Vitahanya could save his life only after transforming himself as a *non-khshatriya*.[22] A chronological list of the dynasty of *Kshatravridha* has been mentioned in *Srimabhagwat*.[23] The rule of this dynasty came to an end about 15 generations before the *Bharat* war. Valmiki's *Ramayana* regard Kashi as a prominent kingdom and mentions that Dashratha, the King of Koshala arranged an *Ashwamedha Yagya* in his capital Ayodhaya where Kings of Mithila, Kashi, Kekaya, Anga, Magadha, Sindhu, Saurashtra and Kings of Southern countries were invited.[24] Besides, the epic *Mahabharata*, too, mentions Kashi as a kingdom in an incident where the Chief Prince of Hastinapur, Bhishma abducted three daughters of *Kashiraj*, namely Amba, Ambika and Ambalika from the *Swayamwar* ceremony, with the object of marrying them off to his foster brother Vichitravirya—who was the grandfather of the *Pandavas*. *Kashiraj* also participated in the *Mahabharat* war in support of the *Pandavas*.[25] His growing eminence and sway can be corroborated by the fact that he has been referred as to *Viryavan* i.e. most powerful and daring and categorized as *Maharathi*. In addition, he was also given position just after Dhristaketu, the Commander-in-Chief of the *Pandavas*.[26] *Kashiraj* who was killed during the war was *Abhibhu*.[27]

In *Devibhagwat Mahapurana*, the *Bishalakshi Devi* at Varanasi has been mentioned as the first among 108 *Siddhapithahs*.[28] In

Padma Purana, Kashi has been included among 135 Northern Indian *Janpadas* (countries).[29] It mentions that Kashi King Paundrak attacked Dwarika, but was beheaded by Vishnu and his head was thrown to Kashi.[30] The same story with a different version has been mentioned in the *Harivansh*, which states that Paundrak tried to establish his sovereignty in the conference of Indian Kings asking them to pay taxes only to him. He explicitly referred to Krishna as an indisciplined man[31] and attacked Dwarika.[32] Krishna, who was in *Badrikashram*, came back to Dwarika for confabulations with Paundrak, but all proved futile. Eventually, Lord Krishna attacked Paundrak and killed him by *Sudarshan Chakra*.[33] As mentioned in *Bhagwat*, Kashi was a well-secured walled city with security gates, conference halls and multistoried buildings.[34] All this is not only in manifestation of the prosperity of the city but also reflect its power and political prominence during the period of Lord Krishna.

Jain literature attaches considerable importance given to the prominence of Kashi Kingdom. According to *Jatakas*, the city extended over 12 *yojanas*[35] and the kingdom of Kasi extended over 300 *yojanas*.[36] Chinese traveller Yuan Chang states *yojana* equal to 8 *krosas*. A *yojana* is regarded as a day's march for an army and a *Krosa* is the hailing distance of the lowing of a cow.[37] The 23rd Jain *Tirthankar* Parsvanath, son of Kashi King Asvasena, was born in Benares 817 B.C. and attained *Kevalya Jnana* on 84th day under a tree near Benares.[38] When 24th Jain *Tirthankar* Mahavira died, 18 confederate Kings of Kasi and Kosala, nine *Mallakis* and *Likkhavis* on the day of new moon, instituted an illumination on the *Poshadha*, which was a fasting day as they said "since the light of intelligence is gone, let us make an illumination of material matter".[39] The *Jatakas* and Buddhist literature gives considerable description on the political and social life of Kashi state. As described in *Angutarnikaya*, Kashi was reckoned among the 16 great *Soasmahajanapada* (countries) during 6th century.[40] At the hermitage called *Migadaya* in Benares, Buddha preached his five *Bhikkchus* for the first time and turned the wheel of the empire of Truth.[41] There is a religious belief that people who die in Benares get *moksha* (Salvation). Even Buddha's favourite disciple Ananda wanted Buddha to die in one of the six cities- Kampa, Ragagha, Savatthi, Saketa, Kosambi and Benares.[42]

Rajovada Jataka reveals that *Mahajanpada* Kosala was contiguous to Kashi.[43] During the period of *Jatakas*, Kashi was called *Rashtra* or Kingdom with Benares as its capital.[44] Other names used for the capital are *Surundhana*, *Sudassana*, *Brahmavaddhana*, *Pupphavati*, *Ramma*.[45] There was incessant animosity persisting between the two neighbours for gaining political ascendancy. As mentioned in *Jataka* stories, before the sixth century B.C., Brahmadatta dynasty ruled Varanasi for a long time.[46] It mentions a King named Bodhisatta, who ascended his father Brahmadatta's throne of Kasi Kingdom and ruled righteously under the title of the great King Goodness. He built six almonries—one each at four city gates, one in the middle of the city and at his palace gate where he distributed 600,000 pieces of money daily and stirred up all India with his alms giving to the deprived and the needy.[47] During his rule, one of his ministers, who was expelled from Kashi for treachery, joined the rival neighbour, Kosala King Dabbasena.[48] Later, when Dabbasena asked him about the power of Kasi, he revealed, "The Kingdom of Benares is like a goodly honeycomb untainted by flies; its King is feebleness itself; and a trifling force would suffice to conquer the whole country". It mentions that the King had 1000 invincible heroes who could not only face even a rut elephant gallantly but also, at the command of their master, could reduce the whole India to his sway.[49]

Kashi King conquered and annexed the entire Kingdom of Kosala and the King was imprisoned.[50] The political ambitions and sway of Kashi ruler becomes more explicit by the fact that he subjugated about thousand Kings of India.[51] Kashi was defeated by three Kosala rulers- Vanka, Dabhasena and Kansa and in sixth century B.C., it was completely annexed by Kosala King Kansa, for which he was called *Baranasiggaho*.[52] Kosala King Mahakosala gave Kashi as dowry to Magadha King Bimbisara to whom the Kosala princess was married, but after the assassination of Bimbisara by his son and successor Ajatshatru and the death of Kosala Ranee, Mahakosala's son Prasenjit explicitly declared battle against Ajatshatru to reoccupy Kashi that produced prodigious revenue. Though Ajatshatru was arrested at the end of this war, but was subsequently married to Prasenjit's daughter Vajira, and Kashi was returned to him as dowry.[53] The immense wealth of Kashi can be surveyed and calibrated by the fact that Ajatshatru, mentioned as the King of Kasi, gave a thousand cows to a man of high learning Gargya Balaki.[54] The travellers were not allowed to enter the city late at night as the four gates surrounding the city were closed for security purposes.[55] Under the kingship of Ajatshatru, a nag principality was re-established in Varanasi. The last King of the lineage of Bimbisara was very incompetent, and the power was usurped by the Governor of Kashi Shishunag, who amalgamated Kashi and Magadh. He gave the onus of the city to his son. After Shishunag, the Nandas occupied Magadha and Kashi became integral part of Magadha Empire.[56]

Benares merited imperial consideration during the reign of Ashoka (third Mauryan king) who built the *Dharma-Rajjika Stupa* in *Sarnath* on the same site where Lord Buddha was believed to have preached his first sermon. Other than this, *Dhamekh Stupa* and *Dhammachakra* pillar surmounted by four lions was also erected.[57] Later, during the period of *Kushanas*, King Kanishka appointed *Mahakshatrapa* Kharpallana and *Kshatrapa* Vanaspar as his deputies to administer Kashi province. After the waning of the imperial *Kushanas*, Benares came under the sway of the *Nagas*, known as *Bharshiva*, who performed ten *Ashvamegha* sacrifices on the banks of *Ganges* after which the site is presently called *Dashashvamedha Ghat.*[58] They performed their coronations at or near Benares where the place Nagwa, the present site of Banaras Hindu University, seems to be associated with their name. Bharshivas rise is dated about 150 A.D.[59] After Bharshiva Nagas, Kashi came under the Gupta rule during fourth and fifth century A.D. No definite reference is found regarding its political sovereignty for a long period,[60] but it was during Gupta reign that Bhuddhist centre at Sarnath entered the golden age of its art and architecture.

Chinese pilgrim Fa-hien visited the holy city (400-411A.D.) and mentioned about four *stupas,* namely *Mulgandh*, *Dhamekh* and two monasteries. A seal bearing Gupta characters *Baranasya Adhisthan-Adhikaranasya* was discovered during excavations at Rajghat site in 1940.[61] During the first half of the seventh century, Harsha established his political ascendancy over Kashi. When Chinese traveller *Yuan-Chang* visited the illustrious and the divine city (630-644 A.D.) he was fascinated by the people's esteemed devotion to learning. He candidly and remarkably describes the prosperous and affluent life of the city. According to him, the Kingdom of Varanasi had a circuit of about 4,000 *lis* or 800 miles with the capital city of *Po-lo-na-se* (Varanasi), which was about 18 *lis* (nearly 3 ½ miles) in length and 5 or 6 *lis* (more than a mile) in breadth. People had plethora of riches and their houses were saturated with real merchandise. There were about 30 Buddhist monasteries with more than 3,000 Brethen and more than 100 *deva* temples, 20 within the capital. He refers to the *Deva* nearly 100 ft high, which was probably *Shiva Linga*; however, there exists a paucity of any reference regarding political status of the city during his visit.[62]

During the ninth and tenth century, Kannauj was occupied by Pratiharas and Pratisthan (present Jhusi) was made the provincial seat.[63] Benares was the district headquarters. Alberuni, who came to India with Mahmud Ghazni also known as 'Ghaznani' gave an invaluable and detailed account of the social, religious, economic and legal life of the Benares city in 1,030.[64] Masnud, the successor to Mahmud Ghazni, appointed Ahmed Nialtigin as Governor of Punjab in 1033 A.D. with directions to commence an expedition against Benares through the route of *Ganges* and capture the amassed wealth stored in its innumerable temples. Eventually, there was a widespread plunder by the Muslim army in this prosperous holy city that was under the possession of *Chedi* King Gangedev. The city was plundered of its riches "from morning to mid-day prayer".[65]

By the end of eleventh century (1,080 A.D.), Kashi regained prominence and became a great political power with the establishment of the *Gharwal* dynasty by King Chandradev with headquarters at Benares. Later, Gharwals transferred their principal seat to Kannauj. In 1193 A.D. Kannauj was invaded by Mahmud of Ghor and mammoth onus of capturing the city of Benares was entrusted to Qutub-ud-din Aibak, his successor in India, who attacked Kashi in 1194 A.D.[66] Inrumerable temples were wrecked and mosques were erected on their foundations with the same material. The prosperity and wealth of the city can be borne out by the fact that Aibak had to deploy about 1,400 camels to carry the booty. Along with a plethora of booty, 300 elephants were also captured, but some say as many as 600-640 elephants were captured including one white elephant.[67] After the Gharwal King Jaichandra, his son Harishchandra ruled over Benares, Mirzapur, Jaunpur and Allahabad, and Kashi flourished as an exemplary city. The royal palaces of *Gharwalas* extended from present Rajghat to Alipur and Adampur. Farishta has described Varanasi as the center of the country of the Hindu.[68] The sovereign rule of a Hindu dynasty in Benares virtually came to an end in 1194 and thus commenced the history of plunder, loot, temple destruction, revolts and religious intolerance that continued for several centuries.

In 1195, Aibak entrusted the administration of Benares to the exalted servants of Muslim rule with strict instructions to administer in compliance with the Islam and repress idolatry.[69] Mohammad Ghori appointed Syed Jamal-ud-din as the first Governor of Benares. A *mazar* known as *Shahi Mazar* situated in *Mohalla Jamal-ud-dinpura* is said to be tomb of this governor. Under Illtutmish reign (1211-1236), Kashi was given status of province with headquarters at Varanasi. During the period of Balban, *Haji Idris* was appointed as the Governor of Benares. Under Gyas-ud-din Tugluq (1221-25), Jala-ud-din was appointed officer-in-charge of Varanasi where a place was established after his name *Jala-ud-dinpura*.[70] In November 1353, Firoz Tugluq marched to quell the rebellion led by Ilyas Hazi of Bengal, who declared himself as Sultan Samsuddin and included Varanasi within his territories. The Sultan himself had to visit Varanasi to collect the Government arrears from the people of Varanasi. During the period of Tugluq Sultans, Mohammad Shah Tugluq conferred Varanasi upon *Khwaja-i-Jahan* in 1394 giving him the title of *Mallik-us-Sar*, Lord of the East, who established an independent Kingdom with

Jaunpur as their political seat. *Sharqi Sultans* were called "great destroyers" by Fuhrer as during their sway every mosque was built on the site of a Hindu temple.[71]

The *Sharqi Sultans* of Jaunpur imposed heavy taxes on pilgrims visiting Varanasi. According to *Eklingi* inscription of 1429 A.D., the Hindu *zamindars* and Kings paid immense chunk of these taxes.[72] The *Sharqi Sultans* built *Lal Darwaza* Mosque at Jaunpur in 1447 A.D. by material obtained from destruction of the temple of *Padmeswar*, which was built in 1296 near *Vishwanath* temple of Varanasi.[73] Due to the military menace of powerful Rajput Chieftains, the *Sharqi* Sultans repaired the old fort of Varanasi in 1465-66. Benares witnessed unrest during the reign of Lodi dynasty. The *Sharqi Sultan* Hussain Shah revolted, but was overwhelmed by the Lodi Sultan, Bahlol Lodi in 1479 in series of battles and appointed Hussain Shah's son Barbak Shah as Governor of Jaunpur and Varanasi.[74] In 1488 Barbak Shah was ousted from Jaunpur, but was subsequently restored to Jaunpur by Sikandar Lodi.[75]

Although Panipat battle of 1526 A.D. ended the Lodi dynasty and commenced rule of Mughals at Delhi, yet it did not put any cessation to the unfortunate time of the holy city. In fact, it became more calamitous as by then the Afghans had shifted to the eastern provinces leading to struggle between the Mughals and Afghans for the occupation of Benares and the adjacent areas, which continued for a long time. Thus Benares, during this time, turned from a holy capital to a battle field for the war between the Mughals and Afghans. In 1527 and 1528.[76] Humayun, son of Babar, subjugated Jaunpur to Gazipur that was plundered by the Mughal army. Sher Shah, the Afghan leader, killed Mughal Governor Mir Fazli with most of its garrison and took possession of Benares in 1538. He rose to prominence after his triumph over the Mughal Emperor in the battle of Chausa in 1538 after which Humayun fled from Chausa and took refuge in *Chaukhandi Stupa* near Sarnath for a single day where Akbar erected an octagonal structure to mark the spot. A stone tablet bearing an Arabic inscription mentioning Humayun's visit has been inscribed there and is still intact.[77]

Even Akbar, who had established his authority throughout the empire and adopted the policy of religious tolerance, had to face tumultous revolts in Benares during his reign. At this time, Benares was under the *Suba* of Allahabad containing 8 *mahals*, 36,869 *bighas*, 12 *Biswas* and revenue to the tune of 8,869,315 *dams* in money with 3,38,184 *Suyurghals* and maintaining an army of 830 cavalry and 8,400 infantry. This figure includes only the city of Benares and not Jaunpur, Gazipur and Bhadohi, which were separate *sarkars* in Allahabad *Suba*.[78] Akbar during his reign had visited many a time this city on one pretext or the other. In 1566, the Emperor himself marched to Jaunpur to suppress the rebellion of Ali Quli Khan, and entrusted the charge of Jaunpur to Ashraf Khan. He then marched for Benares on January 24, 1566 and visited the impregnable fort of Chunar where he captured 10 elephants from the forests in the neighbourhood of Chunar. During his stay at Benares, receiving the intelligence of second revolt by Ali Quli Khan, Akbar marched on February 2, 1566 to chastise him. He rested on his elephant for some time in night.[79] Ali Quli Khan returned to Muhammada-bad and sent troops to Ghazipur and Jaunpur. Iskandar and Bahadur attacked Benares and plundered the whole city.[80]

Akbar decided to stay there till the suppression of the rebellion, but later Quli Khan was pardoned after which on March 3,1566 he marched from Jaunpur.[81] In 1567 he again visited Benares; but this time he issued a general order to plunder the city as the people of Benares had shut their gates against the Emperor. Though subsequently he countermanded the order, yet it was too late by then. He stayed there for three days to maintain peace and proceeded to Jaunpur where he again stayed for further three days. Munim Khan was sent to rule the region.[82] He remained in Benares during his eastern campaign on July 15, 1574.[83] Mint was established at Varanasi for issuing copper coins. During his reign, *Hindu jagirdars* and affluent people in Varanasi built numerous temples. Raja Man Singh of Amer built a temple of *Adi Vishveshwar* near the old pious site. Raja Todar Mal rebuilt the *Vishwanath* temple on a large scale at the request of the famous scholar Narayan Bhatt.

During the rule of Jahangir, Mirza Qulij, *Faujdar* of Benares, rebelled against the Emperor but was killed.[84] Even Emperor's son Khurram (later known as Shah Jahan) also rebelled against his father but in 1624 was compelled to return to Benares.[85] Shah Jahan issued orders that new temples under construction at Benares should be razed to ground without delay, consequent upon which there was demolition of 76 temples in Benares in 1632 as reported by *Subedar* of Allahabad.[86] In 1657 Benares was attacked by Shuja, then incharge of Bengal, but was defeated by Dara Shikoh. Later Shuja did not squander the opportunity when Dara Shikoh was defeated at the hands of Aurangzeb. He seized Benares, ejected Ramdas, the commander of the fort and raised loans of Rs.3 lakhs from the city and then proceeded to annex Jaunpur and Allahabad. In 1666, Shivaji took refuge at Benares with the assistance of local people of Benares, which manifests their hostile feeling for the Muslim ruler. Son of Shah Jahan, Dara Shikoh remained Viceroy of Allahabad Suba for 12 years during which *Sanskrit* learning enjoyed his royal patronage.[87]

The suffering of the Benares city and the people reached its zenith during the reign of Aurangzeb, the most religious intolerant ruler in Indian history, who ascended the throne on May 23, 1658. In 1659, on complaints lodged by some priests of Benares temples about unendurable persecutions meted out by the Muslim officers in performing their religious rites, Aurangzeb issued orders to the *Fauzdar* of Benares that no erection of new temples would be allowed and there should be no unlawful interference in performance of rites by Brahmans and other Hindu residents.[88] This was not because of his religious tolerance, but he could not bear any disturbance from any quarter of his empire during the commencement of his reign. Subsequently, when Aurangzeb established his authority in Delhi, he prohibited Hindu teaching and learning. On April 18,1669, he received reports that, in spite of his orders, people, including Muslims, were going to Benares from far away distance for education. Immediately he issued orders to the Provincial Governors for the demolition of Hindu schools and temples, in compliance with which *Vishwanath* and

Vani Madhav temple were razed to the ground and a mosque was built on the same foundation using the same material; and Aurangzeb was informed of this on September 2, 1,669.[89] The holy Hindu city was rechristened as *Muhammadabad* and coins were issued from local mint bearing that name.[90] The western wall of Gyānvāpī Mosque is still the same of the then original Vishwanāth temple with decorations and Hindu motifs that can be still seen. Due to controversy between two religious communities over this point, law and order problem arises frequently. To meet the problem huge number of Central and State reserve and civil police force are deployed there.

During Mughal period, the scholarship and learning at Kashi was not offered royal patronage. Traveller Bernier gave a detailed account of the education and religion in India during his Benares visit in the middle of 17th century. He considered it general school of the Gentiles and called it the *Athens of India*. He observed that Benares students could entertain no hopes for the reward of extra-ordinary attainments.[91] The period of Aurangzeb was a period of *Muslimization* of the Hindu city that ended with the end of his rule in 1707.

During the reign of Bahadur Shah, Kaswar people rebelled against the Emperor and ousted Mughal garrison from Benares. *Zamindars* of eastern district refused to pay revenue and assumed the title of Raja.[92] In 1712, Farukh Siyar was in need of money to avenge the death of his father and ascended the Imperial throne against Jahandar Shah. On his way to Delhi, he was assigned Rs. 100,000 from a Benares *zamindar* and also prodigious amount from *sahukars* of the city.[93] The Emperor visited Benares in 1713 to impose a levy of Rs. 6 lakhs on Rai Kripa Nath of Benares. In 1713 he sent an army led by Mamur Khan to punish *zamindars*, who were inhumanly slaughtered and women and children were captured. Those persisted were buried alive and those submitted were pardoned and rewarded. This manifests that Benares people were not paying taxes willfully to the imperial treasury.

Benares was not only of political and religious importance but was also the epicentre of trade and commerce in Northern India. Ibn Asir in his writing *Kamil ul-Tawarikh* states, "The King of Benares was the greatest King in India, and possessed the largest territory, extending lengthwise from the borders of China to the province of Malwa, and in breadth from sea to within ten days' journey to Lahore."[94] Bishop Heber found Benares as a clearing house of all commercial goods from Kashmir shawls to Dacca's muslin and jewels of Golcunda. Ralph Fitch in his travelogue described Benares as vast town a manufacturing centre of cotton cloth. *Mahabhasya* mentions that there was a difference in price of cloth manufacture at Kashi and Mathura. This shows that even so early as the second century B.C. Kashi was famous as the center of fine quality cloth manufacture.[95]

Thus we observe that for centuries, under Muslim subjugation, Benares history is full of plunders, temple destruction, revolts that had brought great dissatisfaction among the Benares people.[96] Even Akbar, who was known for his religious tolerance, issued orders for plunder of the city and remained there for days to establish peace and authority. There was great disgruntlement among the people which eventuated in non-payment of taxes. The rebellious leaders against the imperial powers always choose Benares as their base because of the strategic location and, furthermore, they were cognizant of discontentment prevailing among the people against the imperial rulers, who had always plundered the city and wrecked the temples.

Kashi had to weep for her great knowledge, wealth and prosperity, and for being a centre of the country of Hindu. In retaliation of their incessant turbulent and disturbing history of revolt, suppression and pillage, the people of Benares refused to pay the revenue to the Imperial treasury and several times Imperial army was required for revenue collection. The region was very prosperous and fertile and was also the centre of trade and commerce; still collection of revenue became a herculean task for the Mughals. The people of Benares tacitly supported every rebellion against the imperial authority. The feeling of insecurity developed a strong and intense desire among the people of Benares to emerge as a political power as it was in ancient time. They realized that their own wealth, power and resources were enough to establish their own rule. Time provided them an astute and insightful diplomat, Mansaram, who stepped forward according to the place, time and condition and was accepted by the people as the Raja of Benares, which eventually led to the foundation of the new dynasty of Benares in the 18th century.

References

1. Nevill, H.R., *Benares: A Gazetteer*, District Gazetteers of U.P. of Agra and Oudh, Vol. XXVI, Allahabad Government Press, 1909, p.183. It mentions that *Kas* is a type of grass about 5 ft high, which is still available in the entire region of Benares and Oudh after which it is called Kashi.
2. *Vaman Purana*, chap. III, Vishnu says to Hameshwar:

   यो सो ब्रह्माण्डके पुण्ये मदशं प्रभवो व्ययः।
   प्रयागे वसते नित्यं योगशायीति विश्रुतः।।
   चरणाद्दक्षिणातस्य विनिर्गता सरिद्वरा।
   विश्रुता वरणेत्येव सर्वं पाप हरा शुभा।।
   सव्यादन्या द्वितीया च असिरित्येव विश्रुता।
   ते उभे च सरिच्छेष्ठे लोकपूज्ये वभूवतुः।।

   तयोर्मध्येतु यो देशस्तत क्षेत्र योगशायिने।
   त्रैलोक्य प्रवरं तीर्थं सर्व्वपापविमोचनम्।।
   न तादृशं हि गगने न भूम्यां न रसातले।
   तत्रस्ति नगरी पुण्या ख्याता वारानसीशुभा।।
3. *Padma Purana, Kasi Mahatmaya, shalok* 58.

   दक्षिणोत्तर दिग्भागे कत्वासिं वरणां सुराः।
   क्षेत्र्स्य मोक्ष निक्षेय रक्षारिव त्तिमाययुः।।
4. *Skand Purana, Kashi Khanda*, XXX, 20, 21:

   दक्षिणोत्तर दिग्भागे कत्वासिं वरणां सुराः।
   क्षेत्रस्य मोक्ष निक्षेय रक्षारिव त्तिमाययुः।।
5. Nevill, H.R., *op.cit*, p.1.
6. Fisher, F.H. and Hewett, J.P., *Statistical, descriptive and Historical Account of North West Provinces and Oudh*, Vol. 14, part-I, Benares, NWP and Oudh Government Press, Allahabad, 1884, p.2; also see *Imperial Gazetteer of India*, Vol. VIII, New Edition, Published under Authority of HM's Secretary of State for India in Council,

Oxford, 1908, the area given is 1,008 sq miles.

7. Nevill, H.R., *op.cit*, p.183.
8. *Rigveda*, 3/30/5 "मधवन्कशिरित्ते"
   7/104/8 "आप इव काशिना संगृभीता"
   8/78/10 "पूर्धि यवस्य काशिना"
9. *Atharvaveda*, v/22/14, English translation by Ralph T.H. Griffith, Vol. I, E.J. Lazarus and Co., Benares, 1916.
   गंधारिभ्यो मूजवद्भ्यः काशिभ्यो मगधेभ्यः
   प्रैव्यथ्श्जनमिव शेवधितस्मानं परिदवासि।।
   Sacred Books of East (henceforth SBE), *The Satpatha Brahmana* Vol., XLIV, Part V, Motilal Banarasidas, Varanasi, first published in 1881 by Oxford University Press, 13/5/4/19, 13/5/4/21.
10. SBE, *op.cit.*, *Atharvaveda*, Vol. XLII, 4/7/1.
    वारिदं वारयातै वरणावत्यामधि
    तत्रम तस्यासिक्तिं तेनाते वारये विषम्।।
11. SBE, *op.cit.*, *Shatpath Brahamana*, Vol. XLIV, Part V, 13/5/4/19, 13/5/4/21
12. *Gopath Brahmana*, 1/2/9.
13. *Sankhayan Shrautsutra* 16/19/5.
14. *Baudhayana Shrautsutra* 21/30.
15. SBE, *op.cit.*, *Brihadaranyaka Upanishad*, 2/1/1, 3/8/2.
16. *Ashtadhayayi* 4/2/116, 113.
17. Vidyalankar Jaychandra, *Bhartiya Itihaas Ki Rooprekha*, Vol. I, p. 128-129, Pratisthan has been identified with Pihar, a village near Prayag, (Allahabad).
18. Majumdar, R.C., *History and Culture of Indian People*, Vol. I, Bhartiya Vidya Bhavan Series, 1996, p. 277.
19. *Vayu Purana*, 92/21
20. *Skand Purana*, *Kashi Khand*, Chapter 62, 94.
21. *Brahama Purana*, 11/44/47.
22. *Mahabharata*, *Anushashan Parva*, Chapter V, 55.
    एवमत्यस्मि भगवन् कृतकृत्यो न संशयः
    य एष राजवीर्येण स्वजातिं त्याजितो मया।।
23. *Srimatbhagwat*, 9 *Skanda* (Skanto), chapter 17, Shlokas 1-10 (p. 77- Geneological table of Raja Shatravridha to be drawn.)
24. *The Valmiki Ramayana*, *Balkand*, Vol. I, Oriental Institute, Baroda, 1960, 12/20,
    तथा काशिपतिं स्निग्धं सततं प्रियवादिनम्।
    सद्व्रतं देवसंकाशं स्वयमेवानयस्व ह।।

25. *Mahabharata*, *Parva*, chapter 102, vv 56, 64,65.
26. *Gita* 1/5

    धृष्टकेतुश्चेकितानः काशिराजश्च वीर्यवान्।
    पुरुजित्कुन्तिभोजश्च शैव्यश्च नरपुङ्गवः।।
    Gita 1/17
    काश्यश्च परमेश्वासः शिखण्डी च महारथः
    धृष्टद्युम्नो विराटश्च सात्यकिश्चापराजितः ।।

    Also see *Mahabharata*, *Bhishma Parva*, Vol. VII, Bhandarkar Oriental Research Institute, Poona, 1947, Chapter 23, sl. 17.
27. *Mahabharata*, *Karna Parva*, chap VI
28. *Devibhagwat*, 7 Skanto, chapter 30.
29. *Padma Purana*, *Swarga Khand*, *Bharatvarsha Varana*, p. 292.
30. *Padma Purana*, *Uttar Khand*, p. 874.
31. *Harivansh Purana*, *Bhavishya Parva*, chapter 91, Shlokas 1-16.
32. *Ibid*, chapter 93-96.
33. *Ibid*, chapter 101, 1040.
34. *Bhagwat*, 10th *Skanto*, chapter 66, *Shaloka* 41.
35. Cowell, E.B. (ed.), *The Jataka or the Stories of the Buddha's Former Births*, *Rajovada Jataka*, No. 151, Vol. II, Low Price Publications, first published in 1895-1905, Delhi, 1997, p. 1-4.
36. Fausboll, *Tra Jataka*, V, p. 41; III, pp. 304, 391.
37. Beal, S., *Buddhist Records of the Western World*, translated from Chinese of Hiuen Tsang A.D. 629, first published in 1884, Munshiram Manoharlal Publishers Pvt. Ltd, New Delhi, 1983, p. 70.
38. SBE, *op.cit.*, Jain Sutras, Vol. XXII, Part I, p. 271.
39. *Ibid*, p. 266.
40. SBE, *op.cit.*, *Vinayatext*, Vol. XVII, Part II, VII Khandhaka, 1, 1, p. 146.
41. SBE, *op.cit.*, *Buddhist Suttas*, Vol. XI, p. 146, p. 154.
42. *Ibid*, p. 99.
43. Cowell, E.B., *op.cit.*, *Rajovada Jataka*, 151, Vol. II, p. 1-4.
44. Cowell, E.B., *op.cit.*, *Cullaka-Setthi Jataka*, No. 4, Vol. I, p. 19; also see *Devadhamma Jataka*, No. 6, p. 24. *Kasiratthe Baranasiyam Brahmdatte rejjam Karente* is mentioned usually.
45. Cowell, E.B., *op.cit.*, *Yuvanjaya Jataka*, No. 460, Vol. IV, p. 75-76.
46. Cowell, E.B., *op.cit.*, *Tilamutthi Jataka*, No. 252, Vol. II, p. 193; *Althana Jataka*, No. 425, Vol. III, p. 282; *Samkicca Jataka*, No. 530, Vol. V, p. 135.
47. Cowell, E.B., *op.cit.*, *Mahasilava Jataka*, No. 51, Vol. I, p. 128-29;

Janasandha Jataka, No. 468, Vol. IV, p. 109-10.
48. Cowell, E.B., *op.cit.*, *Ekaraja Jatakas*, No. 303, Vol. III, p. 9.
49. Cowell, E.B., *op.cit.*, *Mahasilava Jataka*, No. 51, Vol. I, pp. 129-30.
50. Cowell, E.B., *op.cit.*, *Brahachatta Jataka*, No. 336, Vol. III, p. 76.
51. Cowell, E.B., *op.cit.*, *Dhonasakha Jataka*, No. 353, Vol. III, p. 106.
52. Cowell, E.B., *op.cit.*, No. 282 and No. 521.
53. Majumdar, R.C., *op.cit.*, Vol. II, pp. 22-23.
54. SBE, *op.cit.*, *The Upanishads*, Vol. I, Part I, *Kaushitaki Upanishad*, 4/1, p. 33.
55. *Ibid*, p. 155.
56. Majumdar, R.C., *op.cit.*, Vol. II, pp. 29-30.
57. *Ibid*, p. 507.
58. Jayaswal, K.P., *History of India 150 A.D. to 350 A.D.*, first published in 1933, Low Price Publication, New Delhi, 1990, p. 5.
59. *Ibid*, p. 31.
60. Altekar, A.S., *History of Benares*, published in the *Journal of BHU*, Vol. I, 1937, pp. 64 65.
61. Banaras District Gazetteer, Govt of India, 1963.
62. Watters, T., *On Yuan Chwang's Travels in India*, (A.D. 629-645), Vol. II, originally published in the *Journal of Royal Asiatic Society*, 1904-1905, Munshi Ram Manohar Lal Publishers Pvt. Ltd., 1973, p. 46-47
63. Jhusi plates issued by Trilochan Pal, *Indian Antiquerry*, XVIII, p. 84.
64. Sachau, Edward, C., *Alberuni's India*, Vol. II, Atlantic Publishers, New Delhi, 1989, pp. 146-147.
65. Baihaki, *Tarikhu-s-Subuktigin*, Elliot and Dowson, *The History of India as told by its own Historians*, Vol. II, first published in 1867, Low Price Publication, New Delhi, 2001, pp. 123-124.
66. Nizami, Hasan, *Taju-l Ma-asir*, Elliot and Dowson, *op.cit.*, Vol. II, p. 222; also see, Briggs, J., *History of the Rise of Mahomedan Power in India*, p. 101.
67. Minhaj ud-din, *Tabakat-I-Nasiri*, English translation by Raverty, Vol. I, Oriental Reprint, New Delhi, 1970, originally published in 1881 by Asiatic Society of Bengal, p. 470.
68. Nizami, Hasan, *op.cit.*, p. 223; also see, Briggs, Col. J., *Tarikh-I-Farishta*, Vol. I, Editions Indian, Calcutta, first published in 1829, p. 101.
69. Nizami, Hasan, *Taju-l Ma-asir*, Elliot and Dowson, *op.cit.*, Vol. II, p. 224.

70. Fisher and Hewitt, *op.cit.*, p. 132.
71. Fuhrer, A., *The Monumental Antiquities and Inscriptions of North Western Province and Oudh*, Vol. II, Government Press, North Western Province and Oudh, Allahabad, 1891, p. 179.
72. *Ibid*, p. 201.
73. Fuhrer, A., *The Sharqi Architecture of Jaunpur*, p. 51.
74. Nizam-ud-din-Ahmad, *Tabaqat-I-Akbari*, Asiatic Society of Bengal, 1973, first published in 1911, pp. 349-353.
75. *Ibid*, p. 357-358.
76. Babar, *Tuzuk-e-Babari*, Elliot and Dowson, *op.cit.*, Vol. IV, p. 266.
77. Sherring, M.A., *The Sacred City of the Hindus*, London, 1868, p. 255.
78. Fazl Abul, *Ain-I-Akbari*, English translation by Jerret, 1st published in 1927, Low Price Publication, Vol. II, 2001, p. 173.
79. Fazl, Abul, *Akbarnama*, English translation by Beveridge, Vol. II, published by Asiatic Society of Bengal, Rare Books, Delhi, 1972, pp. 392-95.
80. Srivastava, A.L., *Akbar The Great*, Political History (1542-1605), Vol. I, Shiva Lal Agarwal and Co., Agra, 1972, p. 94.
81. Fazl, Abul, *op.cit.*, p. 397-399.
82. *Ibid*, p. 435.
83. Srivastava, A.L., *op.cit*, p. 101.
84. Sam-ud-Dowlah Shah Nawaz Khan, *Nassir-ul-Umra*, Vol. I, p. 434.
85. Hadi, Mohammad, *Tatimma-I-Waki'at-I- Jahangiri*, Elliot and Dowson, *op.cit.*, Vol. VI, p. 394.
86. Lahori, Abdul Hamid, *Badshahnama*, Elliot and Dowson, *op.cit.*, Vol. VII, p. 36.
87. Sarkar, J.N., *History of Aurangzeb*, Vol. III, Orient Longman Ltd., New Delhi, 1972, first published in 1928, p. 258.
88. *Ibid*, p. 185.
89. Mohd. Saki Musta'idd Khan, *Ma-Asir-I-Alamgiri*, Elliot and Dowson, *op.cit.*, Vol. VII, pp. 183-184; original *firman* of Aurangzeb of 1669 is preserved in Bharat Kala Bhavan, Banaras Hindu University, Varanasi.
90. Altekar, A.S., *op.cit.*, p. 250.
91. Bernier, Franscois, *Travels in the Mughal Empire A.D. 1656-1668*, originally published in 1934 by Oxford University Press, London, Oriental Reprint, 1983, p. 334.
92. Irwine,W., *Later Mughals*, Vol. I, pp. 212-13.
93. Alam, Muzaffar, *The Crisis of Empire in Mughal North India*, Oxford

University Press, Delhi, 1986, p. 247.

94. Asir, Ibn, *Ka milu-T Tawarikh*, Elliot and Dowson, *op.cit.*, Vol. II, p. 251.
95. *Imperial Gazetteer of India, op.cit.*, It has been mentioned that Benares enjoyed a period of peace until the 18th century.

Chapter 2

Mansaram: The Founder of the Ruling Dynasty of Benares

For centuries, Benares under the Muslim subjugation witnessed innumerable revolts, though it was quelled by strong Imperial power at Delhi, but neverthless, there was persistent discontentment and disgruntlement in the minds of the people of Benares and non-payment of taxes ends credence to this fact. The people were profound apprehensive of high insecurity prevailing in their city, especially concerning their lives, property, prosperity, religion and even the day-to-day lifestyle. Due to the religious importance, the Kings, Queens and the Queen's mother of ruling dynasties of different states of India frequently visited the city of Benares. Most of the members of the royal families endeavoured to remain in Benares city during their old age that could develop high political sensitivity in case of any serious activity of the Mughals in Benares and affect the entire Hindu mind of India. Ebbing of Delhi throne and escalating menace of the Marathas made Benares and its surrounding areas even more politically sensitive. Being a border region of Oudh Suba and Hindu dominated area it could have been a door left ajar for the Marathas leading them to Delhi. The Marathas' interest in Benares can be corroborated by the fact that in 1736 Peshwa Baji Rao demanded from the effete

Mughal Emperor Muhammad Shah to give the religious places of Benares to him as *jagir.*[1] The *zamindars* and nobles of Benares availed themselves of the then existing political condition and "began to beat the drum of independence."[2] It was same Benares where even the popular Emperor Akbar was not allowed to enter the city with welcome doors and he had to remain there for 37 days to re-establish the sovereignty and suzerainty of the Mughal paramount power. All this prompted among the people of Benares for establishing their rule.

As a seque to the assassination of the Emperor Farrukh Siyar, Mohammad Shah was installed on the throne in September 1719. Consequent upon the wrecking of the great *Kashi Vishwanath* temple at Benares, the collection of the revenue from the area became an onerous task for the Mughals. So, Mohammad Shah found it convenient to give the *sarkar* of Benares, Jaunpur, Chunar and Ghazipur to one of his courtier Murtaza Khan as *jagir.*[3] The whole area is analogous to the present districts of Benares, Jaunpur, Gazipur, Azamgarh, Ballia and northeastern portion of Mirzapur district.[4] Murtaza Khan, whose original name was Hifzullah Khan, was appointed *fauzdar* of Saharanpur during the reign of Farrukh Siyar and in 1719, he assumed the office of the *qurbegi* (head of armoury) at the court. During the reign of Rafiud-Dowla, he received the title of Murtaza Khan and was given the *niyabat* of *Mir Atish*. Again, during the reign of Mohammad Shah he held important positions in the court.[5]

Murtaza Khan entrusted the onus of managing these four *sarkars* to one of his relatives Mir Rustum Ali, for an annual consideration of Rs. 5 lakhs with the right to retain the surplus for himself,[6] but Rustum Ali could not remit the sum regularly. Being a person suffering from inertia and incapability, he failed to discharge his duties and collect revenue from far and wide. He could neither keep big *zamindars* in check nor make them pay the annual revenue in time.[7] Eventually, in 1728, Murtaza Khan was very glad to lease his *jagir* to Saadat Khan in consideration of an annual sum of Rs. 7 lakhs, who further allowed Rustum Ali to continue to manage the *sarkars* for Rs. 8 lakhs annually.[8] Though some *zamindars* like Fateh Singh, *zamindar* of Jakkhini, Berisal

Singh and Dariao Singh, *zamindars* Manjhawa, who held the highest place among *rissaldars*, paid their revenue regularly,[9] yet Rustum Ali was mostly dependent for the management on his deputies among whom most prominent was Mansaram,[10] who, later on, became the founder of a new dynasty at Benares, which passing through many vicissitudes continued till its integration in India in 1949.

Mansaram, a *Trikarma Brahman* or *Gautum Bhumihar*,[11] was originally a *zamindar* of village Tetharia, later known as Gangapur, in *pargana* Kaswar.[12] Mansaram's father Miranji was a *zamindar* of few hundred *bighas* of land in the village Gangapur.[13] This land was the nucleus of the later *zamindari* of Benares that measured about 59 square miles [14] covering about half the village of Gangapur[15] and was situated at a distance of four *cos* i.e. 12 miles from Benares city and few miles from the north of the river Ganges. *Bhuimhars* are *Brahmans* living mostly in areas where *sarvariya* or *saryuparin Brahmans* were living and marry in both castes *Brahmans* and *Kshatriyas*. This community resides mostly in the present districts of Varanasi, Vindhyachal dham, Azamgarh, Basti and Gorakhpur and some portions of Allahabad district. They are densely populated in the districts of eastern Uttar Pradesh and western Bihar in the both sides of the *Ganges* and used the titles of *Brahmans* like *Pandey, Tiwari, Dixit, Misra, Upadhyay* etc. and *Singh*, *Shahi* of *Kshatriyas*. They belong to *Kashayap, Vatsa, Shandilya, Bhardwaj, Garg, Gautum, Shavarnaya, Vashishtha, Parasar, Kaushik, Shankrit gotras*. Some Upadhyay Brahmans are living in the present-day Nepal.

This community neither takes donations from anybody nor asks for money from anyone because of which they are called *ayachak* Brahman. Generally speaking, they are good fighters and diplomats and perform half of the prescribed Brahmanical duties. They give alms, but do not receive them; they offer sacrifices to their idols, but do not perform the duties of priesthood; they read the sacred writings (the *Vedas* and *Puranas*), but do not teach them. Sir Henry Elliot mentioned about the indications of the origin of *Bhuimhars* in the names of *Gargbhumi* and *Vatsabhumi*, mentioned in *Harivansha Purana* as *kshatriya brahmans*. They were called as descendents of *Kasiya* Princes. This makes indications about their living at Kashi. The idol worshipped by this community is *Bhagwan* Parshuram. They perform all the rituals of different *Vedas* but mostly observed the rituals of *Yajurveda*.[16]

The origin of the family of Mansaram dates back to the time of Raja Banar of Benares during eleventh century A.D. whose *Purohit* Kithoo Misr was the well-known ancestor of the family. Being very altruistic and content to Kithoo Misr, Raja Banar accorded him various offers, which was never accepted by the latter. Eventually one day, without the knowledge of Kithoo Misr, Raja Banar tied up a paper of a rent-free land in his favour to his turban. Knowing the deed of the Raja, the *Brahman* prognosticated that the Raja's rule over Benares would one day end and pass on to the hands of his (Kithoo Misr's) lineage. The saying of Kithoo Misr came out to be true with the attack of Mas'ud Ghazi in 1029 A.D., who was sent by the order of Mehmood Ghaznawee to devastate Benares.[17]

Miranji had four sons, namely Mansaram, Mayaram, Dasaram and Dayaram.[18] After the demise of Miranji in 1721,[19] the *zamindary* passed on to his four sons under the management of his eldest son, Mansaram. This *zamindary* gave an annual income of about Rs. 5,000 at that time. Later on, in 1724 Mansaram started his work under Berisal, who was the *zamindar* of Kaswar. Deeply impressed by the zeal and adeptness displayed by Mansaram, Berisal deployed him as his *Vakeel* to Rustum Ali to negotiate various matters. His continued success and acceptance yielded him the opportunity to serve not only as *vakeel* of his master but also for some other *zamindars* in course of time.[20] Mansaram availed himself of this opportunity and became the favourite of Rustum Ali, who soon made him his *diwan*.[21] This created a cleavage between Berisal and Rustum Ali, which widened day by day and eventually, led to battle where Mansaram took the side of Rustum Ali against his master, inflicted a crushing defeat and expelled him from the *zamindary*. Later, he procured a farm of Rs. 4-5 lakh from Rustum Ali.[22] Rustum solicited the Emperor through Murtaza Khan to confer upon Mansaram the title of *Rajabahadur*.[23] Mansaram supplicated the title for himself and his son, which was granted by a *farman* issued in 1730 by the Emperor Mohammad Shah himself.[24] Mansaram proved to be very successful in collecting revenues from the region.[25]

It goes without saying that Mansaram's instantaneous rise in position and increasing sway over Rustum Ali raised a number of enemies, who were expelled from their *zamindary* by Mansaram with the help of his master's forces. Mir Rustum Ali, who was squandering his time in pleasure, handed over the onus of the management of *sarkars* into the hands of Mansaram.[26] Being extremely ambitious, Mansaram began to increase his power and leverage day by day without dissipating any opportunity. Rustum Ali, with the assistance of Vikramajit, the Raja of Mariahu and Mansaram, commenced his expedition against the refractory *zamindar* of Kantit (in Mirzapur). Though Kantit *zamindar* decided to surrender, but was incessantly and surreptitiously being instigated by Mansaram due to which he continued fighting. At this crucial juncture, Mansaram, put a condition to surrender the Mariahu fort for continuing his assistance to Rustum Ali or he would retreat. Knowing the dire need of his aid at this crucial time, Rustum Ali induced Raja Mariahu to surrender the fort to Mansaram. Eventually, Mansaram joined the expedition and after quelling the rebellion, he took possession of the fort in Jaunpur in 1737.[27] Mansaram acquired a series of minor *zamindars* within the district through the favour of Rustum Ali, and some by his ambitious plans of expelling for forced disobedience or non-performance.[28]

Meanwhile, Rustum Ali's enemies at the Court of Safdar Jang, deputy of *Burhan-ul-Mulk.* Saadat Khan, made complaints against the administration of Benares asserting that Rustum Ali was negligent of state affairs, squander time in pleasure and entertainment, besides nurturing enmity towards the servants of the State. Moreover, Saadat Khan, who was engaged in Delhi, left Safdar Jang as Deputy in his absence and directed him to call Rustum Ali to account. All this made Safdar Jang to leave Faizabad for Jaunpur to punish Rustum Ali in 1738.[29] At this time, the enemies of Mansaram availed themselves by instigating Rustum Ali against him saying that Mansaram had excited Safdar Jang against him. When Rustum Ali was informed about the evil designs of Mansaram, he called him for an explaination of his conduct. Rustum told him that it was through him that Mansaram was raised from a *vakeel* to a position of power and influence.

Mansaram said that the allegation against him was calumnious[30] and proposed to go to Jaunpur to negotiate with Safdar Jang in favour of Rustum Ali to prove his fidelity. The latter being too afraid to appear in person before the Deputy Nawab accepted the proposal of Mansaram and deputed him for negotiation.[31] Mansaram influenced Mohammad Quli Khan, one of the courtiers of Safdar Jang, and through him managed to obtain audience of the Deputy Nawab.[32] He gave him presents on behalf of Rustum Ali and induced him to continue the *zamindary* of four *sarkars* under Mir Rustum Ali proffering an increase of revenue by four lakh i.e. 12 lakhs annually, but *sarkar* of Ghazipur was taken away. Taking advantage of this situation, Mansaram's enemies revived Rustum Ali against him. Reacting to this, Rustum Ali called back Mansaram and appointed another envoy to negotiate with instructions not to brook Mansaram's interference in the matter. In retaliation to this, Mansaram changed his attitude and offered Rs. 13 lakhs revenue for the grant of *sunnud* of three *sarkars* of Benares, Jaunpur and Chunar in name of his son Balwant Singh.[33] Safdar Jang at that time found Mansaram, the most suitable man, who was no more a novice to the revenue administration and the system of management of the *zamindary*. He accepted the proposal of Mansaram while Sheikh Abdullah was made *Fauzdar* in the Ghazeepur *sarkar* on payment of Rs. 3 lakhs annually.[34]

Rustum Ali was taken as prisoner on the grounds of arrears of revenue due to the *Kotwal* of Benares, where he committed suicide. His funeral was attended by Mansaram and Balwant Singh formally, where Mansaram proffered Ibrahim Ali, son of Rustum Ali, to stay in Benares and three villages along with Rs. 50,000, but he spurned the offer and went to Ghazipur where Fazl Ali gave him village of Saidpur for his maintenance. Safdar Jang issued the *sunnud* for the three sarkars of Benares, Jaunpur and Chunar in the name of Balwant Singh under the authority of Saadat Khan that made Balwant Singh the Raja of Benares.[35] This grant did not include the *kotwal* of Benares, governorship of Jaunpur fort and mint at Benares. The *Kotwal* of Benares was directly appointed by Nawab himself, both because of the religious and commercial importance of the sacred city, as well as, to act as his agent in Benares to watch and report surreptitious designs and actions of the ambitious Raja, but Mansaram could not enjoy the rights for long and soon died of illness in 1740. His son Balwant Singh succeeded him with all his powers and possessions. At the time of death, his possessions included 18 *mahals* with the total revenue of Rs. 24, 50,881.[36]

Balwant Singh was extraordinarily ambitious and posterior to the death of Mansaram he sought to obtain recognition directly from the Emperor of Delhi Mohammad Shah. Through Amir Khan, *Subedar* of Allahabad, he deputed a *vakeel* to the Imperial Court with a *nazr* of gold *mohurs* of Rs. 21,775. A *sunnud* declaring Balwant Singh as the exclusive beneficiary of his father, title of Raja and also the *zamindary* of *pargana* Kuswar, Afrad, Kutehar and Bhugwunt under the seal of Grand *Vizier* Kumar-ood-deen Khan was conferred upon him.[37] In 1740, till the death of Mansaram, the *zamindary* of Benares had extended to 18 *mahals* with revenue as follows:

Sircar Benares

1.	*Havillee* Benares, with the zemindary of Soorhy, Chietpoor, & c., to Pertab Rooder	1, 02,700
2.	*Sayer* of the city, &c. farmed by Chiet Rai, & c.	1, 35,000
3.	*Pergunnah* Kettehur, with the town of Sheupore, to Ragoobynsy Rajepoot	1, 65,905
4.	*Pergunnah* Kesswar, with Chekny, the zemindarry of Aley Singh, &c.	87, 522
5.	*Pergunnah* Afrad, the zemindarry of Ragoo Bynsy	55, 611
6.	*Pergunnah* Punderha, the zemindarry of Ruber Baboohar	75, 309
7.	*Pergunnah* Byalsy, the zemindarry of Ragoo Bynsy	51, 200
8.	*Pergunnah* Kole Asselah, zemindarry of Kerpanaht taken from Townpoor	82, 107

9.	*Pergunnah* Ahtgong Kerowa, the zemindarry Soorwar Rajepoot	63, 042
10.	*Pergunnah* Keryat Seekim, zemindarry of Ainder Singh, the half of which to Chuner	85, 752
		9,04, 148

Sircar Allahabad

11.	*Pergunnah* Bhudorn, zemindarry of Holas Rajepoot	5,06, 400
12.	*Pergunnah* Mutafurukat, *jageer* villages of the same *pergunnah*	1,22, 115

Sircar Townpoor

13.	*Pergunnah* Murriahoo, divided in farm to Amrow Singh, & c.	5,17, 504
14.	*Pergunnah* Gurwara, zemindarry of Doorgbynsy Rajepoot	1,07, 005
15.	*Pergunnah* Moongera Santere, in farm	60,822
16.	*Pergunnah* Keerakut, zemindarry of Raggobynsy	55,005
17.	*Pergunnah* Meypoora Lanel, zemindarry of Bhirhar	1,03,500
18.	*Pergunnah* Goushia, or Muchli Sher, zemindar Afghan	74,382
	Total acquisitions of Mansaram	Rs. 24, 50, 881

Benares was strategically significant first, because of being a border district of Oudh *Suba* and secondly due to its trade route, both land and sea passes through the district. The commercial significance of Benares can be visualised by the fact that in 1582, during the reign of Akbar, cotton, sugar, indigo and cloths were manufactured mostly in Benares for export and was returning Rs. 20 lakhs annual balance of trade to Allahabad *Suba*.[38] More revolt meant more loss of revenue. Earlier, the Mughals were strong enough to suppress the rebellion that occurred from time to time, but in the eighteenth century the imperial authority was ebbing and so they did not prefer to assume any risk of confronting further revolts and anarchy in Benares, particularly at a time when the Marathas were posing a great challenge for them who could use this discontentment prevailing amongst the people against the Mughals.

The cardinal question that arises here is that why the Emperor selected only Mansaram for the management of the *zamindary*. The truth is that no one was able to collect the revenue from the people of Benares. The long history of Benares manifests that since the end of the reign of the *Gharwal* dynasty, the people of Benares never paid their revenue willfully. Mansaram was the only person who could collect the revenue as he was the head of the ancient and powerful clan of *Trikarma Brahmans*, a caste that shared a big chunk of the population of the Benares region due to which he enjoyed great influence. Moreover, the ancient royal family had been extinct.[39] Rustum Ali himself too, was unable collect the revenue and so he transferred the onus of the administration to Mansaram. This is manifestsed by the fact that total revenue collection from *Khalisa* (*pargana* Haveli) was Rs. 42,248/7 ½ in 1731, which rose to Rs. 49,246/7½ in 1737 when revenue collection was the onus of Mansaram and finally, it increased to Rs. 75,000 in 1741 during the time of Balwant Singh. Mansaram paid Rs. 5, 00,000/- as an *ijaradar* of the *pargana* under Rustum Ali, but his collection was as much as Rs. 20,00,000.[40] It was this dominant factor that gave him the encouragement and instilled confidence in his mind to step forward towards his ambition. The table of the comparative study of the revenue of the Benares region in different period makes this fact incontrovertible.[41]

Region	*Jama in dams in Ain-i-Akbari*	*Jama in dams in mid-18th century*
Sarkar Jaunpur	5, 63, 94,107	9, 27, 02,303
Sarkar Benares	88, 69,315	1, 93, 38,895
Sarkar Ghazipur	1, 34, 31,308	3, 42, 30 204
Sarkar Chunar	58, 10,654	2, 88, 36,578

In true sense, Mansaram was cognizant that he was accepted by the people of Benares otherwise it would have never been possible for him to directly proffer an increase of Rs. 5 lakhs in the annual revenue, in spite of the fact that Ghazipur region had been taken away from the *zamindary*. While working as *diwan* of Rustum Ali, Mansaram must have unequivocally realized the objective of support lent, and acceptance by the Benares people who were eager to have their own ruler. The *zamindary* that earlier, yielded Rs. 8 lakhs annually was none contributing Rs. 16 lakhs (including Ghazipur) i.e. double the previous amount. Mansaram was not only the founder of the new dynasty in 1738, but he was also the *de facto* ruler of Benares even before of the grant of the *sunnud*. The author of the *History of the Province of Benares* regarded Mansaram as the real ruler from 1730 to 1738.[42]

References

1. Malik, Z.U., *The Reign of Muhammad Shah 1719-1748*, Centre of Advanced study, Aligarh Muslim University, p. 131.
2. *History of the Province of Benares*, Medical Hall Press, Anonymous, Benares, 1882, p. 1, held at U.P. State Archives.
4. Nevill, H.R., *Benares: A Gazetteer*, District Gazetteers of U.P. of Agra and Oudh, Vol. XXVI, Allahabad Government Press, 1909, p. 198 (Chunar is not mentioned); also see Benares Gazetteer, *op.cit.*, p. 59.
5. Benares Gazetteer, *op.cit.*, p. 59.
6. Alam, Muzaffar, *The Crisis of Empire in Mughal North India*, Oxford University Press, Delhi, 1986, p. 129 fn.
7. Srivastava, A.L., *The first Two Nawabs of Oudh*, Shiva Lal Agarwal and Co. Ltd., Educational Publishers, 2nd edition, Agra, 1954, p. 42.
8. Benares Gazetteer, *op.cit.*, p. 60.
9. Nevill, H.R., *op.cit.*, p. 198 and Altekar, A.S., *History of Benares*, Journal of B.H.U., Vol. I, Banaras, 1937, p. 59, the year mentioned is 1722.
10. Srivastava, A.L., *op.cit.*, p. 42.
11. Benares Gazetteer, *op.cit.*, p. 60.
12. M.A. Sherring, *The Sacred City of Hindus*, Trubner and Company, London, 1868.
13. Nevill, H.R., *op.cit.*, p. 282.
14. *Calendar of Persian Correspondence* (henceforth CPC), Vol. V (1776-

1780), Central Publication Branch, Government of India, Calcutta, 1930, No. 1407 dated March 23, 1779, p. 306.

15. *Imperial Gazetteer of India*, VII, published under the authority of His Majesty's Secretary of State for India in Council, Oxford, at the Clarendon Press, 1908, p. 182; also see, Nevill, H.R., *op.cit.*, p. 283.
16. Firminger, W.K., *Affairs of the East India Company,* Being 5th report from the select Committee of House of Commons 28 July, 1812, Vol. II, B.R. Publishing Corporation, 2001, p. 468, Appendix.
17. Khairuddin, Fakhir, *Tohfa-i-Toza,* translated in English y Ansari and Qureshi, New Royal ook Company, Lucknow, 2009, p. 1, Also see Sherring, M.A., *Hindu Tribes and Castes As Represented in Benares*, Trubner and Co., 1872, pp. 39-42.
18. Family Domains of Maharaja Benares, File No. 112, Box No. 77, Regional Archives, Allahabad (henceforth RAA).
19. Letter No. 1407, March 23, 1779, CPC, V.
20. Firminger, *op.cit.*, p. 468.
21. Letter No. 1407, March 23, 1779, CPC, V.
22. Gleig, *Memoirs of Life of Rt. Hon. Warren Hastings*, Vol. I, London, 1841, p. 338.
23. Letter No. 1407, March 23, 1779, CPC, V.
24. Mill, James, *History of India*, IV, London, 1858, p. 361.
25. *History of the Province of Benares*, *op.cit.*, p. 3.
26. Cohn. B.S., *Political System in Eighteenth Century India: The Banaras Region*, Journal of the American Oriental Society, Vol. lxxxii, July-September, 1962, pp. 312-319.
27. Gleig, *op.cit.*, p. 338; also see, Nevill, H.R., *op.cit.*, p. 198, "It is probably true that this Mansaram became the actual ruler of the province."
28. Oldham, Wilton, *Historical and Statistical Memoir of Ghazeepur District*, pt I, Allahabad, 1870, p. 99.
29. Firminger, *op.cit.*, p. 468.
30. Srivastava, A.L., *op.cit.*, p. 186; Proceedings of Indian Historical Records Commission, Vol. XIV, 1937, p. 65.
31. Letter No. 1407, March 23, 1779, CPC, V; also see Nevill, H.R., *op.cit.*, p. 198.
32. Nevill, H.R., *op.cit.*, p. 198.
33. Khairuddin, Fakhir, op.cit., pp. 8-9. Also see Letter No. 1407, March 23, 1779, CPC, V.
34. Letter No. 1407, March 23, 1779, CPC, V.

35. Nevill, H.R., *op.cit.*, p. 198; Proceedings of Indian Historical Records Commission, *op.cit.*, p. 65.
36. BCO, DR, Basta 8, Vol. 46, RAA.
37. Firminger, *op.cit.*, p. 469; Benares Gazetteer, *op.cit.*, p. 60, it is mentioned that Balwant Singh got the *sunnud* in 1739 conferring the title of Raja and in 1740 the *zamindary* of four *purgunnah.*
38. Benares Gazetteer, *op.cit.*, p. 60.
39. Firminger, *op.cit.*, p. 464.
40. *History of the Province of Benares*, *op.cit.*, p. 4.
41. Alam, Muzaffar, *op.cit.*, pp. 251-52.
42. Fazl Abul, *Ain-I-Akbari*, English translation by Jerret, 1st published in 1927, Low Price Publication, Vol. II, 2001, p. 173-76, p. 184, pp. 293-96; also see Alam, Muzaffar, *op.cit.*, p. 253.
43. *History of the Province of Benares*, *op.cit.*, p. 2.

Chapter 3

Raja Balwant Singh
Strategies for Expansion and Consolidation

With the demise of Mansaram and succession of Balwant Singh in 1740, Benares entered into a new phase where it witnessed politics and struggle between powers—Nawab of Oudh and the East India Company headquartered in Calcutta. During this time, when the air was fraught with unforeseen circumstances, Balwant Singh with his great political acumen, prescience and sterling qualities not only extended his possessions from inherited 18 *parganas* to 96 *parganas* but also protected it from getting sandwiched between the two – Muslim power in the west and Christian power in the east.

The *Farman* had already conferred upon him the right to rule in Benares during his father's lifetime. With the exception of minting money coins, a prerogative of the Emperor, and the administration of criminal justice in Benares city, Balwant Singh enjoyed all the powers within his dominions.[1] He selected Tetharia, his grandfather's village for residence and built a mud fort the was later rechristened as Gangapur, the name by which the place is still known.[2] During the incipient period 1740-48, he regularly paid the annual tribute with 'commendable punctuality'[3] and tried to establish his authority firmly by suppressing any probability of local resistance. Pursuant to this policy, he first induced Sheo Baksh Singh, the Monas Raja, to surrender *pargana* Kutehar that was granted to the Raja by Mughal Emperor.[4] He ousted his Uncle Dasa Ram as he was claiming his share in Mansaram's estate. Dasa Ram endeavoured to seek the protection of the Marathas in 1747 during pilgrimage of Kashi Bai, mother of Peshwa Balaji Baji Rao. The Raja put forth the matter in Imperial Court. Though the affairs became political, but resulted to no political turnover and the matter fell into oblivion.[5] Raja Balwant Singh availed himself of the opportunity stemming from the demise of Mughal Emperor Mohammad Shah in 1748 and absence of *Vizier* Safdar Jang who was engaged in imperial affairs. He endeavoured to augment his political authority by refusing to pay the revenue and impelled Nawab's *sazawal* Numkin Khan and Rup Singh to leave Benares.[6]

When Safdar Jang was engaged to subdue Bangash Pathans of Farrukhabad, Balwant Singh with the assistance of Raja Prithvipath Narayan of Pratapgarh attacked Bhadohi *pargana* [7] under Daswant Singh and occupied the *pargana*. This brought Balwant Singh into direct animosity with Ali Quli Khan, Deputy Governor of Allahabad, as the *pargana* was under his authority. With the march of Ali Quli Khan towards Benares, Raja Balwant Singh fled away and sued for peace proffering a substantial amount in expiration of his offence. While negotiations were yet to be concluded, Balwant Singh colluded with some Hindu officers of the opponent and made an instantaneous attack where these Hindu officers offered no resistance. Eventually, Balwant Singh came out to be victorious and Deputy Governor fled in ignominy to Allahabad.[8] Thus, by 1750 Raja Balwant Singh had became so powerful as to defeat none other than the Deputy Governor himself.

This spectacular victory of Balwant Singh incensed Safdar Jang, but he failed to take any stringent measure as he was defeated by Bangash Pathan leader Ahmad Khan in a battle at Ram Chatauni, 7 miles east of Sahawar on September 20, 1750. On the call of Ahmad Khan, Raja Balwant Singh met him in Jhusi and presented Rs. 1 lakh and received *khil'at* with the confirmation of half of his territory and the other half was conferred upon Sahib Zaman Khan, cousin of one of Ahmad Khan's wife. Raja Balwant Singh was directed to encamp across Arail and break the supply line to the Allahabad fort. Ahmad Khan appointed Mohammad Amir Khan, *Fauzdar* of and Zaman Khan, *Dilazak* of Jaunpur and his Viceroy in Jaunpur, Azamgarh, Akbarpur, Mahaul and other places. surrendered without any resistance as its *Fauzdar* Fazl Ali fled away. Raja Balwant Singh vehemently rebuffed to surrender his territory, after which Zaman Khan was directed to expel him. He got re-enforcement and was joined by Akbar Shah, Raja of Azamgarh and Shamsher Jahan, *zamindar* of Mahaul, 23 miles north-west of Azamgarh.[9]

The strength of force thus assembled at Akbarpur, 32 miles south-east of Faizabad, was 1,700 horse and 10,000 infantry.[10] They occupied the fort of Sarhanpur after a seize of 15 days. Subsequently, Jaunpur was also occupied after a feeble resistance of six hours. Zaman Khan instead of marching towards Benares moved to Nizamabad, 32 miles north-east of Jaunpur. It is said that the leading moneylenders of Benares proffered prodigious amount of Rs. 2 crores to the Pathans on the condition that they would not enter the city, which was accepted by them and they retraced their steps. Soon, Ahmad Khan retreated to Farrukhabad with the approach of Safdar Jang and the Marathas. At this turnover of events, Raja Balwant Singh marched to Mariahu, 12 miles south of Jaunpur and demanded Zaman Khan to surrender the territory. Zaman Khan fled to Bettia and consequently Raja Balwant Singh recovered all his possessions by April 1751.[11]

After Ahmed Khan's retreat, Nawab turned to Benares to avenge Raja Pratapgarh and Raja Benares for their support to the Bangash Pathans. At Sultanpur, 36 miles south of Faizabad, Raja Prithvipat was stabbed during his meet with the Nawab.[12] Subsequently, he marched to Benares and detached a contingent across *Ganges* to pursue the Raja, who fled to Mirzapur. Safdar Jang plundered the fortress and town of Gangapur. The Raja made overtures through his confidant Lal Khan, who was sent with a present of Rs. 2 lakh and offer of revenue increase by Rs. 2 lakh.

Safdar Jang agreed to pardon him after his appearance, but in spite of so much insistence and assurance of safety, the Raja evaded his appearance with great astuteness and farsightedness. Meanwhile, impelled by the Imperial summon to return to Delhi because of Abdali's invasion, the Nawab accepted to make peace with the Raja by end of March 1752 and send a *khil'at* that confirmed the possessions under the Raja on the condition of Rs. 15 lakh annual revenue and appointed Narul Hasan Khan Bilgrami as *sazawal*. On April 3, 1752, Nawab commenced his march to Delhi.[13] All these developments and perpetual success "taught the Raja his power, and his aggrandisement processed rapidly to the intense dismay of the Oudh government, which was now powerless to resist him."[14]

During Abdali's invasion, Balwant Singh strategically used the time in consolidation of his power. Giving effect to this policy, he first shifted his residence from Gangapur to Ramnagar across the *Ganges* where he constructed a stone fort in 1752.[15] Fuhrer described the fort in words, "The structure raises loftily on the banks of the *Ganges*, and is the picture of a feudal castle."[16] He adopted an expansion policy towards south of Benares, surrounded by *Ganges* in north, *Karamnassa* in east, river Sone and Kaimur hills in the south and a chain of hills in the west.[17] He had covetous eyes over impregnable hill fort of Bijaygurh, 50 miles from Chunar, which was almost inaccessible to an invader as described by Popham in his report to Hastings, "so exceedingly steep, that it must be very difficult, to ascend, and if assailed should act resolutely, next to impossible to annex."[18]

The Raja planned to first capture the fort of Pateeta and Lateefpur situated between Chunar and Bijaygurh. Both the forts were not only strategically important, but also secured from enemy's attack. Hodges, during his travel in 1781, described the Lateefpur fort, "The fort of Lateefpore is made from the singularity of its situation, being immersed in a thick wood of bamboos and other trees close to the foot of the ditch and only one direct avenue to the fort which might be secured with a few men; if resolutely defended."[19] Regarding Pateeta fort, Hastings himself wrote to Wheeler, "The fort, though small, is of stone with four towers, a parallel rampart and a ditch, a great depth surrounding them and the town itself guarded by an entrenchment extending far beyond it and the space between the hills and jungles almost impenetrable."[20] Though these forts were situated within his territory, yet the actual possession was under the subordinate *zamindars*. He effortlessly took the possession of Pateeta and Lateefpur by September 1753.[21]

After the occupation of these two forts, Balwant Singh commenced negotiations with Vijay Singh, the Governor of Bijaygarh fort. Unable to offer firm resistance, Vijay Singh acquiesce in Raja's proffer to purchase the fort on payment of Rs. 50,000 in December 1753. In 1754, he also took the possession of fort of Agoree, which extended its boundaries to the bank of *Sone*, 12 miles to the south of Bijaygarh.[22] Safdar Jang again marched to Benares on February 17, 1754 to chastise Raja Balwant Singh for his incessant extensions, but the Raja fled to Chandrauti, 12 miles north-east of Benares. The Nawab without taking any stringent measure moved back to Delhi impelled by the perplexing affairs in the Imperial Court.[23] It was the same time when Gaziuddin superseded Nawab as the *Vizier* of the Empire. This made the circumstances propitious for the Raja to plan for the possession of the impregnable fort of Chunar, situated on *Ganges*, 20 miles east of Mirzapur.[24] The possession of this fort was of considerable significance because of its strategic importance, commanding the trade route, both land and sea, and was the only place within his territory that was not under his authority. Safdar Jang obtained the possession of the fort from the Emperor during his march to Bengal to support Ali Wardi Khan from the Marathas aggressions in 1742.[25]

In 1754, Raja Balwant Singh occupied the *pargana* of Kera Mangroor and proffered a payment of Rs. 7000/- as annual revenue to the *Naib Subedar* at Patna. The possession was soon legalized by the Emperor Alamgir I, who conferred a rent-free grant of the *pargana,* and was subsequently confirmed by Emperor Shah Alam II.[26] After the demise of Safdar Jang in October 1754, Raja Balwant Singh enticed Agamir, the *Qilladar* of the Chunar fort, to hand over the fort in return of Rs. 1 lakh. This collusion posed a great challenge to Nawab Shuja-ud-daula who proceeded to Benares in November 1756, but Balwant Singh soon fled away to Lateefpur. The mother-in-law of Balwant Singh, widow of Bariar Singh, *zamindar* of Pindra,[27] offered a resolute resistance, at a place 19 miles north-west of Benares, to the forces of the Nawab, who knowing that a the resistance was offered by a lady admired her courage and resumed the march of his army. Nawab took the possession of all the belongings of the late *killadar* of Chunar, which included Rs. 7 lakh cash and other valuable worth Rs. 4 lakh and appointed a new *killadar*. Shuja-ud-daula now directed his operations against the Raja in December 1756. The Raja, who was in the fortress of Bijaygarh, sent an envoy to the Maratha Chiefs for their assistance. Even Shaikh Ali Hazin, one of the holiest men of the time, advised him to patch up with the Raja, but the Nawab refused. He summoned Fazl Ali, *Fauzdar* of Ghazipur and expressed that he want him to replace Balwant Singh. Fazl Ali, who was cognizant of Raja Balwant Singh's power, proposed to the Nawab that he could undertake the onerous task of extirpating him provided, he was put in command of a force of 10,000 cavalry at least for a year, and exempted from the payment of Rs. 10 lakh that was current year's revenue. These exorbitant and outrageous terms were a terrible shock for Shuja-ud-daula. Mohammad Ali Khan, one of his courtiers, suggested that it would be highly imprudent to struggle with the Raja as this would result in great disturbance throughout the region and would indubitably affect Faizabad, too.[28]

Further, he was advised not to depose and replace the Raja, as no one else was locally so entrenched or commanded enough public and army support to be able to pay annual revenue into the treasury regularly. Even Fazl Ali had to counter many obstacles to pay regularly the revenue of Ghazipur and his exorbitant demands would cost more than the revenue paid.[28] It was the same time when Abdali had entered Delhi. Raja Balwant Singh sent his envoy Lal Khan with a *peshkash* of Rs. 5 lakh and also put forth an enticing offer to augment the tribute by Rs. 5 lakh, and that he may be allowed to continue to rule.[30] Nawab confirmed him in all his possessions and conferred upon him the *pargana* of Bhadohi as *jagir* in February 1757.[31] Nawab's prompt assent to this settlement was because of inescapable circumstances—firstly, Ahmad Shah Abdali's second invasion of Delhi and secondly, the Raja had made a religious appeal to the Marathas for military assistance. Though the Marathas did not respond by the time, but Shuja-ud-daula knew that they had interest in upbringing pilgrimage centers under the direct control of Hindu rulers.[32] In addition, Fazl Ali could not pay the revenue regularly. He oppressed the people to such an extent that eventually in 1757, Shuja-ud-daula sent Beni Bahadur and Raja Balwant Singh to Ghazipur to expel him. Fazl Ali offered armed resistance, but was defeated and fled to Patna. Eventually, having no viable alternative, Ghazipur was given to Raja Balwant Singh on an annual tribute of Rs. 8 lakhs.[33] By the time of Plassey, despite incessant antagonism and constant resistance of Nawab, Raja Balwant Singh extended his sway to 96 *parganas*.[34] Quite apart from the inherited 18 *parganas*, Raja Balwant Singh acquired many *parganas* some of which are enumerated below:[35]

Sircar Chunar

1.	Agory Bijeygar, a hill zamindary to Rajpoots	70,312
2.	Singrory, another hill zamindar	4,109
3.	Bhagwut, or Pattuta to an Afghan zamindar	62,203
4.	Lutteefpoor, in zamindarry to Syed	40,975
5.	Bhooly, zamindary of Daim Khan Afghan	80,609
6.	Dhoos, farmed by Tokrai Amroro Sing	45,112
7.	Mowy....Ditto....	51,745
8.	Muchwar, Mowary	80,307
9.	Nerome Ram Town Sing	96,208
10.	Mehach or Danapoor, Baboo Doorybzey Sing	61,905
11.	Burhul, farmed to Dhoonda Baghet	35,107
12.	Ragoopoor, or Ramnagur	60,300
13.	Havilla Chunar in several villages	26,572
14.	Kera Mungrove, formerly belonging to Chainpoor Circar, Shahabad Soobah Behar, now attached to Chunar	1,15,300

Sircar Ghazipur

Obtained from Shuja-ud-Dowla, first in farm, then in zamindary, through means of Raja Beni Bahadur, on the dismission of Fazl Ali

15. Haville and the town of Ghazipur, Mehal And Sayer to Aga Mehndi	1,51,000
16. Seydpoor Phittree to Oussan Sing, fixed 73,000	92,700
17. Behryabad to Bukhshi Sadanund now to Beniram Pundit	20,000
18-21 Shadiabad, Bhadowan, Zahoorabad and Bahadurgunge	1,90,000
22-27 Belliah, Pachooter, Lucknisser, Kharced, Secondapoor, Gossah, in five pergs. The three last formerly annexed to Townpoor, and now altogether composing Meer Serif Aly's districts	5,36,000
28. Zemaneah	2,00,000
29. Chounsah	1,15,000
30. Kurindah	58,000
31-32 Gundeah and Dahnea	50,000
33-34 Kerryat Pallee and Mahomedabad	1,25,000
35. Chandpore, formerly in Circar Townpoor, to Baboobeem Sing's	18,000
36. Boorgan and Burragong Nugrah Zemindarry	25,000

Sicar Townpoor

37-41. Havillee, the city, Hajeypoor, Mulhee, and Seopoor, five Mehals obtained from Safdar Jang	3,00,000

Sicar Allahabad

42-51 Canteel-Bijeypoor, the Zemindary of Lal Gobind Jeet, subdivided into 10 mehals, of which some belonged to Chunar, Suckteesgur, Chowrasse Agory, Chenahi, and c. obtained from Sujah-ud-Dowla, on the death of Mohammad Kuli Khan, through Beni Bahadur	5,23,212
Total acquisitions of Raja Balwant Singh	Rs. 32,34,676

It also include the *pargana* of Kheirapur, subdivided into five tuppahs of Chowrassi, Dia, Gowherar, Tandeh, and Budooghur, of which part to Chunar, formerly taken in farm from Shah Alam, whole in possession of Allahabad, now transferred to the *Vizier*. Its total revenue collection was Rs. 2,52,207.

By the sixth decade of the eighteenth century, the emergence of East India Company from a trade to political power brought about great political changes in northern India, which immensely escalated the prominence of Benares and its Raja, as the territory was contiguous to both the powers- the Oudh in the west and English in the east. Moreover, it was mere 60 miles beyond the limits of the English authority,[36] with *Caramnassa* river as the line of demarcation. The tremendous potential of Raja Benares was first perceived by the English in 1757, when Monsr. Law,[37] Chief of French factory at Kasimbazar in 1756, managed to cross Bihar and seek the protection of Raja Benares, in spite of English attempt to distress and impede his way.[38] It was a time when the Emperor was a mere puppet in the hands of the *Vizier* Gazi-ud-din and Nawab Oudh was too sharing overt hostile relations with the *Vizier*. On the other side, the English had proved their military power by firm possession of Bengal Province. Raja Balwant Singh was profoundly cognizant that observing these perplexing affairs at Imperial court, if the English planned to extend towards west, then he would be the first to confront with them and indubitably, the immense riches of Benares would entice them for loot and plunder. All these escalating threats roused his profound interest in Patna, which becomes more apparent by the letter of Mir Jaffer's agent at the Court of Shuja-ud-Daula to Umar Beg Khan, "The Raja Benares has wrote several times to Shuja-ud-Dowla to enter the country or that Patna is empty."[39]

Shahzadah Ali Gauhar commenced his eastern expedition in 1759 and was joined by Quli Khan. In this expedition Raja Benares offered him Rs. 2 lakh[40] and any further assistance in his power,[41] and *Shahzadah* conferred him with *Khil'at*,[42] but the Raja did not join the march because of the menace from the Nawab, who also had not joined the expedition. This proved to be a sagacious decision as the Nawab availing himself of the absence of Quli Khan took the possession of Allahabad fort. Quli Khan, aloof the Emperor in between and instantly moved towards Allahabad, but was impeded in Benares as Shuja-ud-Daula all directed his deputy Beni Bahadur and Raja Balwant Singh to prevent him from crossing Benares. The joined army was deployed about two *cosses* below Ramnagar. Quli Khan after making abortive attempt to cross *Ganges* encamped in Saidraja where Raja Balwant Singh's army narrowly watched him and any person crossing *Ganges* was being plundered. Quli Khan applied both the Raja's to allow him to move towards Allahabad with few servants, which was accepted after the Nawab's assent, but the Nawab also directed them to seize all the effects of Quli Khan, plunder his camp and strip of his troops.[43] Balwant Singh's sagacity and farsightedness saved him from this fate.

During the expedition of Emperor Shah Alam II in 1761, the English asked Raja Benares to assist Major Carnac otherwise, his territories, too, would suffer the same harm that was previously done to Bengal and Bihar.[44] Though the Emperor's eastern expeditions abortive, but the upper echelon in Fort William were cognizant of an impending war with the Nawab and perceived that it would be an arduous task for them to extend their political leverage beyond Bengal and Bihar without the support of the Raja who was a "man of wide range of experience and broad horizons." They wanted to make optimum use of the overt hostility between the Raja and the Nawab, as articulated in a letter to Carnac, "In case of your carrying the war into Shuja-ud-daula's country, we believe that Balwant Singh, the Raja of Benares, will gladly join you."[45]

The political affairs became more perplexing when Mir Qasim, the deposed *Subedar* of Bengal decided to move towards Benares at the invitation of the Nawab Oudh.[46] Captain Jennings, who was camped at Sasaram, candidly expressed his inability to shun the army of Mir Qasim from joining the *Vizier*, "Upon enquiry I find there is no way of preventing this Party but by crossing *Caramnassa*, their rout being round the hills through Balwant Singh's Country which brings them to the Western gate of Rotas Gur without entering the Nawab dominions."[47]At this political spectrum in the end of 1763, Raja Balwant Singh was in as situation, in which he found himself seized by unavoidable danger prudent and felt the imperative need for doing something prudently were as on one side English had deployed an army at the banks of *Caramnassa*, which included 800 infantry rank and file, 140 artillery,[48] 140 cavalry and on the other side Mir Qasim had entered Benares with an army of 15,000 men and prodigious wealth.[49] Turning against any power meant a direct confrontation and he would be the first and foremost to suffer the casualty.

It was for this reason that when 150 Frenchmen headed by Serjeant Delawar deserted the English army, they were supported and guided by the Raja to join the Nawab, in spite of his assurance to Captain Jennings to return those deserters.[50] Mir Qasim entered into an agreement with the *Vizier*[51] and in March 1764, the joint army of Shuja-ud-daula, Emperor and Mir Qasim commenced the march towards the English army.[52] Where on one hand the Nawab wanted the revenue of Bengal and Bihar to be paid to the Emperor, the English wanted that the deserters should be handed over to them.[53] At this juncture, the English policy was very lucidly enunciated in one of the letters of Raja Shitab Roy, which was passed by Fort William authorities, "We think it our duty to form against him (Shuja-ud-daula) all the enemies we possibly can that the proposed alliance with Balwant Singh will, therefore, be a proper measure and prove as well now as in all time to come a strong barrier and defence to the Bengal Provinces."[54] In March, Fort William authorities gave their assent to the proposal of Major Carnac to enter into a treaty with Raja Balwant Singh and "to protect and maintain Balwant Singh's independence both now and hereafter."[55] The Bengal Nawab and Raja Benares were already in negotiations and on March 18, 1764, the Raja consented to enter into an agreement with him on the condition that the territory, which he hold under Shuja-ud-daula would be granted to him as *jagir* and it must be endorsed by Carnac on behalf of the English Company.[56]

With the march of joint army of the Emperor, the Nawab and Mir Qasim, Raja Balwant Singh fled to Lateefpur fort and sent Lal Khan to negotiate with the Nawab. The Nawab's army was preparing a bridge across *Ganges*.[57] Major Carnac knew that the entry of Nawab's army in Benares would encumber their negotiations with Raja Benares. In the meantime, the bridge over the river *Ganges* broke down, which gave them enough time to negotiate. This breakdown of bridge was not by fluke, but premeditated. This can be determined by the fact that Fort William explicitly consented to the Major that Nawab's army should be prevented from crossing the river by destroying any bridge being constructed.[58] The Nawab's army reached Benares on March 26, 1764, and encamped at *Balwar Ghat*, on the banks of *Ganges*, waiting for the Raja's appearance.[59] The significance of Raja's support for the Nawab can be assessed by the fact that Nawab sent his son to persuade the Raja. This made the Raja to appear surrounded by two-three thousand horses and several thousand men of infantry.[60]

While the Nawab was waiting for the Raja, the Emperor wrote to the President that he was not in favour of marching in support of Mir Qasim, but "was unable of himself to prevent it."[61] It can be envisaged how arduous it was for the Raja to save himself from being sandwiched between the two opposing powers on both sides of his territory along with the armed forces, when the Emperor himself was impelled to march forward with one power and ready to give his tacit support to the other. The English army encamped at Sasaram in March,[62] retired towards *Sone* in April because of the dire need of grain.[63] At this Fort William authorities pointed him for not providing any satisfactory information from his side regarding the amount of stock of Provisions available in the city.[64] The upper echelon of the English Company were incessantly giving instructions to carry war into Shuja-ud-daula's country[65] that would not only break the supply line, but also induce Raja Balwant Singh to come to Company's interests overtly. Major Carnac never abided by these instructions. It seems that his ulterior reason was to confirm Balwant Singh to their side as he had joined the Nawab's army even after an agreement with the English.

Major Carnac and Bengal Nawab sent Mir Ashruff, Shahbauz Cawn and Mir Ahmed Ali to induce the Raja to join them. The Nawab and Mir Qasim received the information of these clandestine negotiations[66] Despite this, they adopted no stringent measure against him, as they did not want to trigger the Raja to stand against them, thus making the circumstances favourable for the English. Under constraining circumstances, Raja joined the Nawab's army on April 23, 1764 at Daudnagar, situated on the bank of *Sone* with 2,000 horses and 5,000 soldiers.[67] On May 10, 1764, the English asked Carnac to send a Company to induce Raja Balwant Singh to join "their side and trouble Shujuddaula by jeopardizing his line of supply".[68] Where as on one side the Raja was in agreement with the Company, on the other, he was compelled to join the Nawab's army. The Nawab was always suspicious of him and even during the Buxar battle he directed him to remain along with his troops across the *Ganges* in Ghazipur. Thus during the battle, the Raja was at Amla, a village in *pargana* Mohammadabad of Ghazipur district[69] and remained inactive on the pretence of illness.[70]

Benares was very significant for the English because of plethora of wealth, as their military expenses doubled, imposing an enormous amount of Rs. 7 lakh monthly.[71] So Council ordered Officer- in-Commanding on June 11, 1764 to take possessions of Ghazipur and collect its revenue with strict orders "to prevent any ravages being committed on the Country or injuries being done to the inhabitants, on contrary, all manner of encouragement and protection be given in order to gain their affection."[72] On 23rd October the English inflicted a crushing defeat over the joint army in the battle of Buxar. Forthwith upon this, Raja Balwant Singh unequivocally proposed that if intended the English to take the possession of Shuja-ud-daula dominions, then Benares, Ghazipur, Jaunpur and Bijaigarh, the *Zamindary* might be given to him and also the management of Azamgarh and two or three of the districts paying customary rent,[73] on the same terms as he hold them under Shuja-ud-Daula and payment of revenue amounting to Rs. 24 lakhs per annum with Rs. 1,70,000 monthly installments.[74] Major Munro gave his assent to grant him *sunnud* and establish his authority in the territories under his jurisdiction until the conclusion of negotiation with the Nawab.[75]

The moot question is what prompted Major Munro to be so impetuous to accept everything that the Raja demanded in spite of Board's instructions not to repose any confidence in the Raja. The letters asserted, "With respect to Balwant Singh Rajah of Benares and zamindar of Gauzeepoor Country, the double part he acted in the beginning of the war sufficiently warns us to put no confidence in him and therefore if he has not already been permitted to join you or you have entered into no engagement with him we would have him dispossessed of his Country and his person if possible secured."[76] When the army encamped at Benares, Major Munro knew its immense wealth might tempt the sepoys. So he gave strict orders against pillaging or plundering the inhabitants.[77] At a time when Company was emerging as a political power, he did not want to create anti-feeling among the Hindus as the city was known for its antiquity and held sacred in the eyes of the whole country.[78]

The merchants of the city had promised to give him Rs. 4 lakhs for protection, which they accepted.[79] Thus, doing this where on one hand he would get money and confidence of the local inhabitants; he would also be able to get the support of the Raja. Moreover, the Emperor was still there at Benares.[80] When Munro reached Benares, he desired to meet Raja Balwant Singh, but latter refused to appear in person unless signed articles were not delivered to him. Major immediately sent the articles as it would be highly imprudent to leave a disgruntled Raja with 15-20,000 horses[81] at a place from where he could effortlessly break the line of communication and supply while the army would march to Allahabad.

It was an onerous task for the English to drive out the Raja because that would involve a protracted deal with him. At this juncture, when *Vizier* was reviving against the English with Pathans joining him and army totaling strength upto 30,000,[82] the English army would not be able to march forward to Chunar or Allahabad for the siege of the strategic forts that were still under the *Vizier*. How the English were impelled to accept Raja Balwant Singh with no viable alternative as had been candidly articulated by Major Munro in one of his letters, "...there are very few people in the country who had any appointments. But such as have been turn'd out formerly by Balwant Singh and have no weight in the Country or troops at Command, so that consequence of putting any of them as *Phousdars* or *Jemadars* to collect the revenue and assist the King against any of his enemies would be keeping the army here I don't know how long and would require at all time a stronger detachment of the troops remaining in the Country..."[83]

It was only after this above-mentioned letter of Major Munro that the Fort William authorities perceived the significance of Raja Balwant Singh and vested Munro with full authority to come in terms with Balwant Singh as he may deem prudent with instructions that the power and authority over the Raja and his territory be vested in the Company by *sunnuds* from the Emperor and the rents amasssed should be appropriated for the Company and wrote off from the Royal Book of Revenue. The letter of Munro suddenly brought a perceptible change in the opinion of the English authorities sitting at Fort William and London regarding Raja Balwant Singh and Benares. Immediately, they thought it prudent to intervene in the matter with high hands. Earlier the upper echelon had no objection to accepting the ransom of Rs. 4 lakhs from the inhabitants of the Benares and regarded it as a "reward to the Army" and "compensation for the Loss", but now they changed their stand regarding the people of Benares and instructed Major Munro that "no further considerations of this kind should be demanded from the inhabitants or expected by the army but every care taken to conciliate the affection of the people. We would consider the Country not as a conquest but belonging to the King whom we have engaged to support against the common enemy."[84]

Moreover the demands of the Raja was highly recommended by none other than the Emperor himself who expressed that the Raja would never present himself without the attainment of his desires and completion of his business[85] and also advised the English that "he once got Beni Bahadur and Balwant Singh to come in, Vizier would leave the Country immediately and never make any head again if once we get Iliabad and Chunar Fort..."[86]

After the acceptance of all demands, Raja Balwant Singh was asked to give the first collection of revenue amounting Rs. 7 lakh[87] to the Emperor on account of having no other support.[88] It was only after the receipt of the articles that Balwant Singh stopped the grain supply line to the Chunar fort and ordered his people to seize *Vizier*'s troops within Benares and also assured that he would proceed with the detachment to seize Chunar whenever called.[89] The Emperor sent a signed article to the English by which Benares was given to the Company in same manner as it was under *Vizier* as compensation of the expenses of the war and consequently, the Raja was to pay the revenue to the Company and the amount would be expunged from the Book of Royal revenue.[90] Major Munro made an agreement with Raja Balwant Singh appointing him in Benares on payment of same annual amount to the company as was being paid to the *Vizier*.[91]

On 5th January Raja Balwant Singh fled to Lateefpur as on the very next day i.e. 6th January Major Munro, with whom he was in agreement, was replaced by Carnac and the command of the army devolved upon Fletcher.[92] Another reason for the Raja to go to Lateefpur was the *Vizier*'s proffer of friendship to the English through a letter which states, "If the English will now enter into friendship with me, I will immediately dismiss their enemies and withdraw my protection from them and this friendship being confirmed, I will join with the English army…"[93] The Raja was full of apprehensions and speculations of the oscillating political conditions as apparently mentioned by General Carnac in his letter, "… Balwant Singh's having eloped from our army and desiring an explicit account of our plan and views in the prosecution of the war that he regulate his conduct accordingly but offering it at the same time as his opinion that we have engaged ourselves too far with the King unless it be our determined resolution to pursue Shuja-ud-daula to the utmost and to decline all further reconciliation with him."[94] Forces were sent under Major Stibbert to besiege Chunar on 22nd January and Major Fletcher himself marched towards Allahabad on 24th January. Knowing the support of the Raja was indispensable, Major Fletcher asked the Emperor to write to the Raja to join the English and left one and a half battalion for protection of Benares.[95]

Raja Balwant Singh not only got an assurance from the English, but an agreement was signed on 6th February by the Emperor and sealed by Mr. Marriott (English Chief of Benares) and Major Fletcher stating, "Whatever may be conducive to the daily increase of his (Balwant Singh) honour and reputation shall be done. This we swear to by God and the Prophet Jesus. This agreement shall by no means be deviated from."[96] Soon, Balwant Singh sent an army under the command of his brother to join the Imperial troops in surrounding the fort[97] and another under Babu Samir Singh, his brother's son to Allahabad.[98] On 8th February, both the forts surrendered.[99] Though the Raja's force assisted the English army still Fort William authorities instructed General Carnac and Mr. Marriott to keep strict eye upon his conduct and correspondence and that he may not be allowed to maintain such a body of forces that may prove detrimental to the English in any occasion.[100]

Though, every step of Raja Balwant Singh was being noticed by the English, but they never looked forward to adopt any measure against him even after the surrender of forts, as it would take a protracted period for completion of actions and, in the meantime, this would create disturbances in that corner, while the army was planning to march to Lucknow and if Shuja-ud-Daula again turned against the English, then Balwant Singh's situation would automatically place him between their Provinces and the army. It is of decisive importance to note that the English could never ignore the colossal amount they were receiving from Benares that was fixed as follows:

Total amount of the revenue	Rs. 20,86,607
Sundrys to be deducted	
Pymahly or destruction occasioned by the troops of Shuja-ud-Daula in spoiling the crop	Rs. 2,00,000
Nuncar or allowance of his zemindary	Rs. 15,800
Total (Rs. 20,86,607-Rs. 2,15,800)	Rs. 1870,807

Sundry Expenses deducted till the resolution of the Board is known on the following heads:-

Jagheer of Boydway	Rs. 1,35,000
Kirat to sundry people agreeable to their *sunnuds*	Rs. 93,306.10
Total	Rs. 2,28,306.10

Total revenue to be paid *Hussun* Rs. 16, 42,500.6 in monthly installments of Rs. 1, 36, 875 and 6 *anna* in the last month.[101]

The Fort William authorities themselves expressed their need of money in a letter to General Carnac stating, "We are glad to find payments already made from Balwant Singh collections, proved so reasonable, a supply, but as it appears we may still continue in want of money."[102] Raja Balwant Singh sent an *arzee* to Fort William requesting that as far as his districts extend, no other person should be placed to interfere in his business.[103] How much the Raja was important for the English at the time of agreement when they were still in hostility with the *Vizier* can be aperantly observed in the Consultation of April 18, 1765 of Fort William where on one hand they instructed General Carnac to keep strict vigilance over Balwant Singh's conduct and correspondence and on the other side, they had given up the articles amounting to Rs. 2, 28, 306.10 (*Jagheer* of *Boydway*-135000 and *Kirat* and allowance Rs. 93306,10) which was earlier left to be determined by Fort William.[104] East India Company was basically a trading Company whose every policy and course of action was mostly guided by the monetary factors and at a time when they were going through pecuniary exigencies on account of the war, giving up their claim over such a substantial amount was only "in hopes of making it his (Balwant Singh) interest to remain faithful by the advantages he will reap from his connection with us the security that We look for from extending our frontiers being great object than any increase of our revenues."[105]

Despite stringent instructions of Board against pillaging, the sepoys could not shun themselves from the enticing wealth of Benares city as Clive himself confessed to the Court of

Directors, "How much must the expectations of your army be raised, when they are suffered, without control, to take possession for themselves, of the whole booty, donation, money and plunder, on the capture of a city. This, I can assure you, happened at Benares..."[106]

The Court of Directors repudiated the transfer of Benares and Ghazipur because their policy was not to extend the possessions of the Company.[107] Moreover, by taking the possession of Benares, high revenue producing region, they did not want to give the Nawab any reason to revive against them, as articulated by the Court of Directors in a letter, "... the war with Shuja-ud-Daula ended so conformable to our wishes. We always esteemed the power of that Soubah the strongest barrier we could have against the invasions of the northern powers, and of the Morattas which have so long laid desolate the northern provinces..."[108] Carnac, too, articulated in a dispatch of April 1, 1765, "the security we look for from extending our frontier was at this time, a greater object (or the Company) than any increase of our revenues."[109] Eventually, after protracted negotiations, treaty of Allahabad was executed between the Nawab Shuja-ud-Daula of Oudh, Nawab Nundjum-ud-daulah of Bengal and the English Company at Allahabad on August 16, 1765 and sealed and approved by the Emperor. The articles apropos to Raja Balwant Singh are enumerated below:[110]

Article V -"His Highness Shuja-ud-dawlah engages in a most solemn manner to continue Balwant Singh in the zamindaries of Benares, Ghazeepur and all those districts he possessed at the time he came over to the late Nabob Jaffier Aly Cawn and the English on condition of his paying the same revenues as heretofore."

Article VII-"It being firmly resolved to restore to His Highness the country of Benares and the other districts now rented by Bulwant Sing, not withstanding the grant of the same from the King to the English Company, it is therefore agreed that they shall be ceded to His Highness in (the) manner following viz. They shall remain in the hands of the English Company with their revenue till the expiration of the agreement between

Bulwant Sing and the Company, being on the 27th of November next; after which His Highness shall enter into possession, the Fort of Chunar excepted which is not be evacuated until the 6th article of this treaty be fully complied with."

By this treaty, Benares was restored to Shuja-ud-Daula but Balwant Singh was to continue to rule within his territories with assured safety from Nawab's vengeance. The Court of Directors expressed their sheer gratification regarding the articles of the treaty concerning Balwant Singh, "We are equally pleased to see the care that has been taken of all those who showed their attachment to us, in the course of the war, Balwant Singh's joining us at the time he did was of signal service, and the Stipulation in his favour was what he was justly entitled to."[111] The Court of Directors wanted a buffer state between the Nawab and the English with a favourable Raja so that he could be used against the Nawab in case of any attack in future as the Nawab was still a great power and *Vizier* of the Empire. The English knew that the Nawab's obstinate hostility with the Benares Raja would always be propitious for them.

By giving Raja Balwant Singh the same status, which he had before the Buxar battle, the English not only assured amiable relations with the Raja but also procured adequate grounds to enter and intervene in the matters of the Nawab. Raja Shitab Ray articulated in his letter to Cartier, "The sole object of Lord Clive in concluding the Treaty which he did between the Vizier and Balwant was to place his *zamindary* under the Company's protection in order that since the boundaries of Behar and Benares are contiguous, it may prove serviceable to the English in times of need."[112] This treaty marked the inception of the legal entry of the English in Northern India. On the other hand, by taking Benares under direct administration they did not want to vex Nawab Shuja-ud-Daula, who was also *Vizir* of the Mughal empire and command enought political and religious sway and the Maratha power that were day-by-day enhancing their leverage in Delhi and had profound interest in Benares. Since the territory under Raja Balwant Singh was mentioned in the article, so it also curbed the limits of the ambitious Raja. Raja Balwant Singh still had covetous eyes over the Chunar fort and had, times, asked Mr. Marriott to handover the fort of Chunar but the Governor, as expected, doggedly rebuffed stating that he should not think of any such proposal and "Were the English thus to violate their engagements with the Wazir, what reliance could be placed upon them..."[113] The treaty replaced the Nawab's interference by the English interference in Benares.

In June 1766, Chapra Conference was held and was attended by Clive, Carnac, Nawab, Raja Balwant Singh, agent of the Emperor, and representatives of the Rohillas, the Marathas and the Jats.[114] Nawab showed his resentment towards the Raja and demanded Rs. 3 lakh as *peshkash* that was accepted by the English.[115] A covenant assuring non-intelference of the Nawab was signed and sealed. The English always had strict eye over the Nawab as he was in correspondence with the Marathas. Fort William informed to the Court in December 1767, "Altho we are induced to treat Shujah-Doula with great Delicacy and carefully to conceal every suspicion of fidelity, we think it requisite to observe his conduct with circumspection and check in the beginning those symptoms of Ambition that may in Time become dangerous."[116] All these prevailing circumstances made them to support the Raja and pay no heed to any grievances of the Nawab against him. On September 1, 1768, Shuja-ud-Daula complained Fort William that the Raja had not paid Rs. 3 lakhs as settled in the Chapra Conference, but the English immediately repudiated his demands on October 23, 1768, stating that "should this be a new Demand, we should not approve of it, as it is directly contrary to the Tenor of the Treaty, where it is particularly provided that no Increase whatever should be demanded by the Nawab on the Rent of Bulwand Sing's country."[117]

With the possible invasion of Mir Qasim, Sikhs and Marathas, the importance of Raja Balwant Singh immensely increased, which can be envisaged by the fact that they regarded Raja's loyalty "clearer than the sun" and their alliance with him "one in a thousand." The Raja was asked to report precise information regarding the movements of Mir Qasim, Sikhs, Marathas, and the attitude of Allahabad and Faizabad courts and was authorized to correspond directly with Cartier. The Raja was directed to augment his troops and collection of war material and to enter into negotiations with neighbouring Rajas through whose territories the enemy was likely to pass.[118] Instantaneously, the Raja reported all the information required by the English about the enemy and his intercourse with Rajà Hindu Pat, principal *zamindar* of Bundelkhand. He assured to oppose any passage of enemy in Bengal and the safety of his frontier by the service of 3,000 horses and 1,000 infantry, which could further be augmented by including personnel engaged in police work.[119] The Nawab, who was always vexed by the Raja, sent 200 sepoys to Benares to oppress the inhabitants and merchants. On complaints preferred by Raja Balwant Singh about incessant oppression since last two months,[120] the English instantly asked the Nawab to cease any such oppression and recall his sepoy.[121]

The extension of the Raja's sway from inherited 18 *parganas* to 96 *parganas* itself manifests his tenacious will, political ambitions and sagacity. Raja Balwant Singh was precisely and with great circumspect walking on a difficult tightrope where any decision could be perilous for him and Benares. He tried to balance both the powers anyhow, as his guiding principle was to maintain his authority and independence of Benares and protect it from being sandwiched between the two. It was not only the time but also the Raja's sterling qualities that increased his prominence. It was his political astuteness that though both Nawab and English were suspicious of him and desired to replace him still they were impelled to accept him as the Raja of Benares. The security guaranteed by the English to the Raja in 1765 gave them a sufficient ground to interfere in the Nawab's matter. The events mentioned in chapter four would more lucidly manifest how the English used this treaty to grab every opportunity in increasing their influence in the politics of northern India.

References

1. Mill, James, *History of British India*, Vol. II, Associated Publishing House, New Delhi, 2nd reprint, 1978, p. 817.
2. *History of the Province of Benares, op.cit.*, p. 3. Gangapur is 7 miles south-west of Benares. The remains of the mud fort had been in 2008, bulldozed for construction of a Medical College.
3. Fisher and Hewett, *Statistical, Descriptive and Historical Account of North Western Provinces of India*, Vol., XIV, Part I, Benares, North Western Provinces and Oudh Government Press, Allahabad, 1884, p. 106.
4. Crookes, W, *The Tribes and Castes of North Western Provinces and Oudh*, Vol. IV, pp. 1-2.
5. Qunungo, K.R., *Some Sidelights on the History of Benares*, Proceedings of the Indian Historical Records Commission, Vol. XIV, 1937, pp. 65-66.
6. Crookes, W., *The Tribes and Castes of North Western Provinces and Oudh*, Vol. IV.
7. Nevill, H.R., Gazetteer of Benares, Allahabad, 1909, p. 199.
8. Oldham, *op.cit.*, p. 100.
9. *Journal of Asiatic Society of Bengal*, The Bangash Nawabs of Farukhabad, A Chronicle (1713-1857), William Irwine, Part II, Vol. xlviii, 1878, pp. 75-80.
10. Srivastava, A.L., *The First Two Nawabs of Oudh*, Shiva Lal Agarwala and Co. Ltd, Educational Publishers, Agra, 1954, 2nd ed., p. 161.
11. *Journal of Asiatic Society of Bengal*, The Bangash Nawabs of Farukhabad, A Chronicle (1713-1857), William Irwine, Part II, Vol. xlviii, 1878, pp. 81-82.
12. *Ibid*, p. 87.
13. Srivastava, A.L., *The First Two Nawabs of Oudh, op.cit.*, pp. 166-67
14. Fisher and Hewett, *op.cit.*, p. 106.
15. Oldham, *op.cit.*, p. 101.
16. Fuhrer, A, *The Monumental Antiquities and Inscriptions in North Western Provinces and Oudh*, Indological Book House, Delhi, 1969, p. 212.
17. Srivastava, A.L. *Shuja-ud-daula*, Vol. I, Shiva Lal Agarwal and Company Limited, Delhi, 1961, p. 25.
18. FPD, 5 November 1781, No. 2, letter from Popham to Hastings.
19. Hodges, William, *Travels in India*, London, 1794, 2nd edition, p. 55. Pateeta was 4 miles north of Chunar and Latefpur 10 miles beyond in the same direction.
20. FPD, 18 October 1781, No. 10, letter from Warren Hastings to

Wheeler, 22 September 1781.

21. Srivastava, A.L. *Shuja-ud-daula, op.cit.*, p. 25.
22. Barnett, Richard.B., *op.cit.*, p. 39.
23. Srivastava, A.L. *Shuja-ud-daula, op.cit.*, pp. 26-27.
24. Hodges, William, *op.cit.*, p. 52.
25. Srivastava, A.L., *Shuja-ud-daula, op.cit.*, p. 25.
26. FPD, 22 April 1775, No. 2, Copy of the *farman*.
27. Fuhrer, A., *op.cit.*, p. 213.
28. Khairuddin, Fakhir, *op.cit.*, pp. 35-36.
29. *Ibid.*
30. Barnett, Richard, *op.cit.*, p. 47; also see Srivastava, A.L., *Shuja-ud-daula, op.cit.*, p. 31, mentions Balwant Singh paid Rs. 25 lakhs to the Nawab.
31. *Status of Maharaja of Benares*, Box 47, File 24, Department XIV Political, United Provinces, Proceedings 4, November 1907, p. 4, Regional Archives, Varanasi. This document mentions that Balwant Singh secured Badohi pargana in 1755 and half of it was given to him as jagir.
32. Barnett, Richard, *op.cit.*, p. 47.
33. Oldham, *op.cit*, pp. 91-92.
34. Fisher and Hewett, *op.cit.*, p. 106; also see *Seir Mutaqherin, op.cit.*, II, pp. 288-90.
35. Firminger, Walter Kelly, *Affairs of the East India Company* (Being the 5th Report from the SC of the House of Commons 28th July, 1812), Vol. II, B.R. Publishing Corporations, reprint 2001, pp. 469-70.
36. PD, letter from Clive to the Court, August 6 1757, National Archives of India (henceforth NAI).
37. Fort William-India House Correspondence, Vol. II, NAI, New Delhi, p. xxxiii.
38. PD, letter from Clive to Court, August 6, 1757.
39. Fort William-India House Correspondence, Vol. II, *op.cit.*, p. xxxiv.
40. Calendar of Persian Correspondence (henceforth CPC), Vol. I, No. 58, News from Lucknow, February 24, 1759, p. 5.
41. FPD, SC Pr., 15 January-2 November 1759, Vol. 10, letter dated September 6, 1759, pp. 85-86, NAI.
42. PD, letter to Court, March 12, 1759, enclosure No. 12.
43. Seid Gholam Hussein Khan, *Seir Mutaqherin*, II, Low Price Publication, New Delhi, 1990, pp. 317-324.
44. Letter to Raja Balwant Singh, February 12, 1761, No. 915, CPC.
45. FPD, SC Pr., letter from SC to Carnac, February 13, 1761.

46. Letter from Vizier enclosed in a letter from Shakiru-d-daulah, January 10, 1764, No. 2017, CPC, Vol. I.
47. FPD, Sec. Pr., January-July 1764, Vol. 3, letter from Jennings to President Vansittart, March 12, 1764, February 20, 1764, p. 77.
48. FPD, Sec. Pr., 8 December 1763-12 July 1764, Vol. 2, December 30, 1763, p. 12.
49. FPD, Sec. Pr., 8 December 1763-12 July 1764, Vol. 2, December 8, 1763, p. 2.
50. FPD, Sec. Pr., January-July 1764, Vol. 3, letter from Jennings to Board, March 1, 1764, pp. 64-65.
51. News from Benares, March 8, 1764, No. 2092, CPC, Vol. I,; also see *Seir Mutaqherin*, II, *op.cit.*, p. 524.
52. FPD, Sec. Pr., January-July 1764, Vol. 3, letter from Major Carnac to Fort William, March 26, 1764, p. 89.
53. FPD, Sec. Pr., 24 July- December 1764, Vol. 4, September 8, 1764, p. 518.
54. FPD, Vol. 3, letter from Raja Shitab Ray to Major Carnac, March 29, 1764, p. 97.
55. FPD, Sec. Pr., January-July 1764, Vol. 3, letter from Fort William to Major Carnac, March 29, 1764, p. 97.
56. FPD, Sec. Pr., January-July 1764, Vol. 3, March 29, 1764, letter from Carnac to Board, March 18, 1764; also see FPD, Sec. Pr., 24 July- December 1764, Vol. 4, Mir Ashraff's Narrative, October 11, 1764, p. 597.
57. FPD, Sec. Pr., January-July 1764, Vol. 3, letter from Major Carnac to Fort William, April 9, 1764, p. 112; another letter from Major Carnac, April 3, 1764, pp. 101-102.
58. FPD, Sec. Pr., January-July 1764, Vol. 3, letter from Fort William to Major Carnac, June 20, 1764, p. 298.
59. FPD, Sec. Pr., January-July 1764, Vol. 3, letter from Major Carnac to Fort William, April 9, 1764, pp. 112-113.
60. Seir Mutaqherin, *op.cit.*, pp. 25-26.
61. FPD, Sec. Pr., January-July 1764, Vol. 3, letter from Emperor to President and Council, April 3, 1764, p. 108.
62. Letter from Raja Shitab Ray, March 17, 1764, No. 2114, CPC, I.
63. FPD, Sec. Pr., January-July 1764, Vol. 3, letter from Major Carnac to Fort William, April 16, 1764, p. 117.
64. FPD, Sec. Pr., January-July 1764, Vol. 3, letter from Fort William to Major Carnac, May 10, 1764, p. 176.
65. FPD, Sec. Pr., January-July 1764, Vol. 3, letter dated March 29,

1764, p. 99.

66. FPD, Sec. Pr., 24 July- December 1764, Vol. 4, Mir Ashraff's Narrative, October 11, 1764, p. 597.
67. FPD, Sec. Pr., January-July 1764, Vol. 3, letter From Major Carnac to Fort William, April 26, 1764.
68. FPD, May 10, 1764, letter from Board to Carnac, May 10, 1764.
69. FPD, Sec. Pr., January-July 1764, Vol. 3, letter from Resident at Durbar to Fort William, June 29, 1764.
70. Letter from Khiali Ram to Raja Shitab Ray, No. 2459, CPC, I.
71. FPD, Sec. Pr., 24 July- December 1764, Vol. 4, letter dated July 24, 1764, p. 428.
72. FPD, Sec. Pr., January-July 1764, Vol. 3, letter dated June 11, 1764, p. 261.
73. FPD, Sec. Pr., 24 July- December 1764, Vol. 4, Translation of proposal from Raja Balwant Singh to Munro, November 21, 1764, p. 716.
74. FPD, Sec. Pr., 24 July- December 1764, Vol. 4, Translation of letter from Raja Shitab Ray, November 21, 1764, p. 717.
75. FPD, Sec. Pr., 24 July- December 1764, Vol. 4, Munro's reply to Raja Balwant proposal, November 21, 1764, p. 716.
76. FPD, Sec. Pr., 24 July-December 1764, Vol. 4, Instructions to Major Munro for further operations of the army, November 6, 1764, p. 661-63.
77. FPD, Sec. Pr., 24 July-December 1764, Vol. 4, letter from Major Munro to Vansittart, President Council dated November 22, 1764, December 6, 1764, p. 732.
78. FPD, Sec. Pr., 24 July-December 1764, Vol. 4, Instructions to Major Munro for further operations of the army, November 6, 1764, p. 663.
79. FPD, Sec. Pr., 24 July-December 1764, Vol. 4, letter from Major Munro to Vansittart, President Council, November 22, 1764, December 6, 1764, p. 732.
80. Letter from Major Munro to the King, November 16, 1764, No. 2474A, CPC,I.
81. FPD, Sec. Pr., 24 July-December 1764, Vol. 4, letter from Major Munro to Vansittart, President Council, November 22, 1764, December 6, 1764, p. 732.
82. *Ibid*, pp. 733-34.
83. FPD, Sec. Pr., 24 July-December 1764, Vol. 4, letter from Major Munro to Vansittart, President Council, November 22, 1764,

December 6, 1764, pp. 734-35.

84. FPD, Sec. Pr., 24 July-December 1764, Vol. 4, letter from Fort William to Major Munro, December 6, 1764, pp. 739-43.
85. Calendar of Persian Correspondence, *op.cit.*, letter from the Emperor to Major Fletcher dated February 13, 1765, No. 2556, p. 379.
86. FPD, Sec.Pr., 24 July-December 1764, Vol. 4, letter from Fort William to Major Munro, December 6, 1764, p.739.
87. FPD, Sec. Pr., 24 July-December 1764, Vol. 4, letter from Messrs. Billers and Dacres to Fort William, dated December 31, 1764, p. 789.
88. FPD, Sec. Pr., 24 July-December 1764, Vol. 4, letter from Messrs. Billers and Dacres to Fort William, dated December 27, 1764, p. 786.
89. FPD, Sec. Pr., 24 July-December 1764, Vol. 4, letter from Munro to Vansittart dated November 22, 1764, December 6, 1764, p. 734.
90. FPD, Sec. Pr., 24 July-December 1764, Vol. 4, translation from Persian-The Article mentioned in the letter to be executed by the King, December 6, 1764, pp. 745-46.
91. FPD, Sec. Pr., 24 July-December 1764, Vol. 4 letter from Messrs Billers and Dacre to Fort William, December 27, 1764, pp. 785-86.
92. FPD, Sec. Pr., 3 January-29 April 1765, Vol. 6, letter from Fletcher to Fort William, January 6, 1765, January 21, 1765.
93. FPD, Sec. Pr., 3 January-29 April 1765, Vol. 6, letter from Shuja-ud-daula to Munro, January 3, 1765, January 17, 1765, p. 11.
94. FPD, Sec. Pr., 3 January-29 April 1765, Vol. 6, letter from Major Carnac to the Council, January 5, 1765, pp. 36-37.
95. FPD, Sec. Pr., 3 January-29 April 1765, Vol. 6, letter from Fletcher to Fort William, January 23, 1765, February 4, 1765, p. 77; also see letter from Major Fletcher to King, January 23, 1765, February 28, 1765, No. 2573, CPC, I.
96. Letter from Major Fletcher to King, February 6, 1765, February 28, 1765, No. 2584 and Agreement with Raja Balwant Singh, No. 2584A, CPC, I.
97. Letter from the King to Major Fletcher, February 28, 1765, No. 2583, CPC, I.
98. Letter from Raja Balwant Singh to Major Fletcher, February 28, 1765, No. 2585, CPC, I.
99. FPD, Sec. Pr., 3 January-29 April 1765, Vol. 6, letter from Stibbert

to Fort William, February 8, 1765, February 19, 1765 and letter from Fletcher to Fort William, February 8, 1765, February 19, 1765, pp. 129-130.

100. FPD, Sec. Pr., 3 January-29 April 1765, Vol. 6, letter from Fort William to General and Mr. Marriott, April 18, 1765, pp. 291.
101. FPD, Sec. Pr., 3 January-29 April 1765, Vol. 6, Account of the revenue of Balwant Singh, Fort William, March 21, 1765, Statement No. 1 given by Balwant Singh under his seal, p. 244.
102. FPD, Sec. Pr., 3 January-29 April 1765, Vol. 6, letter from Fort William to General Carnac, March 21, 1765, p. 237.
103. FPD, Sec. Pr., 3 January-29 April 1765, Vol. 6, Account of the revenue of Balwant Singh, Fort William, March 21, 1765, Statement No. 6 given by Balwant Singh, p. 249.
104. FPD, Sec. Pr., 3 January-29 April 1765, Vol. 6, Consultation of Fort William, April 18, 1765, p. 291.
105. *Ibid.*
106. PD, letter from Clive to the Court, September 30, 1765.
107. PD, letter from Court Fort William, December 24, 1765.
108. PD, letter from Court to Fort William, May 17, 1766, para.6.
109. SC, 1 April 1765, SC to Carnac and Marriott, April 1, 1765.
110. Aitchison, C.U., *A Collection of Treaties, Engagements and Sanads relating to India and Neighbouring Countries*, Mittal Publications, Delhi, 1983, p. 99.
111. PD, letter from Court to Fort William, 17 May 1766.
112. Letter from Raja Shitab Ray, No. 377, September 21, 1770, CPC, III.
113. Letter to Raja Balwant Singh, October 31, 1765, No. 2733, CPC, I.
114. PD, letter from Fort William to Court, September 8, 1766; also see Srivastava, A.L., *Shuja-ud-daula*, Vol. II, *op.cit.*, pp. 27-32.
115. Letter No. 741,CPC, II; also see Phairuddin, Fakhir, *op.cit.*, p. 53.
116. PD, letter from Fort William to Court, December 16, 1767.
117. Letter No. 1108, CPC, II.
118. Letter to Raja Balwant Singh, No. 97, February 22/23, 1770, CPC, III.
119. Letter from Raja Balwant Singh, No. 128, March 16, 1770, CPC, III.
120. Letter from Raja Balwant Singh, No. 121, March 14, 1770; No. 161, April 7, 1770, CPC, III.
121. Letter No. 154, April 1770, CPC, III.

Chapter 4

Raja Chait Singh
Transfer of Benares to East India Company

Raja Balwant Singh throughout his life span struggled to make Benares less and less dependent on the Nawab, but during the fag end of his life he was fettered by grave illness and the question of succession assumed serious proportion and was constantly pertaining him. He was a man of great farsightedness and knew pretty well that both the Nawab and the English would make continued endeavours to penetrate into the internal affairs of Benares, and, therefore, his successor would need to walk a more difficult tightrope than what he did during Buxar battle. In the absence of male issue from his wife Rani Gulab Kunwar the succession issue was all the more exacerbated and he had three options before him for determining the succession.

1. Mahipnarain, the son of his daughter, who was married to a *zamindar* of Pindra named Bariar Singh.
2. Raja Chait Singh, son of Raja Balwant Singh from his Rajput wife Pannakunwar. She was a daughter of a *zamindar* of Bijaigarh in Mirzapur district.
3. Muniyar Singh, grandson of Mansaram's brother Daya Ram and an adopted son of Raja Balwant Singh.

Realizing the imminence of death, he wrote a letter to the English just prior to his death on August 23, 1770,[1] expressing his desire to lead a retired life in Benares and solicited Governor's favour to be extended to his son Chait Singh, who was now mature enough to attend to state affairs.[2] But the royal family and *Brahmans* bolstered the case of Maheep Narain, as he was the grandson of *Brahman* wife Rani Gulab Kunwar.

The demise of the Raja created great political activeness in the neighbouring states. The English were cognizant that if they did not place Chait Singh on the same footing as his father the Nawab around promptly place his "rapacious favourite" that would prove highly detrimental to the commercial interests of the Company, as their Europe an exports as well as the articles of trade from these provinces hinges on the treatment of the Mirzapur and Benares merchants. The most experienced people of Patna, too, opined that there would be decline in prosperity if Benares is "left to the uncontrolled disposal of Shuja Dowla" and their commerce with these regions would be much impeded.[3] The English had already experienced how worthwhile it was to maintain affable relations with Raja Balwant Singh considering Nawab and Maratha powers which have to be reckoned with, especially because the buffer *Zamindary* ruled by Raja Balwant Singh was of strategic importance to the English Army. The military power of Raja Benares could be used for the defense of their boundary without an iota of financial burden on the Company. Chait Singh solicited the Governor for his favour and protection[4]. Even James Alexander, Supervisor at Patna and Raja Shitab Ray, *Naib Nazim* of Bihar, expressed their overwhel-ming support for Chait Singh.[5] The English discerned that favouring Chait Singh 'in some measure independent of the Nabob' would prove serviceable to them in times of need.[6]

The English were fully aware of the fact that the Nawab would never acquiesce in giving Raja Balwant Singh's son the possession of Benares with the same authority "either in country or forces"[7] and "it was a delicate point to accomplish with the Vizier."[8] The English, ostensibly, supported Chait Singh's claim on two bases, first *Gentoo* laws, according to which right of inheritance belong to the issue of male line to "utter exclusion of that of the female"[9] and secondly, their principle that "when they form friendship with a person, they treat as friends his children and his children's children".[10] The Nawab did not want to dissipate the opportunity and decided to set out to settle the affairs in his favour. On 25th August he ordered Captain Harper to march with 19th battalion to Benares, which the Captain complied with to deviate him from taking any inimical measures unless the Company issues some orders.[11]

On 26th August, the Nawab ordered his minister Elich Khan to march to Benares with 800 cavalry to assure the inhabitants that "they need not be under any apprehension in consequence of the Rajah's death and also to prevent the family of Balwant Singh from desponding too much." Chait Singh along with his family fled to Lateefpur.[12] The English resolutely recommended conferring upon Chait Singh the territory of Raja Balwant Singh.[13] Their staunch support for Chait Singh was not merely because of being a frontier territory or commercial interests. It was the same time when the Marathas were escalating their leverage in Delhi and making the utmost endeavours to extend their power and authority. The English received an intelligence that the Emperor, influenced by "the insinuations of artful and designing men", had entered into an alliance with the Marathas and now intends to move to the capital to join the Marathas.[14] The Nawab, too, deviated from taking any stride against the English wishes because of escalating Maratha menace and the treaty of 1765 and 1768, by which Nawab and the English were bound for military assistance in case of any outside attack.

The Nawab planned to leave for Benares on 1st October as his tents were pitched on the road, but on resolute recommendation from the President he directed Harper to attend the conference between Elich Khan and Chait Singh regarding the fixation of *nuzzrana* and increase of revenue and defer his departure with an ostensible reason of wound on his leg and that the march of his retinue through the country might be detrimental to the new crop.[15] Elich Khan interceded with Chait Singh on behalf of the Nawab for more than a month[16] and demanded Rs. 20 lakhs as *nuzzrana* and increase of revenue by Rs. 5 lakh per annum. Chait Singh was determined not to accept any further demand of the Nawab as the English were in favour of his succession and the Nawab would never be averse to their wishes in the present political spectrum. For the English, "this matter was of utmost political import to the Company's affairs" and they could not admit of any delay, as "the neighbouring provinces are such commotion".[17] Eventually, on 8th October, with the arbitration of Harper, both reached to an amicable solution of revenue increase by Rs. two and a half lakhs per annum and 17 lakh as *nuzzrana*. This amount was to be paid in two installments—Rs. 10 lakhs immediately and remaining 7 lakhs in twelve months. After signing the agreement Chait Singh was delivered customary *khil'at* and elephant.[18]

The English policy was guided by the concurrent political developments in northern India and they endeavoured to settle the matter with the gratification of both the parties. Where, on one hand, they wanted an amiable person as Raja Benares, on the other hand, they could not nettle the Nawab and make conditions propitious for the Marathas as they had asked the Nawab to assist the Rohillas in expelling the Marathas.[19] Thus, the English were very silently preparing a confederation against the impending danger from the Marathas. On October 10, 1770, Chait Singh was fully vested with the power and authority held by his father. A salute of 15 guns was given by the artillery of the 19th battalion "in order to make the young man of more consequence in this Government and to convince the people that it is through your (English Governor) mediation he has attained to the succession."[20] The *Pottah* was issued by the Nawab in the name of Raja Chait Singh dated November 22, 1770, by which the new Raja was to pay annual revenue of *Benares Cum Sunna Rupees* 22, 48,449 in equal *kists* (instalments). The particulars of revenue to be paid by the new Raja as mentioned in the *Pottah* were as follows:

Revenue paid by Raja Balwant Singh:

Benares	Rs. 12, 00,607
Buddohy	Rs. 1, 30,000
Lucknesegur	Rs. 16,000
Bejeypoor	Rs. 2,00,000
Gazepoor	Rs. 5,00,000
Shadeyabad	Rs. 40,000
Total revenue	Rs. 20,86,607
Deduct nankar, half of the jaghire of Buddohy and Altemgah, etc.	Rs. 88,158
Net Revenue paid by Rajah Bulwunt Sing	Rs. 19,98,449
Increase settled with Rajah Cheyt Sing	Rs. 2,50,000
Net Revenue to be paid by Rajah Cheyt Sing	Rs. 22,48,449

Though the Governor had countersigned the agreement and also affixed his seal still he gave a separate written assurance to the Raja that if he would regularly pay the revenue to the *Vizier* "the Company will always attend to your welfare, and afford you their care and protection, and in the Agreements aforementioned there shall never be any breach or deviation."[21] The numerous multitude and gun salute was less in the respect of the new Raja and more to exhibit their influence in the region as alluded in a letter, "The Vizier's readiness in complying in this our earnest recommendation and request is a circumstance the more pleasing as it must give strength to the opinions of the several powers of Hindostan, of the strict friendship subsisting between us and the Vizier's having considered Captain Harper as a necessary witness to the negotiation carrying on between his agent Allage Cawn and the young Rajah Cheyt Sing will serve as a proof to the world, that he meant not to take any measures therein, that might give the least cause for suspicion of our part."[22] Even the Court of Directors were most gratified, "It affords us great satisfaction to find that the succession of the late Balwant Singh's son to the *zamindary* of Benares met with no opposition from the Vizier."[23]

Though Raja Chait Singh was invested with authority, he was in full apprehensions and trepidation. He gave affirmative response to the Nawab's invitation for the marriage of his son

Mirza Amany in November 1770, but evaded on ostensible grounds.[24] The Raja sent number of *arzis* and *nazr* to the Governor soliciting for a separate treaty with the English under the royal seal.[25] Probably, the Governor evaded responding to these *arzis* because of imminent meeting of the Nawab with General Barker in Benares to discuss on the escalating menace of the Marathas and Rohillas. The Nawab set out for this meet on February 1, 1771.[26] It was only after this meet that Governor decided to respond to the *arzis* of the Raja. He benignly rebuffed the solicited fresh treaty as his father had been promised for protection by the treaty of 1765. He assured that his engagements with the Nawab and the English would be conducive to the interest and welfare of the Raja. He sent a *khil'at* with an elephant through the Raja's *vakeel* Shaikh Ali Naqi.[27] On the advice of Harper the Raja met the Nawab on February 8,1771, in Phulpore, 10 *cos* from Benares where the Nawab bestowed on him *khil'at, jagir, sarpunch* and a sword. General Barker also reached Benares on 10th February.[28] On 20th February, the Nawab visited the Raja's palace at Ramnagar where he was presented with money, cloth, elephants, horses and jewels. The Nawab fastened his turban on the Raja's head and honoured him with a sword.[29]

The English refrained from getting into the intricate matters by evading to answer to the Raja's *arzis* because they received intelligence about clandestine negotiation between the Nawab and the Marathas where the former accepted to pay Rs. 80 lakh on the stipulation that he would get the possession of the country of the Rohillas and Kora and Allahabad.[30] The Marathas were grave peril for the Nawab until the negotiations were not productive and in any such case the English were the lone power from where the Nawab could get succour. The English were moving ahead with great circumspect to pervert the menace and not to exacerbate the difficulties. Fundamentally, both endeavoured to gratify each other, as both were in need of each other's support in these exigent circumstances. President Cartier asked the Raja to keep him precisely informed of events that happen in his quarter.[31] The Raja too was maintaining amiable relations with the English, as he was full of trepidation due to the Nawab. It was a time when volatile political equations were guided by the apprehension about the Marathas. Where, on one hand, the Raja was persistently paying the revenue to the Nawab, on the other hand,he also rendered many services to the English. Warren Hastings assumed the charge as Governor and President of the Bengal Council on April 28, 1772. The Raja sent a congratulatory letter and *nazr* of gold *mohurs* to the new Governor.[32] Hastings continued the policy of his predecessor and advised the Raja to follow his father's footsteps, "who was famous throughout India for his administrative ability, breadth of vision, and discernment".[33]

Discerning the intricate political state of affairs in northern India, the Court of Director in April 1771 directed the Bengal Council to procure the territory of Raja Balwant Singh for the provinces of Kora and Allahabad. They divulged motive behind the decision to the Council, "our frontiers would be more easily defended, a greater influence would be preserved by us over the neighbouring powers, and we might possibly be relieved from the necessity of keeping up so large and expensive a military establishment as we have at present in Bengal."[34] The Court of Director knew that complexities might crop up in negotiations, so they advised the Company servants to "avail themselves of the circumstances which may occur either in the situations, desires, projects, temper or wants of this prince" and recommend to seize "every opportunity which may offer for accomplishing by friendly negotiation so desirable an end."[35] These instructions manifest the avidity of the higher echelons to procure the Benares territory under their direct administration, whatever the circumstances may be, but prudently deviating from any direct confrontation with the Nawab.

The Bengal Council first mooted somewhat similar proposal in 1769[36] as the Emperor abandoned the possession of Kora and Allahabad to the Marathas, which the English assigned to him in 1765. It was suggested to sell them to the Nawab whose avidity to recover those ancestral dominions was well known.[37] The Council approbated Hastings negotiations with the Nawab at Benares and vested him with full authority. Hastings left Calcutta on June 24, 1773, accompanied by Middleton to meet the Nawab and reached Benares on August 19, 1773.[38] During the conference, Shuja-ud-daula was "inflexibly averse" to Hastings proposal of exchanging Benares for Kora and Allahabad. Even Hastings upheld this decision in his report that "if I insisted upon it, he had not the power to dispute and must of necessity submit but that he would never willingly consent to part with a span of his territory... he could have no reason to give up a valuable part of his country, with a certain revenue, for a district which even in time of peace would not yield him near so large net revenues as was paid him by Raja Chait Singh and in war or nothing besides his being continually exposed to the invasions of Mahrattas." Hastings could not repudiate such cogent reasons. Since his purpose was to confirm and strengthen the alliance between the Nawab and the Company, any further insistence upon it would have been productive of contrary effect and so he thought it prudent to drop the proposal.

The Nawab insisted to demand from Raja Chait Singh Rs. 10 lakhs and forts of Bidjeygur and Lateefpur. The Governor rebuffed the proposal stating that a treaty already exists between Clive and the Nawab including Raja Benares assuring protection to him and his family and stated that it had been "inviolably maintained by Lord Clive, Mr. Verelst and Mr. Cartier. If I would break them what faith would he himself place in my engagements with him." Hastings refused without cogitating as the English interest lies in the protection of the Raja from the Nawab. Hastings avowedly articulated, "His (Raja Chait Singh) country is a strong barrier to ours without subjecting us to any expense, and we may depend upon him as a sure ally, whenever we may stand in need of his services."[39] The Nawab asserted that the treaty was only with Raja Balwant Singh and never extended to the posterity. Hastings opined, "it is true did not mention Chait Singh by name or family of Balwant Singh but was certainly understood both by my predecessor in administrative and beyond Company themselves as including whole family and posterity of Balwant Singh."[40]

Hastings induced Nawab to confirm Benares in favour of

the Raja and his posterity on the same terms as was granted to Raja Balwant Singh in 1765. The Nawab acquiesce in confirming it as he had already given the Raja a *Pottah* in 1770 through solicitation of Captain Harper.[41] On September 6, 1773, *Kowlnama* or Agreement was conferred on Raja Chait Singh with assurance that "no increase shall ever hereafter be demanded, and if you remain firm and steady in your obedience and in the payment of your rents, no harm shall, by any means, happen to your *ryots* or country...this agreement is made between me and my heirs, and you and your heirs, and it shall never be deviated from." Hastings also gave a written assurance to Chait Singh on the same day that if he regularly paid the stipulated amount the Company would always afford their care and protection and there shall be no breach.[42]

Hastings proposed the Nawab for free trade, which the latter rebuffed resolutely. Hastings thought it imprudent to insist upon the demand as the same profit could be achieved by an agreement with the Raja for Mirzapur, the epicenter for the merchants of Bengal, Bihar, Deccan and other regions of Hindustan, was within Benares dominions.[43] Being a Governor General of a trade company, Hastings instantly availed himself of this opportunity and made an agreement with the Raja that articles of Broad cloth, copper and lead bought at the Company's sales should pass duty free through his territories to Mirzapur and on all other goods he should levy equal duties on all merchants European or Native or other indiscriminately.[44] Earlier the native merchants were levied double of the English. This equal duty, as seems, was not for equitable trade, but for general encouragement to the exports of Bengal goods and thus promoting Company's sales. These negotiations were focused to make the Raja less dependent on the Nawab, and more arduous for the Nawab to depose the Raja as the new *Kowlnama* was extended to his posterity.[45]

Raja Chait Singh desired that general residence of Europeans in his country should be prohibited and any particular person to whom an indulgence might be granted should be restricted to Benares. He also informed that Messrs Fowke, Motte and Scott had conducted themselves so entirely to his satisfaction that he had no objection to their residing in Benares. This request was put forward as Europeans employed forced labour without payment in the Raja's territories. Hastings promptly ordered the Europeans to quit by the year end, after which they would not be under Company's protection, and if proved refractory, they might be expelled by force. On September 10, 1773, both Nawab and Hastings departed from Benares.[46]

During the conference the Raja also agreed to Hastings's proposal to raise 500 horses for the Company's assistance. The amiable relation between Raja Chait Singh and Hastings continued unabated. The Raja rendered many services to the Bengal Government and even personal affairs of Hastings. Hastings formed a Body Guard at Benares in September 1773 with 50 troopers. By the end of the year, its strength was augmented by adding 50 horses supplied by the Raja and the establishment consisted of 1 Captain, 1 Lieutenant, 4 Sergeants, 6 *Duffedars*, 100 Rank and File, 2 Trumpeters, 1 *Farrier*. It was this Body Guard that later became the nucleus of President's Body Guard of the present day.[47] The Governor's prompt consideration of every grievance from the Raja manifests his importance in the eyes of the English. In November 1773, Raja Chait Singh complained to Hastings that Colonel Wilding and Colonel Muir had taken possession of few villages in Chunar. These places were not of much importance, for revenue collection hardly exceeds Rs. 1000/- annually, but it was immensely important for his prestige and solicited to give up those villages.[48] Even Hastings accepted that these villages were not included within the boundary of Chunar and directed Muir to restore them soon.[49]

Sidi Mohammad Basir Khan, at the Nawab's direction, took possession of 19 villages in Jaunpur and the *pargana* of Garwara, which was given to Raja Chait Singh by the Emperor himself for Rs. 1,75,000 annually. During the conference at Benares, the Nawab assured that those villages would continue under the Raja on the same terms. The Raja wrote to Hastings in 1774 that it had not yet been relinquished, and now the Nawab was demanding an increase of Rs. 75,000 more.[50] Hastings promptly asked the Nawab to restore the villages and that he should adhere to the terms of *Kowlnama* granted to the Raja in 1773.[51] The Nawab returned the *pargana* Garwara and 19 villages to please the Governor though it was of great advantage to him.[52]

The incessant amicable relations between the Raja and the English brought more and more acrimony between the Raja and the Nawab. Hastings was proceeding with great circumspection to widen the cleavage between the Nawab and the Raja to make space for the English and he knew the Raja could prove a barrier against the impending inroads of the *sanyasis* for which he had already demanded 500 horses under the command of Captain Toon in December 1773 on the payment of Rs. 20 per *sawar* per month.[53] In February 1774, Raja Chait Singh sent Hazi Nazib Ali Khan with 500 horses under Captain Toon and directed them to assert utmost in the Company's service.[54] In March 1775, when the Bengal government received intelligence of armed *sanyasis* proceeding towards Benares, they asked the Raja to make his utmost endeavour to oppose their entry in concert with Muir.[55] The Raja directed all *fauzdars* and *zamindars* on the frontier of the *zamindary* to keep vigilant eye over the movement of the *sanyasis* and to disseminate any information about their plans and movement, which forced the *sanyasis* to disperse.[56]

In June 1774 Shahab Khan, a dismissed *vakeel* of Raja Chait Singh, was granted *sunnud* of Jaunpur by Shuja-ud-dowla and further endeavoured to procure a *khil'at* from the King.[57] The Raja brought the matter under English consideration, after which Hastings wrote to the *Vizier* to promptly revoke the *sunnud*.[58] Though the Raja paid the revenue of the year 1181 *fasli,* still in November 1774 the Nawab demanded a *tunkaw* of Rs. 5 lakhs to be paid to the Company and deduct Rs. 50,000 from his monthly *kist*, till the sum was recovered. The Raja refused to pay the *tunkaw* unless he was assured that no further *tunkaw* would be demanded, but the Nawab rebuffed.[59] Later in January 1775 the Raja paid the amount to Motte on request of the Governor General and solicited him to ask the Nawab not to make any further demand.[60]

While the Raja was oscillating between the English and the Nawab, he was also facing escalating internal discontentment because of being an offspring of a *Rajput* lady. Moreover, the other two claimants were serious menace to him. Muniyar Singh harboured evil designs against the Raja and entered into a clandestine agreement with a man to give him Rs. 10,000 and two villages for the assassination of the Raja, but the collusion was exposed in June 1774, and Muniyar Singh fled to Durgakund.[61] Hastings wrote to Raja Chait Singh assuring Company's support against any evil designs fostered by Muniyar Singh.[62] The Raja invited prestigious public figures in the obsequial feast of his brother Sujan Singh's wife, but Ausan Singh rebuffed to come under the pretence of illness. The Raja, highly exasperated with his *dewan's* inexcusable conduct, summoned *durbar* next day, took the management of affairs in his control and established his full authority.[63]

Perceiving the impending danger, Ausan Singh entered into an agreement with Muniyar Singh in October 1774 and plundered some villages within the Raja's territory. The Raja, in retaliation, sent troops under his brother Sujan Singh and solicited Col. Muir for two companies and two guns[64] and with the assistance of the English troops, Muniyar Singh was defeated.[65] On this achievement, Raja Chait Singh sent a *nazr* of 21 gold *mohurs* to Hastings and latter on Raja's solicitation asked the Nawab not to give his protection to the rebels and to direct Nauroz Ali Khan, *amil* of Pratapgarh and *Naib Suba* of Allahabad to expel them from their districts.[66] The *Vizier* still continued to avail himself by encouraging the Raja's enemies and summoned Muniyar Singh from Allahabad and Ausan Singh from Bundelkhand. The Raja wrote to Hastings to use his leverage on the *Vizier* to desist him from motivating his enemies and expel them, as their presence impeded the work of collections,[67] but by the time there was demise of Shuja-ud-daula and was succeeded by his son Asaf-ud-daula.

The new Nawab pursued the same policy of his father as on March 15, 1775, Raja Chait Singh reported to Hastings that Muniyar Singh was still in service, and Ausan Singh had moved to Allahabad with an intention to harm two-three *mahals* from Nauroz Ali Khan, adjacent to the territory of the Raja. He solicited Hastings to write in his favour to the new Nawab.[68] Thus, during this time, very affable correspondence prevailed between Raja Chait Singh and Hastings. Every second of time, Raja Chait Singh received a staunch support from Hastings because the Governor did not want to squander any opportunity to procure Benares after the demise of Shuja-ud-daula, for which he was silently waiting since long.

Asaf-ud-daula imposed a *tunkaw* of Rs. 6 lakh on Raja Chait Singh to be paid to the Company. The Raja was cognizant of the fact that if he consented to pay the *tunkaw* it would be considered as a precedent and if in case he refused the demand he would come under Governor's vexation. Raja Chait Singh immediately brought the matter into the notice of the Bengal Council explaining that the previous demands of Rs. 5 lakh was discharged because of the Governor's pressure and he had raised the sum by loans with great difficulty and any further payment was beyond his power. He requested the Governor not to give consent to this *tunkaw* and ask the Nawab to desist from any such further demands.[69] The Bengal Council bolstered the Raja's case and not only wrote to the Nawab to deviate from making such demands, but also instructed Bristow, Resident in Oudh, to remonstrate to the Nawab against such proceedings that were contrary to the engagements with the Raja of which they were "the Guarantee".[70]

Bristow when intimated these instructions to the Nawab, the latter expressed his resentment at the Board's protecting the Raja on the ground that that Raja Chait Singh was his *zamindar* and he had the right to demand rents in advance, and Company was not authorised to make any representation to him. There was protracted conversation, in which the Nawab confessed that he had no means of discharging money due from him to the Company and last time the Raja had paid Rs. 5 lakh *tunkaw*. Bristow explained him that the Raja was induced to pay the last *tunkaw* and he did it to avoid any altercation and now the Nawab should not "by a repetition establish a precedent so disadvantageous to himself and contrary to the terms of the treaty." Due to the Company's pressure the Nawab assured not to impose *tunkaw* in future. Bristow lucidly expressed to him that "Board would never suffer the rights of their dependents to be infringed; Rajah Chyte Sing was to be considered in this light, and he was not to be put upon a footing with his other zamindars."[71] The Raja expressed the gratitude *tunkaw* just to oblige the Governor General, which the latter promptly accepted.[72]

In 1775, Raja Chait Singh lodged a complaint with Hastings about the loss of revenue due to the stationing of *harkaras* by Colonel Muir (officer commanding, the garrison of Chunar) in different *Chowkeys* (stations/posts) of Chunargur, Benares and Mirzapur to seize the cattle of Biharies laden with goods and brought them by road of Chunargur and levy duty on pilgrims who come to Benares to worship.[73] Hastings directed Colonel Muir to check no obstructions thrown in the way of the pilgrims.[74] On 19th June, Muir met Raja Chait Singh where latter admitted that he had brought these charges on misrepresentation of the facts by his officers and so the dispute was solved amicably.[75]

With the demise of Shuja-ud-daula's and accession by an effete Nawab Asaf-ud-daula circumstances became propitious for the Council and they decided to enter into a new defensive treaty putting forth the reason that the previous treaty expired with the demise of Nawab. The English were resolute to procure Benares under direct control and on February 13, 1775 the Council members had protracted deliberations on the question of Benares where Governor-General candidly expressed, "The Raja of Benares from the situation of his country, which is a frontier both to the Province of Oude and Bahar may be made a serviceable Ally to the Company whenever affair shall require it...to ensure his attachment to the company his interest must be connected with it, which cannot be better effected then by freeing him totally from the remains of his present Vassalage under the guarantee and protection of the company at the same time guarding him against any apprehensions from this Government by thus pledging the faith that no encroachment shall ever be made its rights by the company."[76]

Eventually on March 3, 1775, the Council resolved that Raja Chait Singh should exercise "free and independent authority in his Dominions subject only to the payment of his tribute".[77]

The decision taken by the Council regarding provision of Benares in the defensive treaty was communicated to the Court of Directors that "it should be an article in the new treaty with him, that the Rajah of Gauzipore should be rendered totally independent and left to exercise a free authority in his own dominions subject only to the payment of his tribute" and "that in return for the guarantee and protection which we thus agreed to afford the Nabob we should demand from him the cession in favour of the Company, of the Tribute now paid to him by the said Rajah of Gauzipore."[78]

Bristow was empowered to propose the treaty to the Nawab and communicate if he does not acquiesce in the proposal, English troops would be withdrawn from Oudh and he would be left on his fate.[79] Draft of the proposed treaty was prepared, which lucidly mentions in article 5, "to grant the revenue and perpetual jurisdiction of Raja Chait Singh's *zemindary* to Company on concession of their protecting his country."[80] The Nawab, having no viable alternative, signed a treaty on May 21, 1775 the 5th article, which mentions, "The said Nabob, for the defence of his country, as above specified, declares that he has given up of his own free will and accord, unto the English Company, all the districts dependent on the Rajah Cheyt Sing, together with the land and water duties, and the sovereignty of the said districts in perpetuity; That the English Company shall, after one month and a half from the date of this Treaty, take upon them the sovereignty and possession of the districts under Rajah Cheyt Sing," as hereunder specified, viz—

Sircar Benares	The districts of Juanpore.
Sircar Chumah	Bijehpore Bahdore
Suktessgur	Mulboss Kawss
The Sircar of Gawzypore.	

The *Pargana* of Seekundapore, Jeride, Shaay, Abad, Toppa, Surchchur, and as formerly; the Mint and Kutwally of Benares.[81] On the same day, he also signed an agreement that all the dues, *tunkaws* etc. on the Raja would now be due from himself and would be given up to the Company after one and half months *i.e.* on July 4, 1775.[82] Bristow also took *parwanas* in the name of Raja Chait Singh on the *kotwal* and Mint master at Benares.[83]

Now the Company had to determine in what manner the transfer was to be implemented and the regular payment of revenue due from the Raja. The Governor General and Council decided that a plan of settlement should be approved with Raja Chait Singh without encroaching upon his rights or breaching his engagements with the Government. On June 12, 1775, Hastings submitted a plan of settlement with the Raja, the proposals of which are enumerated below[84]

1. The Raja shall pay the yearly revenue of Rs. 22,48,449 in the Patna treasury of the Company.
2. The Raja shall be empowered to exercise a complete and uncontrolled authority under the acknowledged sovereignty of the Company.
3. The *sunnuds* shall be granted to the Raja conferring upon him the power of appointing officers to the charge of *kotwali* and mint of Benares, the latter to be subject to such orders and regulations as the Governor General and Council shall at any time deem proper to decree.
4. The Raja shall maintain a body of 2,000 horses for immediate service on such a fixed establishment as shall be prescribed by the Governor General and Council, and whenever the service of the corps shall be required it shall be consigned to the command of such officer or officers as the Council shall appoint and will be paid from the Company a gratuity of Rs. 15 monthly for each private man, and in proportion for the officers of the said corps during the time of such service.
5. While the Raja shall continue faithful to these Engagements and pay due obedience to the authority of this Government, no more demands shall be made upon him by the Company, of any kind, nor in any pretence whatever and no person shall be allowed to interfere with his authority or to disturb the peace of his country.

Hastings observed, "By encouragement and protection, he may prove a profitable dependant, a useful barrier and even a powerful ally to the Company; but he will be neither, if the conditions of his connection with the Company are left open to future variations".[85] This acquisition was of immense importance as had been stated in a letter of the Council to the Court of Directors dated August 3, 1775, "The cession of Benares, and the other Territories of the Rajah Cheit Sing to the Company, we flatter ourselves will prove perfectly agreeable to your ideas, as it conveys a valuable acquisition to the Company, without encumbering them with any new Engagements, or loading them with additional Expenses, nor indeed, is it liable to the Objection of involving them in the trouble of new collections, and new establishments, with all the disorders which attend them. The Revenue which accrues from this acquisition amounts to Rupees 23,72,65612 and will be paid by the Rajah in monthly payments as a neat Tribute, without rendering any accounts of his Collections, or being allowed to enter any claim for deductions."[86]

The plan of settlement was placed in the Council on 5th July for scrupulous discussion. It was also attended by the *vakeel* of the Raja. The decision taken regarding the five proposals with some alterations[87]—

1. First proposal of the plan agreed, but proposed that tribute was to be paid at Calcutta instead of Patna.
2. Second proposal was agreed, but a compensation be demanded from the Raja for *kotwali* as the Raja was not enjoying this right under the Nawab.
3. Agreed to the third proposal on the Raja's paying an annual compensation to the Company for the *kotwali* and mint and obliging himself to coin money of precise standard only, which shall be fixed by the Board. Though yearly revenue could not be fixed for want of informa-tion, but was tentatively fixed at Rs. 23,72,656.12.
4. Fourth proposal was agreed that Raja Chait Singh will maintain a body of 2,000 cavalry disciplined after the European manner, but there was no obligation for him to do so.

5. The fifth proposal was accepted as proposed in the plan.

On August 16, 1775, the Council met for the consideration of the settlement to be made with Raja Chait Singh for his annual Tribute. It was unanimously agreed that the demanded sum should not exceed the sum being given to the Nawab. Clavering placed some information regarding the revenue being received by the Nawab from the *Cutwally* (Kotwali)and the Mint of Benares and Jaunpur fort. As per the information Mint master pays-Rs. 36-40,000 p.a. by the collection of duties upon the following articles.

Gold or silver coins 1%

Gold thread

Jewels, Colts, Mats, Basket,

Elephant Teeth, Lac-Lead, Old Arms, a kind of lightwood used for they make boxes, and all new religious places, buildings for Hindu worship. The *kotwal* pays about Rs. 12, 000 annually. The duties collected by the *kotwal* and Mint Master were so small, that it appears to be more with a view to keep up the Nabob's authority than any real advantage as on most articles they do not collect even 20th part of what the Raja does. The account of revenue given by the *Vakeel* of Raja Chait Singh was as follows.—

Net revenue paid by Raja Chait Singh to the Late Nabob Sujah-ul-Dowlah	Rs. 23, 72,656.12
Cutwally at Benares	Rs. 5000
Cutwally at Jaupur	Rs. 10,000
Mint, coinage @ 2 ½ alloy	Rs. 16000
Sungwuzunee or Controller of weights and measures	Rs. 300
Yetesaub or Clerk of the market	Rs. 250
Mokkumee or Broker	Rs. 600
	Rs. 32,150
	Rs. 24,04,806.12.0

He also told that the payment by the Mint master Doollob Dass Taoksally was Rs. 1600 but Asaf-ud-Dowla increase the alloy of the coinage from 2 ½ to Rs. 5 and so the annual revenue rose to Rs. 25000. Hastings proposed that Rs. 23, 72, 656 should be fixed as the yearly revenue to be paid by the Raja. The majority of the Councillors were not satisfied with the information given by the *Vakeel* of Raja Chait Singh. General Clavering mentioned that the amount stated by the *Vakeel* that the Nawab received from *kotwali* and mint do not include the sums paid by them as presents and other donation to the Nawab's ministers, which according to him amounted more than Rs. 50,000 annually. Eventually, it was decided that the proposed amount of Rs. 32,000 annually by Raja Chait Singh would not be accepted as compensation for the mint and *Kotwali* and to appoint a covenanted servant.[88]

It was resolved, after protracted deliberations, to appoint a covenanted servant enquire so that the Board may come to a final settlement to with the Raja. For this purpose Francis Fowke was appointed with detailed instructions and a letter of credence to the Raja was prepared. He was instructed to present the Raja *sunnuds* of investiture, *khil'at* and to receive a *nuzarana* of Rs. 10,000 in the name of the Company for the acknowledgment of his vassalage. The instructions given to him are as follows:[89]

1. To inform the Raja that he was not to enter into any engagement with any foreign Prince on pain of forfeiting his zamindary.
2. To assure the Raja that the Council do not want to increase his tribute but require the exact sum and in same species of rupees as was paid to the late *Vizier* Shuja-ud-dowla and the equivalent amount fixed for the grant of mint and *kotwali.* Suitable deduction will also be allowed to him for expense and risk of transporting the revenue at Calcutta.
3. He will enjoy free and uncontrolled management of internal government and collection of revenue as long as he adheres to the engagement and they would never demand any augmentation other than the fixed annual tribute.
4. The Raja was to be resolutely recommended to maintain a body of 2,000 horses disciplined after the European manner and the Company will pay a gratuity of Rs. 15 per month for each private man when they will be under Company's employment but he was not be insisted upon for compliance

with this demand.

5. The Raja was to be informed about the condition for giving the management of the mint that the Company shall fix was the weight and standard of the coins and on proof of any deviation from them or of coining any other specie in the mint the grant of it shall immediately become void.
6. He was asked to enquire following matters:
   i. What sum the present incharge of the mint paid directly to the Nawab or in presents to his Ministers for that farm.
   ii. What is the exact standard and weight of the Rupees coined in the Mint in last 12 months.
   iii. What was the exact standard weight of the Rupees coined since 1765.
   iv. What quantity of bullion had been coined since 1765.
7. He was also directed to enquire about the presents and the sum that was paid to the Nawab by the *Cutwals* for the privilege of holding those Courts.
8. To report about the exact state of trade and the comparative account of the exports made to those parts by different European nations settled in Bengal.
9. To take from the Raja an oath of alliance to the Company on being invested with the grant.
10. To endeavour to engage the Raja to prevent Europeans particularly foreigners to travel through his district if not furnished with proper passports from this Government.

The Council informed the Raja that Fowke had been deputed on their behalf to take the possession of territories for him, on payment of annual tribute of Rs. 23, 72,656.12.0 with regular monthly *kists* of Rs. 1,97,721.6.4 and *nuzarana* of Rs. 10,000 on the occasion of investiture. Fowke would deliver him *sunnud and khil'at*. The Raja was asked to take an oath of allegiance to the Company, which means forming any alliance with any foreign power or acting in any manner contrary to the fidelity towards the Company all his rights and privileges would be forfeited. He was also asked to make a public proclamation of these transactions so that the natives, as well as, the Europeans might be fully informed of the grant made to him with the reservations of the rights of sovereignty to the Company.[90]

On 23rd October ceremony was held on western outskirts of the city of Benares, where Raja Chait Singh gave a *Tahund* under his signature and took an oath of fidelity to the Company swearing upon his sword to observe "inviolably his allegiance" and not to enter into any engagement with any power. At this occasion he received a sword, shield, and elephant and a horse.[91] He got *sunuds* and *khil'at* along with following articles:[92]

5 pieces of cloth	Rs. 367.8.0/-
1 pair of *sarpunch*	1575.0.0/-
1 Elephant	3675.0.0/-
1 Horse	630.0.0/-
Total	Rs. 6247.8.0/-

The Raja had presented a number of articles to Parker, Lt. Col. Commanding 3rd Brigade, near Allahabad on 20th November during his visit to Benares, but when considered by the Board, it was decided that all presented articles should be returned to the Raja, as by the decree of the King of England and by the orders of the Company, all the servants were forbidden from receiving presents. The Council resolved regarding the status that the Raja was not to make first visit to any person appointed by this Government except the Governor General, members of the Board or persons introduced by a recommendation from this Government. In case of Colonels, Commanding Brigades and persons deputed y the Government, he should send persons of credit to meet them on their arrival. The Raja was declined to receive from any other British subject except those introduced by a recommendation from the Governor General or the Board.[93] Lt. Colonel Parker, as directed by the Council, returned the presents to Raja Chait Singh.[94]

On November 16, 1775, Fowke submitted a scrupulous report to the Council. As per the report the Mint Master had paid Rs. 25,000 and stamp Rupees of 10 *Massahs* with an alloy of 4 *rutties* and 4 *chawls* or 05625 decimal parts of a Rupee per rupee. He gave a present of Rs. 10,000 to the Nawab. Regarding *kotwali* he reported that there were two *kotwal* one in Benares and other in Jaunpur both appointed by the Nawab. The *kotwali* of Benares was given by the Nawab as *jagir* to his minister Elich Khan who appointed a *Naib* as *kotwal*. The *kotwal* remained only for last months during which more than Rs. 6000 was collected of which only 700 was transmitted to Elich Khan and rest was charged as wages of the Officers and other expenses. Amount collected by fine was about Rs. 10,000 annually. Fowke did not provide any information of the *Kotwali* of Jaunpur as the *kotwal* refused saying that he need to apply to the Nawab Asaf-ud-Daula for his orders.[95]

On December 13, 1775, the Board settled yearly revenue as per the resolution. Raja had to pay an annual tribute of 23,40, 249 *muchhlidar* rupees of weight 10 *massa* and an alloy of 2 *rutties* and 2 *chowls* [96] or Calcutta *sicca* Rs. 22,66,180.

Stipulated revenue paid by Raja Chait Singh	Rs. 22,48,449
Amount paid as *Nuzzurana*	Rs. 90,000
Amount settled with *Sung Wazunnaee, Yestsaub* and *Moceemee*[97]	Rs. 1800

The Board resolved to relinquish free and entire direction of the Mint to the Raja without any acknowledgment and compensation from the Raja, but he must enter into an obligation with this Government that rupees shall weight each 10 *massa* and contain 2 *rutties* and 2 *chowls* of alloy according to the regulation of the Mint of 1766. The Board decidedly expressed that in case of any deviation from the fixed standard, such fine would be imposed as the Board may deem prudent on the first instance of deviation from the standard hereby established. The Board gave its assent to deliver the *Kotwali* of Benares and Jaunpur to the Raja without any payment, but no profit could be yielded by the Courts except the amounts of their charges levied unless by the oppression or sale of justice. They also lucidly expressed that they would "not furnish the Raja or his Ministers with pretence for introducing or continuing a system of penalty in his Courts" and, for this purpose the Board ordered Mr. Bristow, Resident at the Nawab's Court, to ask the Nawab to recall his officers from the *Kotwali* at Jaunpur so that it may be handed over to the Raja. It stated, "In return for these concessions to Raja Cheyt Sing and for the very grant advantages which he will derive by being thus secured in the free and independent Government of his Country, we expect his ready compliance with the other terms proposed for the settlement of his tribute, and that he will consent to under moderate and reasonable terms."[98] On January 1, 1776, Fowke received Nawab's *parwana* to the *Kotwal* and *Killadar* of Jaunpur directing to consider themselves as Company's servants.[99]

In January, the Raja made another representation that the Raja's tribute in *muchhlidar* Rs. 23, 40,209 would be equivalent to Calcutta Rs. 21,66,860,3. As per the Company's orders the Raja was to issue for the coinage of Rupees of 10 *massa* weight while since past years the Rupees coined at Benares were deficient of that weight and so the difference would be a considerable increase of the tribute. He requested that in case the standard established, he must be allowed a deduction of Rs. 38, 835.13.3 being the difference in the amount of his tribute between *muchhlidar* Rupees at the present weight and that of full weight 10 *massas*. Even Fowke in his letter suggested, "This deduction will make no difference in the annual amount of Calcutta Sicca Rs. 21, 66, 860.3." In this representation, the Raja also desired to get *sunnud* signed by the Board for the offices of mint and *Kotwalies*.[100]

On February 1, 1766, the Council decided that the fixed tribute would be Calcutta *Sicca* Rs. 22, 66, 180. However, the Raja was given the option to pay the sum either in *muchhlidar* Rupees at Benares or in *sicca* at Calcutta. In case, he agrees to the latter, he would be allowed a premium of 2% for remittance of regular payment and insisted upon the Raja to pay the tribute regularly to prevent it running into arrears, in which case Company would be impelled to take stringent measures that would be "disagreeable to the Raja".[101] The Raja soon accepted all the terms and that in case of any deviation the Board could impose a fine on him.[102] Though Raja accepted all terms of the Company, but he showed great reluctance in accepting the terms regarding the maintenance of a body of 2,000 horses disciplined after the European manner. He represented to Fowke that the body of horse in his service was mainly composed of his own relatives and faithful adherents and they made the collection of revenue in the whole country, in which case, he could not discharge them. He also expressed his inability to make any addition to the establishment of horse.[103]

Though the *sunnuds*, *pottah* and *kowlnama* were already given to the Raja in October 1775, but fresh negotiations regarding the exact amount of the tribute and the kind of currency to be minted and paid as tribute had changed many things. So fresh documents incorporating new resolutions regarding settlement agreed both by the Raja and the Board was ordered. On April 15, 1776, *sunnud* was granted to Chait Singh confirming him in four *sarkars* together with the *Kotwalies* of Benares and Jaunpur and the Mint at Benares and *kabuliyat* was executed by Raja Chait Singh.[104] On 20th April, the Board sent the *sunnud* and *pottah* together with the *Kabuliyat* and *Muchulka* (obligation) to be executed by the Raja to Fowke.[105] The Raja firmly objected to the provision of the *Muchulka* according to which he was to pay a penalty of ¼% or 4 *annas* in a rupee for any delay in the payment of the monthly *kists* after the expiration of the 51 days grace, from the date the *kists* fell into arrears, on the ground that no *zamindar* or *Taluqdar* had ever agreed to or executed such a *Muchulka*. He gave him the sincerest assurances of punctuality.[106] He also objected to the use of word *Muchulka* in his *sunnud* and *Pottah* and the phrase "and all former *sunnuds* to become null and void"[107] thereby indirectly asserting his rights to possess, exercise and enjoy all the rights, privileges and powers, the Rajas of Benares had acquired from time to time at different stages by the Emperor, the Nawab of Oudh and the Company.

The Governor General and Council in their letter 30th May to Fowke consented to exempt the Raja from the execution of the *Muchulka* and on use of the term in *sunnud* and *pottah*,[108] but the Raja was to be told that the Government would implement these conditions if payments run in arrears. On June 24, 1776, the Council authorized Fowke to erase the penalty clause from the *pottah* and *sunnud*.[109] But the Raja refused to accept the corrected documents, for the reasons "that any harassment in a *sunnud* or public deed is totally unprecedented in the usages of this country, that the clause in the *sunnud* by which the former *sunnuds* are declared to be null is likewise contrary to custom and practice, and further that in the above clause the word "*sunnuds*" being used in the plural numbers, the *Kowlnama* which he received with the former *sunnud* and *Pottah* is thereby likewise rendered void and of no effect." Fowke intimated further that "The Raja objects to the execution of the *Kabuliyat* on account of the clause it contains by which the former *sunnuds* are annulled. He declares himself ready to return the old *sunnud* and *Pottah* on receipt of the New Ones."[110] This was brought under consideration of the Bengal Government, which on July 29, 1776 ordered the Secretary to prepare a new *sunnud* and *pottah*, to omit the word '*Muchulka*' and the sentence "all former *sunnuds* to become null and void".[111]

Thus finally and mutually approved *sunnud*, *pottah* and *Kowlnama* was issued fresh by the Board. The Raja now sought to obtain an observance of the ceremony of the annual grant of *Farighkatti* or the Quit Receipt by the Company in acknowledgment of full receipt of the annual revenue from the Raja. This was a custom under Nawab's sovereignty, which the Raja wanted to continue accompanying the grant of *khil'at* and the payment of *nuzarana*. On July 29, 1776 the Bengal Government acquiesce in to grant him *khil'at* after the completion of all annual payments, but the Raja was required to pay to the Company a *nuzarana* equal to the value of the *Khil'at*.[112] Fowke transmitted the corrected *sunnud* and *pottah* to Chait Singh on September 4, 1776.[113] On 7th September, *farighkhatti* was granted to him on the completion of the payment of revenue for the first year.[114] On 22nd September, the Raja received his *khil'at* with due éclat and pomp.[115]

The fort of Jaunpur and its dependencies were handed over

to the Company by the Nawab on 19th June, but these were not instantly transferred to the Raja in accordance with the terms of the treaty. Fowke was in possession of the fort and district of Jaunpur. When the Council came to know about this fact, it immediately directed him to deliver them upon the Raja[116] and eventually on November 12, 1776, the fort and its dependencies were delivered to the Raja.[117] From 19 June to 12 November 1776, an income of Rs. 15, 918:4 was collected.[118] The Council directed Graham, "As we have on behalf of the Company granted him the possession of all the territories ceded by the treaty with the Nabob we consider the Collections of Jaunpore as a right belonging to him". Graham soon paid the amount to the Raja.[119]

The Raja had following forts within his possessions in Benares[120]

1. Beedijegur in *pargana* Burrere
2. Agoree
3. Cussoombah
4. Lutifpore in *pargana* Aurora
5. Pateetah in *pargana* Pateetah
6. Mungrore in *pargana* Kerah
7. Secunderpore
8. Luttesgur
9. Beejipore, uninhabited and out of repair in *pargana* Kunteet
10. On the borders of Singrany a Guard House at the Gaut of Lal Gunge
11. On the borders of Singrany a Guard House at Halleah
12. Gungapore in *pargana* Kuswar
13. Pindra in *pargana* Coal
14. Juckin in *pargana* Kirriat
15. Seekunt
16. Sagur in *pargana* Mutchilishahar
17. Jaunpur in *pargana* Jaunpur
18. Serinjah in *pargana* Chowsah
19. Oyna in *pargana* Bulleah

Besides these, there were number of mud forts in many *parganas* but were not of much importance.

The Company always had covetous eyes over the Benares

because of its alluring wealth and strategic position. After the demise of Raja Balwant Singh, the English played a cardinal role in Chait Singh's accession to the *gaddi* (throne) much against the will of the Nawab. It was a time when the air of Delhi politics was fraught with Maratha menace, which made both the English and the Nawab to accept Chait Singh as the new Raja, where it was indispensable for the English to place an affable Raja on Benares as it was barrier for the defense of Bengal Provinces, on the other side, the Nawab did not want to nettle the English as he was in defensive agreement with them by the treaty of 1765 and 1768, and in case of any attack the English were the lone power from where he could get military and financial succour. During the ceremony, 15 guns salute was given to the Raja less in respect of the Raja and more to convince the people that it was through English mediation that he succeeded despite of the Nawab's uncrillingness to continue the *Zamindary* under the same family.

Though in 1771 there was a perceptible change in the policy of Court of Directors who directed to procure Benares in return of Kora and Allahabad to Nawab, but it could not materialize as the Nawab rebuffed the proposal resolutely in the Benares Conference of 1773. Hastings, however, managed to extend the *kowlnama* to the posterity as the English policy was to make the Raja more and more independent of the Nawab. With the death of Shuja-ud-Daula, the circumstances became propitious for the English who without losing the opportunity signed new agreement with Asaf-ud-daula and thus Benares came under their direct administration. Though the Council resolved that the Raja would get free and independent authority within his dominions subject only to payment of tribute, but the ensuing events, which I have mentioned in my fifth chapter shows that how the English, after the transfer, made use of every singular opportunity to interfere into the internal matters of the Raja and his administration and how the office of Resident became a tool for the English to fulfill this purpose and to wrung maximum wealth of Benares for the accomplishment of their own political aggrandisement.

REFERENCES

1. PD, letter to Court, September 11, 1770, paragraph 2; also see letter from Raja Balwant Singh, August 6, 1770, No. 320, CPC, III, the date mentioned is 1 September.
2. Letter from Raja Balwant Singh, No. 320, CPC, volume III.
3. SC Pr., 1770, letter from James Alexander, Supervisor at Patna to President and SC, August 26, 1770, September 1, 1770.
4. Letter from Chait Singh, No. 353, September 8, 1770, CPC, III.
5. Letter from Raja Shitab Ray, *Naib Nazim* of Behar, September 21, 1770, No. 377, CPC, III.
6. SC Pr., 1770, letter from James Alexander to President and SC, August 26, 1770, September 1, 1770.
7. SC Pr., 1770, letter from Harper to SC, August 25, 1770, September 25, 1770.
8. PD, letter from Fort William to Court, September 11, 1770, para 2.
9. PD, letter from Fort William to Court, October 31, 1770, para 33.
10. Letter to the Vizier, No. 350, September 4, 1770, CPC, III,
11. SC Pr., 1770, letter from Colonel Harper to SC dated August 25, 1770, September 25, 1770; also see letter from Vizier, September 8, 1770, No. 352, CPC, III.
12. SC Pr., 1770, letter from Harper to SC, August 27, 1770, September 25, 1770.
13. Letter to the Vizier, No. 350, September 4 or 8, 1770; letter to Chait Singh, No. 365, September 15, 1770, CPC, III.
14. Letter from the Emperor, No. 370, September 18, 1770, CPC, III.
15. PD, letter from Fort William to Court, October 31, 1770, para. 30.
16. Letter to Raja Chait Singh, October 12, 1770, No. 415, CPC, III.
17. SC Pr., 1770, letter from Harper to SC, October 4, 1770, October 19, 1770.
18. Letter from Raja Shitab Ray, No. 424, October 22, 1770, CPC, III; also see PD, letter from Fort William to Court, October 31, 1770, para 30.
19. Letter from the Vizier, No. 413, October 10, 1770, CPC, III.
20. SC Pr., 1770, letter from Harper to SC, October 8, 1770, October 19, 1770.
21. FPD, Secret, October 4, 1773, No. 6, Translation of the *Pottah*.
22. PD, letter from Court, October 31, 1770, para 30.
23. PD, letter from Court, August 28, 1771.
24. PD, letter to Court of Directors from SC, December 24, 1770.

25. Letter from Raja Chait Singh, No. 486, December 7, 1770, CPC, III.
26. CPC, III, No. 581, p. 155; No. 591, p. 158.
27. Letter from Governor to Raja Chait Singh, No. 688, April 1, 1771.
28. Letter from Raja Chait Singh to Governor, No. 639, March 3, 1771, CPC, III.
29. Letter from Raja Chait Singh to Governor, No. 644, March 6, 1770, p. 171, CPC, III.
30. PD, letter from Fort William to Court of Director's, October 31, 1770, para 34.
31. Letter to Raja Chait Singh from Cartier, No. 688, April 1, 1770, CPC, III, p. 185.
32. CPC, IV, p. 2, No. 11.
33. Letter from Hastings, No. 42, CPC, IV.
34. PD, letter from Court to Fort William, April 10, 1771, para. 47.
35. PD, letter from Court to Fort William, April 10, 1771, para. 48.
36. PD, letter from Fort William to Court, January 6, 1769, para. 6.
37. Gleig, G.R., *Memoirs of Life of Warren Hastings*, Vol. I, London, 1841, pp. 344-46.
38. Letter from Hastings to Sulivan, October 12, 1773, Gleig, I, *op.cit.*, p. 357.
39. FPD, SC Pr., 31 May-30 December 1773, volume 18, October 4, 1773, No. 2, letter from Hastings to Council dated September 4, 1773, pp. 561-563.
40. BM, Add.Mss 29212, Accession No. 276, Roll No. 276, Diary of Transactions and Occurrences on Voyage to Benares in 1773, p. 72.
41. FPD, SC Pr., 31 May-30 December 1773, volume 18, October 4, 1773, No. 2, letter from Hastings to Council dated September 4, 1773, pp. 567-568.
42. FPD, SC Pr., 31 May-30 December 1773, volume 18, October 4, 1773, No. 5, pp. 586-588.
43. FPD, SC, October 4, 1773, No. 2, Governor General's Report of his negotiation with the Vizier, p. 11.
44. FPD, SC Pr., 31 May-30 December 1773, volume 18, October 4, 1773, p. 576; Translation of Raja Chait Singh agreement relative to the duties, October 4, 1763, pp. 674-675.
45. FPD, SC Pr., 31 May-30 December 1773, volume 18, 4 October 1773, No. 5, Translation of new *Kowlnama*, p. 586.
46. *Ibid*, letter from Hastings to Council, pp. 577-79.
47. FPD, 9 November 1773, No. 2; also see 6 January 1774, Minute of Governor General; letter No. 2602/A from Rastrapati Bhavan

to Shreya Pathak dated 17 May 2007.

48. Letter from Raja Chait Singh to Hastings, No. 674, December 2, 1773, CPC, IV.
49. CPC, IV No. 679, p. 124.
50. Letter from Raja Chait Singh to Hastings, January 2, 1774, No. 735, CPC, IV.
51. Letter from Hastings to the Nawab, No. 805, February 6, 1774 CPC, IV.
52. Letter from the Nawab to Hastings, July 11, 1774, No. 1148, CPC, IV.
53. FPD, December 9, 1773, No. 3; also see January 6, 1774, No. 1; CPC, IV, No. 703, p. 127; No. 706, p. 128; No. 757, p. 146.
54. Letter from Raja Chait Singh to Hastings, February 15, 1774, No. 822, CPC, IV.
55. FPD, March 30, 1775, No. 6, Council to Muir, March 30, 1775.
56. FPD, SC, April 20, 1775, No. 2, letter from Muir to Hastings, April 9, 1775.
57. Letter from Hastings to Raja Chait Singh, No. 1129, June 29, 1774; letter from Makkan Singh, *vakil* of the Raja to Middleton, No. 1155, July 13, 1774, CPC, IV.
58. Letter from Hastings to Shuja-ud-Dowla June 28, 1774, No. 1123, CPC, III.
59. FPD, January 2, 1775, No. 13 and 14.
60. Letter from Raja Chait Singh to Governor General, No. 1533, January 23, 1775, CPC, IV.
61. Letter from the Raja to Hastings, No. 1112, June 19, 1774, CPC, IV.
62. Letter from Hastings to the Raja, No. 1128, June 29, 1774, CPC, IV.
63. Letter to Raja Chait Singh, No. 1317, October 5, 1774; also see No. 1311, CPC, IV.
64. Letter from Raja Chait Singh, No. 1340, October 13, 1774, CPC, IV.
65. Letter from the Raja Chait Singh to Hastings, No. 1357, October 24, 1774, CPC, IV.
66. Letter from Raja Chait Singh, No. 1389, November 8, 1774, CPC, IV.
67. Letter from Raja Chait Singh, No. 1533, January 23, 1775, CPC, IV.
68. FPD, SC, March 30, 1775, No. 2, letter from Raja Chait Singh to Council, March 19, 1775.
69. FPD, SC, March 30, 1775, No. 2, letter from Raja Chait Singh to his *Vakil* at Calcutta.
70. FPD, letter from Council to Bristow, March 30, 1775, No. 3.
71. FPD, letter from Bristow to Council, April 27, 1775, No. 5; CPC, IV, p. 303, No. 1741.

72. CPC, IV, No. 1764, p.306.
73. FPD, SC, June 26, 1775, No. 9, letter from Colonel Muir to Hastings.
74. FPD, SC, May 22, 1775, No. 14, letter from the Council to Colonel Muir.
75. FPD, June 26, 1775, No. 10, letter from Council to Muir.
76. BM, Add.Mss 29198, Accession No. 270, Roll No. 270, February 13, 1775, Minutes of members of the Board.
77. *Ibid*, March 3, 1775, Minutes of members of the Board.
78. PD, letter to Court, March 24, 1775.
79. *Seir Mutaqherin*, III, *op.cit.*, p. 106.
80. FPD, SC, June 6, 1775, No. 3, Draft of the proposed treaty.
81. FPD, SC, June 6, 1775, No. 6, Treaty between the Nawab and the Company dated May 21, 1775.
82. FPD, SC, June 6, 1775, No. 7, Translation of Agreement under the seal of the Nawab.
83. FPD, SC, 6 June 1770, No. 5, letter from Bristow to Council, May 22, 1775.
84. FPD, SC, June 12, 1775, No. 2.
85. FPD, SC, June 12, 1775, No. 3.
86. PD, letter from Fort William to Court, August 3, 1775.
87. FPD, SC, 5 July 1775, No. 2.
88. FPD, August 16, 1775, No. 6 and No. 7.
89. FPD, SC, Draft of the Instructions to Francis Fowke, August 24, 1775, No. 3.
90. FPD, SC, August 24, 1775, No. 4, letter from Council to Raja Chait Singh.
91. FPD, SC, January 8, 1776, No. 22, letter from Fowke to Council dated December 20, 1775.
92. FPD, SC, September 4, 1775, No. 5.
93. FPD, SC, December 6, 1775, No. 16, letter from Council to Fowke, December 6, 1775.
94. FPD, SC, 3 January 1776, No. 1, letter from Col. Parker to Governor General and Council December 21, 1775.
95. FPD, December 13, 1775, No. 2, Fowke to Council, November 16, 1775.
96. FPD, SC, 1 February 1776, No. 5, letter to Fowke.
97. FPD, SC, 30 May 1776, No. 3, letter from Fowke to Governor General.
98. FPD, SC, December 13, 1775, No. 5, Council to Fowke dated

December 13, 1775.

99. FPD, 1 February 1776, No. 1, letter from Fowke to Council, 22 January 1776.
100. FPD, Sec. Pr., February 1, 1776, No. 4, letter from Fowke to Council, January 22, 1776.
101. FPD, SC, February 1, 1776, No. 5, letter from Council to Fowke dated February 1, 1776.
102. FPD, SC, 26 February 1776, No. 5, letter from Fowke to Council, 18 February 1776.
103. FPD, April 3, 1776, No. 1, Fowke to Council, March 19, 1776; also see 26 February 1776, No. 5, letter from Fowke to Hastings, 18 February 1776.
104. FPD, SC, April 15, 1776, Consultation No. 11 (*sunnud*), No. 12 (*pottah*), No. 13 (*kabooleyeat)*.
105. FPD, May 30, 1776, No. 3, Fowke to Council, May 16, 1776.
106. FPD, May 30, 1776, No. 6, Petition of Raja Chait Singh.
107. FPD, June 24, 1776, No. 2, Fowke to Council, June 13, 1776.
108. FPD, May 30 1776, No. 7, Council to Fowke, May 30, 1776.
109. FPD, June 24, 1776, No. 3, Council to Fowke, June 24, 1776.
110. FPD, July 29, 1776, No. 8, Fowke to Council, July 17, 1776.
111. *Ibid*, Order of the Council, 29 July 1776.
112. FPD, June 29, 1776, No. 9, Council to Fowke, July 29, 1776.
113. FPD, October 21, 1776, No. 14, Fowke to Council, September 25, 1776.
114. FPD, October 21, 1776, No. 17.
115. FPD, October 21, 1776, No. 14, Fowke to Council, September 25, 1776.
116. FPD, SC, October 28, 1776, No. 5, letter from Council to Fowke dated October 28, 1776.
117. FPD, SC, January 20, 1777, No. 13, letter from Fowke to Hastings dated November 15, 1776.
118. FPD, SC, January 20, 1777, No. 14, Crown A, letter from Fowke to Council dated December 8, 1776.
119. FPD, January 20, 1777, No. 15, letter from Council to Graham, January 20, 1777.
120. BM, Add.Mss. 29205, Accession No. 273, Roll No. 273.

Chapter 5

Increasing Tribulations of Raja Chait Singh

Interference of The Bengal Council Into Benares

When Benares was transferred from the Nawab to the East India Company, it was avowedly accepted and professed by all the members of the Council that there would be no interference by any person and the Raja would enjoy uncontrollable authority within his dominions except payment of stipulated revenue, which was not to be increased in any case or under any pretence, however, in ensuing years there were encroachments on the just rights of the Raja and high-handed interference. The years were full of duplicity, deceits and breach of the terms of *sunnud* with every person having lone purpose to wrung maximum from the Raja's coffers. The bifurcation of the Council members into two opposing groups, one of Hastings and his adherent Barewell and the other led by Clavering, Monson and Francis, and the acrid relations among them was impinging upon the Raja's relation with the Governor General of Fort William.

The majority of opposing group and their incessant opposition in the Council fettered Hastings to take any wilful measure and implement his plan but this balance changed with the demise of Monson on September 25, 1776. Hastings now commanded the majority in the Council using his casting vote. The first step taken by him was to remove Fowke on December 23, 1776, [1] on pretence that the investiture of the Raja, for which he was sent to Benares was over. On the same day he appointed his adherent Graham for demanding and receiving bills of exchange from the Raja and "for transacting any occasional business" between this Government and the Raja. Though Francis expressed his dissent, considering Fowke more appropriate for the post, but finally acquiesce in Graham's appointment; and only Clavering was averse to the decision.[2] Daniel Barewell was appointed as the assistant Resident, but neither there was additional work nor any special purpose to create a new post of Assistant Resident[3] and even the Court of Directors reprimanded the appointment of Graham and regarded the post dispensable stating, "...two persons appointed immediately afterwards, with two Salaries, to execute an Office which had been filled with reputation by Mr. Fowke alone; and that Mr. Graham enjoys all the Emoluments annexed to that Office of Mr. Fowke, We must be of opinion that Mr. Fowke was removed without just Cause, to make room for Mr. Graham; and that the addition of Mr. Barewell's salary is a clear loss of 300 Rupees P. Month to the Company."[4] The fact that Mr. Barewell was the brother of Councillor Barewell itself manifests the purpose, for which Hastings appointed him.

Although, Hastings staunchly supported the appointment of a Resident at Benares, but previously in his minute of June 12, 1775, when it was proposed that the rent should be received at Patna being the nearest provincial station he demurred, "...it would frustrate the intention of rendering the Rajah Independent if a Resident was appointed to receive the money as it became due at Benares such a Resident would unavoidably acquire an Influence over the Rajah and over his Country which would in effect render him the master of both. This consequence might not perhaps be brought completely to pass without a struggle and many appeals to the Council, which in a government constituted like this, cannot fail to terminate against the Rajah, and by the Construction to which his opposition to the agent would be liable might eventually drawn on him severer Restrictions and end in reducing him to the mean and deprived state of a mere Zemindar".[5] In spite of divulging so deleterious effect of a Resident on the Raja's authority, Hastings within a short span of time manifested a perceptible change in his attitude towards Benares. Thomas Graham assumed the office of Resident in mid January 1777, with an ulterior motive of encroaching upon Raja's inviolable rights as he divulged in his letter to Anderson, "If I have put even a shadow of authority, I will make him feel very sore for his indifference... I shall have it in my power to bring him on his marrow bones".[6] He joined with a pernicious desire to build up the political power of the Residency and interfere in the internal matters of the Raja.

Towards the end of 1776, Ajeet Singh, a Raja on the southern frontier of Benares, started assembling force under command of Govind Singh, one of his vassal, with intention of making incursion into Raja Chait Singh's territories from Mirzapur, but the Raja stoutly resisted any such hostile act and did not asked for any assistance from the Commander-in-Chief, General Clavering who deems this as a part of his duty.[7] On January 13, 1777, Colonel Dow was authorized to comply with any requisition made by Raja Chait Singh for military assistance against invasion, but the Raja was powerful enough to repel the invaders.[8] On March 8, 1777, Graham wrote that Raja Chait Singh was repairing his forts, stocking provisions, issuing orders for the manufacture of gunpowder, assembling forces and moving guns in night.[9]

To comprehend the relation of the Raja with Fort William authorities it is indispensable to know what relation the Coucillors were sharing with each other. Hastings agent in London Mr. Macleane avowed himself to be "authorized, empowered and directed to signify to the Court of Director's his desire to resign his Office of Governor General of Bengal; and to request their nomination of a Successor to the vacancy which would be thereby occasioned in the Council". Before Hastings could acknowledge and confirm the proceedings of his agent, Clavering, being the senior most Councillor, assumed the office of Governor General and directed the Secretary to issue summons in his name as Governor General to Messrs Barewell and Francis for a Council meet and Mr. Barewell concurred this as an "unwarrantable and illegal" act of Clavering.[10] On 20th June, Court of Directors avowed that the office of Governor General could be vacated only by death, removal or resignation and that Macleane's letter was "in fact no Resignation but a notification of Governor General's desire to resign... He neither asserts himself to be authorized nor does he take upon himself in fact to make an actual resignation: he only intimates an intention of the Governor which is to take place in future". The Court in their general letter to the Council stated that they unanimously resolved to accept the resignation, but this intended to accept if there should be any resignation in future and nominated Edward Wheeler to succeed the office "which would become vacant." It was highly misinterpreted by the Councillors who regarded the seat of Governor General vacant.[11]

In retaliation to all these acts of Clavering, Hastings with concurrence of Barewell declared the Offices of General Clavering as senior Councillor and Commander-in-Chief vacant, but without admitting that he had succeeded to the office of Governor General and Barewell was promoted to the vacant office of Senior Councillor. The Court of Directors dubbed this as an act of "indecency" and the resolutions "unwarrantable" and "illegal," as the other Councillors were neither summoned nor informed of this Council meet.[12] On June 24, 1777, the Court of Directors perceiving the perplexing situation of the Council demurred the matter, "We cannot be of opinion (except perhaps in case of legal Conviction of certain crimes) that your Honourable Board can, by its own Authority, either remove any Member from the Council, or declare his seat be vacant". They not only instructed to recede the execution of resolution, which prevented Clavering to exercise his offices but also that each member be placed in the position previously held.[13]

While these frequent political changes were taking place in the Council, Raja Chait Singh sent his *vakeel* to Clavering to congratulate him for becoming Governor General, but knowing that Hastings was still the Governor-General his *vakeel* retraced to Benares. It was never erroneous to send a deputation to felicitate a newly appointed Governor-General, but Raja Chait Singh was now fully trapped in the web of Council politics. This whole incident nettled Hastings who articulated, "It is a fact that when the unhappy divisions of our Government had proceeded to an extremity bordering on civil violence, by the attempt to wrest from me my authority, in the month of June 1777, he had deputed a man named Shambu Nath, with an express commission to my opponent; and the man had proceeded as far as Murshidabad, when, hearing of the change of affairs, he stopped, and the Raja recalled him."[14] It was after this incident that Hastings was bent upon to avenge the Raja.

In 1777, payment of revenue encumbered with the abolition of Murshidabad Mint and the *shroffs* doubled the rate of premium. Due to this impediment in May 1777, the Raja appealed a grace of 15-20 days for payment of tribute and to make the payment in gold *mohurs* coined at Benares with the impression of Calcutta mint.[15] The Council brusquely rebuffed the plea on June 2, 1777, asking Graham to discourage any requisition of the Raja contrary to the agreement with the Government and to insist upon him to make the future payment with strictest regularity.[16]

He took significant stride in this direction by favouring Ausan Singh, an arch enemy and the dismissed *dewan* of the Raja. Ausan Singh was incessantly soliciting Hastings to intercede with the Raja in his favour assuring him of his fidelity. Hastings emboldened him to immediately proceed to Benares without least apprehensions and exhorted to the Raja to receive him and permit him to reside with his family at Benares "unmolested".[17] Previously, in 1777, Hastings appreciated the Raja for his sagacity when he ousted Ausan Singh from Benares and warned the Raja "against the counsels of interested persons who will not hesitate to take advantage of his youth and secure to themselves authority detrimental to the interest of his zamindary".[18] Now after 1777, he exhorted to the Raja regarding his family matters without any scruple, "it is more for the Honour and Interest of your Family, to settle this Matter privately than to make it the subject of public

Notice." Hastings basically had ulterior plans to plant Ausan Singh in Benares so that he could be used as a stooge against the Raja at an opportune time. This is more evident in his letter to Graham where he directed him to use his utmost endeavour to induce the Raja but also stated, "It is necessary to give you a Caution that you do not attend to any Demands of Oassaun Sing... If he meets, with Encouragement he will require stipulations, and claim your support you must flatly refuse to hear the fact and refer him for the last wholly to his master, offering only your good offices to promote a Reconciliation."[19]

By February 1778, Ausan Singh reached Benares with Hastings's assurance of protection of life and honour. There he heard from *Ray Rayan* that it was being contemplated to grant him a land yielding revenue of Rs. 3 lakhs and Rs. 4000 as monthly salary, but it was just heresy. Through the favour of Governor General he was granted a *khil'at*.[20] How far the Raja was being compelled to be favourable to his enemy be witnessed by the fact that both Graham and Barewell asked the Raja to grant Jaunpur to Ausan Singh, but the Raja refused to comply with their request. Eventually, it was agreed to settle *pargana* Saidpur yielding annual revenue of Rs. 65,000 out of which he was required to pay Rs. 15,000 to the Raja and retain Rs. 50,000 for himself.[21] This money, indubitably, was being used against the Raja.

As already mentioned, collection of revenue in Benares was an arduous task. Though Ausan Singh got a residence and high yielding land in Benares still it was not enough to support his expenditure, as he was not able to collect the revenue, which he divulged in a letter to Hastings that he "feels it very difficult to make both ends meet." He even requested the Governor General to either grant him farm in *parganas* of Chainpur and Sasaram in the *sarkar* of Shahabad in Bihar or to write a letter to Middleton, Resident of Oudh, in his favour to grant him a farm of Azamgarh for a term of 10 years. This manifests that Ausan Singh, unable to collect the revenue in spite of being a local and influential person of the region, wanted a farm situated out of Benares.

This was not the end of humiliation that the Raja was

undergoing. Graham and Barewell impelled him to execute a deed of reconciliation with Ausan Singh where the Raja declared that he would support Ausan Singh with honour, would not deceive him in any matter and consider his friends and foes as his own friends and enemies. Ausan Singh also declared he would never be "lacking in the duties of fidelity and zeal to the Raja and will be guilty of no improper action or attempt to deceive him openly or secretly" and consider the Raja's friends and enemies as his own friends and enemies.[22] Hastings had plans to humiliate the Raja by high-handed interference in the administration and encircled him by his enemies. The agreement was implemented on strictest terms only from the Raja's side, but Hastings never adhered to it. Circumstances became propitious for Hastings with the demise of Clavering in September 1777.

In early September 1777, the *shroffs* of Benares refused to arrange for the payment of future *kists* because of detention of their gold in the Calcutta Mint. The Raja made a representation to Graham for saving him from the prevailing circumstances,[23] but the Council paid no heed to the representation and wrote to Graham on September 29, 1777, that they would not brook any breach of the mutual agreement whatever the cause would be.[24] On December 1, 1777, the Council decided not to entertain any representation from Raja Chait Singh. The Raja was communicated that it was his onus to find panacea to his troubles and not the Company's business, and without any scruple they stoop so low to even ask the Raja to coerce the *shroffs* for regular payment of the tribute. Thus the Raja was to bear a loss of at least Rs. 80,000 per annum in uncontrollable circumstances.[25]

Hastings asked the Raja to dismiss his *vakeel* Bhai Ram at Calcutta in December 1777, and permitted to appoint another *vakiee* with warning that he would dismiss new *vakeel* if he does not comply his duties towards the Governor General.[26] By this time the Raja must have perceived the ulterior motives of the Governor General and observing the Resident against himself he thought it prudent to comply with all demands of the Governor General and not to exacerbate his diffliculties by giving him any chance of complaints. On December 11, 1777, Edward Wheeler joined as Councillor on the vacancy of Clavering. Though he joined the side of Clavering, but did not want to break openly with the Governor General.[27]

The Governor General schemed to appoint an officer on his own part to the command of the Raja's forces, but being resolutely opposed by Francis and Fowke he could never implement this. Not only the Resident and the Governor General, but also the so-called well wishers of the Raja in Calcutta were also having the sole purpose to extort maximum wealth. In March 1778, Fowke and Francis advised the Raja to act according to his own will and not to comply with the Governor General's demands, as he was not able to act against the Raja because of persistent opposition from Francis and others. The Raja was also told that Wheeler expects a bribe from him to support his cause. Fowke was playing game by giving a complete misleading picture. He was pretending to be a well wisher of the Raja and instigated him to act against the Governor General. His relation with the Raja should be seen less as his well wisher and more as an enemy of Hastings. He wanted to use this cleavage as a weapon against the Governor General. Hastings was not oblivious of his surroundings as he prohibited the Raja's *vakeel* Hulasi Ram from attending his *durbar* because Hulasi was being helped by Francis and Fowke in the transaction of his master's affair and was a medium of correspondence between the Raja and the opposition party.[28]

In 1778, Graham incessantly expressed his qualms on Raja's probity. He alleged that the Raja was in correspondence with the Marathas and would be the first to join the enemies in case of any serious reverse. Graham also reported that Raja Chait Singh had offered Ausan Singh to restore him as the *dewan* on the condition that he would break all his connections with the English.[29] Firstly, the Raja would never assent to reinstate his arch enemy as *dewan* and secondly, if he did so then this does not in any way raise qualms on his probity to the Company, in fact it was the Council that violated the agreement by interfering into the personal matters of the Raja and emboldening his enemies.

The adversities of Raja commenced with the declaration of war between Britain and France in March 1778. On July 9, 1778, a proposal was put forth in the Council calling for Raja's contribution to the burden of the war by establishment of three battalion of sepoys and its maintenance at his expense. All the Councillors acquiesce to the demand, but the question rose on the Company's right to exact money under duress more than the stipulated sum mentioned in *sunnud*. Hastings adroitly evaded by leaving the decision on the superiors. The question was put in abeyance, to which he remarked, "I must therefore adhere to the question as it stand, wishing to avoid the question of right. If however we cannot agree upon this point, still, I would wish to have the requisition made in the words of the question, and leave the decision of future rights to our superiors." He further reiterated- "I agree to the question in the original terms of it, deeming it a right inherent in every Government to impose such assessment as it judges expedient for the common service and protect subjects, and we are not precluded from it by any agreement subsisting between the Raja and this Government." Francis and Wheeler, though supported the resolution, yet regarded this step as unjustifiable. Francis suggested that the Raja should be informed that no demand would be imposed upon him after the war. Hastings denied this suggestion, but agreed to add to the proposal "and to be disbanded at the end of the war".

Barewell had gone much beyond what the resolution demanded. He regarded military establishment independent of the English administration a great menace for the Company and opined that the Raja's force "be place upon the same footing as the regular Military Force of the Presidency", but this was not accepted. Eventually, the proposal was resolved and the Raja was informed that as a subject he was under obligation to promote the interest of the Company and was asked to intimate his prompt consent.[30] On 18th July, Graham presented a *parwana* of Governor General.[31] On 30th July the Council received Raja's reply that he was contemplating the matter and would promptly reply.[32]

The Raja instructed his *vakeel* Ali Naqi to express to the Governor General his inability to comply with these demands, and make endeavours to know the attitude of the English authorities in England over this issue and then to signify his assent to pay. From certain sections, he was receiving information in his favour. Colonel Dow advised him to wait for Sir Eyre Coote who was expected to join the Council in a month's time and everything would be settled to his gratification. One of the Raja's officers, Ram Singh informed him on July 24, 1778, that Hastings does not enjoy the favour and support of the England authorities. On July 25, 1778, the Raja was also informed by Sambhunath, *munshi* of Fowke, about the reappointment of Fowke as the Resident by the England authorities who was to arrive in Benares within a month and all his affairs would be settled to his gratification.

Before getting this information, Raja Chait Singh endeavoured to get recommendation from Raghunath Rao, the Maratha Chief, but now he became so confident of the support that he wrote to his former *dewan* Bhai Ram that he does not need any recommendation from the Maratha Chief as "Providence was favouring his cause" and also directed to keep strict vigilant eye over Ausan Singh.[33] Hastings cognizant of these developments observed, "I will not conceal from the Board I have expected this evasive conduct in the Rajah, having been for sometime past well informed that he had been advised in this manner, to procrastinate the payment of five lacs to afford time for the arrival of despatches from England, which were to bring orders for a total change in this Government, and this he was given to expect, would produce a repeal of the demand made upon him by the present Government."[34] Hastings even refused to meet Ali Naqi on the pretence that he was too busy.[35]

It was unanticipated that the English were advising the Raja to evade the payment and even the Raja's *vakeel* and other source, too, gave him the information of the change of Government at Fort William with so conformity. It seems that Hastings himself was emanating erroneous information apprehending Marathas interference in the Raja's case. He wanted to shun any possibility of the Maratha joining the Raja's cause as they were the greatest enemy in their way of expansion and if, in any case, they got the Raja's support then the strategic, geopolitical, religious and economic factors of Benares would exacerbate the situation for the Company particularly at a time when English were in a war with the Marathas since 1775.

On August 17, 1778, Hastings met Ali Naqi who expressed that his Raja was "at all times ready to pay obedience to the commands of Board" and consented to pay Rs. 3 lakhs on account of the expenses of three battalions of sepoys. But according to Hastings, the amount of three battalions on double *batta* exclusive of tents, arms and contingents was Rs. 4, 76,000 and fixed the amount as 5 lakh of *muchhlidar* rupees, which was to be paid instantly to the Resident. The *vakeel* contended much for fixing the sum at Rs. 3 lakhs, but Hastings under duress received his consent for Rs. 5 lakhs in his master's name by virtue of the authority that he derived from the Raja. The Governor General opined, "as the Raja's consent has been expressed with such a limitation, and eluded in his written answer, the payment of subsidy ought not to be left subject to your Country which during the course of a year may produce, but immediately demanded."[36] The Raja was asked to make the payment to Graham immediately. Francis opined that the amount of demand should be added to the monthly *kist* of the Raja, but was all in vain.

The Court was informed of this requisition of Rs. 5 lakh on Raja Chait Singh on August 17, 1778, that states, "...but as we think it just, that Rajah Cheyte Singh should contribute his part to the charges of the War, we have determined that 3 of these battalions should be raised and maintained at his expense, by means of a subsidy of Rs. 5 lakhs per annum, which he has agreed to for one year."[37] This letter misguided the Directors about the exact situation, for the Raja was not willing to pay more than Rs. 3 lakhs and Hastings contrained by force the Raja and demanded a total sum of Rs. 5 lakhs on this account. The letter neither expressed about how the Raja's consent to the demand was taken under duress nor stated about controversy regarding the Company's right, which was left to be decided later by the superiors. All this gave an erroneous understanding that the Raja willingly proffered his assistance to the Company. Hastings wrote to Mr. Sullivan, "We have required the Raja of Benares to contribute, as his share of the burden of the War, the maintenance of 3 battalions of sepoys, computed at 5 lakhs of rupees yearly, and he has consented."[38]

On 20th September, Raja Chait Singh appealed that owing to financial distress caused by the extortions of the *Vizier* he was not in a position to pay the prodigious amount at a time and appealed to pay the money in installments in 6-7 months in *samwat* specie, as he was unable to pay in *muchhlidar*, but the Governor General obdurantly rebuffed the request[39] and on 28th September, directed the Resident to demand full payment in *muchhlidar* coins within five days of the communication of the Council's orders and to communicate the Raja that "his evading or neglecting to accomplish payment within that span will be deemed equivalent to an absolute refusal and, in case of his Non compliance with your demand, we peremptorily enjoin you should refrain from all further intercourse with him, until you shall receive further orders on the subject."[40]

Such impudent and rigorous measure keeping the Directors oblivious of the exact situation manifests Hastings intentions against the Raja. He wanted to leave no viable alternative for him other than to make the payment and that too within a short span of time. The Raja predicting the ulterior motive of Hastings paid of Rs. 50,000 a week before this order i.e. September 21, 1778[41] and deeming imprudent to delay it further he made full payment on October 10, 1778.[42] Thus he made full payment before the completion of three months time span from the day when *parwana* was given to the Raja on 18th July. Still Governor General went so extreme to order the Resident to refrain further intercourse with the Raja. Regarding the payment of first subsidy Hastings articulated, "After many excuses, and protestations of inability he at length consented, with a very ill grace to the payment, and with a worse discharged it."[43]

The Raja, through his *vakee* Ali Naqi, not only consented to make the payments but also acquiesce in to accept the amount of maintenance of three battalions to be Rs. 5 lakhs as computed by the Board. There was no alibi or protest from his side regarding the payment except that he appealed to pay the amount in five installments, as it was difficult to pay such a huge lumpsum at once. With this payment the Council's order of 28th September was revoked. By end of September, 200 sepoys with *naiks* and *subadar* ranks were proceeding from Buxar to Allahabad but in the way there was a scuffle with *zamindar* of Raja Chait Singh's territory in which one *subadar* was killed and several sepoys were wounded. Nawab Asaf-ud-daula informed about the siteration to the Governor General and solicited for issue of peremptory orders upon the Raja to deliver the persons who had committed this outrage for punishment.[44]

The Raja was honoured with a *khil'at* and *farighkhati* for the full payment of his tribute for the year 1777-78.[45]. The Raja intimated Hastings about the full payment of Rs. 5 lakhs, which he had raised by disposing of all his belongings, and supplemented the deficit by taking loans, so as to adhere to the time schedule and avoid any default and avert any consequences. Hastings appreciated the Raja for his obedience and assured him continued full support and patronage, to protect the Raja's interests, punish his enemies and settle all his affairs once and for all,[46] but all the assurances of Governor General were only pompous promises as they were to share more embitter relations in future.

The Raja was informed in advance that Graham, who visited Calcutta at the end of December 1778, after his return would be "creating mischief", and his *vakeel* advised the Raja to leave for Lateefpur and Bijaigarh and commenced the fortification of strategic positions so that when Graham arrives with "bad intentions" the Raja would excite a commotion within the country and then retire to the hills from where he could negotiate. On January 1, 1779, there were heavy discussions on the issue, after which on 3rd January Babu Subhan Singh was sent to *pargana* of Chhattisgarh to make necessary arrangements and the Raja left for Lateefpur at midnight on the same day with his adherents Bhagatji, Ghulam Hussain Khan, Faizullah Beg, Bal Kishan Hazari and even asked each to take two reliable horsemen with them. The Raja then left for Bijaigarh and before departure he summoned Jagdeo Singh, Zalim Singh, Diljit Singh and son of Ramroch to return to their *pargana* near the residence of Ausan Singh and kill him as his death was necessary for the peace of the country. They were even provided 100 horsemen and 200 muskets for the accomplishment of the task.[47]

Such high level preparation by the Raja and his leaving for Ramnagar displays that he was well aware of what "bad intentions" Graham had and what "mischief" he was planning in connivouce with Hastings and Barewell at Calcutta that was to be implemented after his arrival at Benares. In any such condition Ausan Singh was a great menace to the Raja so he even planned to kill him, but things were never implemented in such manner, as there were speculations about Sir Coote's view as to which party he would favour as the Councillor. Francis had even moved the Raja's case to the Prime Minister of England on his behalf. The Raja received information from Sambhunath that all the decisions regarding Benares would be put into abeyance till Sir Coote joins the Council, as the Resident would not get the support of the Councillors, other than Governor General and Barewell. He advised that there was no danger to him and he should come back to Ramnagar.[48] Francis assured Ali Naqi that with the joining of Coote; Fowke would replace Graham. During this time Barewell was to leave for Europe, but the Governor General persuaded him to stay.[49] The *vakeel* also endeavoured to meet Mrs. Hastings appealing to exert her influence over her husband (G.G.) in respect of Raja's affairs where she promised to get the matter settled in a satisfactory manner.[50]

Sir Coote joined as Councillor on April 1, 1779, in place of General Clavering. It was highly indispensable for Hastings to get favourable attitude of Coote and so he endeavoured to gain his friendship by an official support of his pretensions, an unreserved surrender of the military department and other more important concession.[51] Instantly after the joining of Sir Coote, Francis moved a resolution on April 5, 1779, for the recall of Graham as Resident, but was not passed as Sir Coote did not support him.[52] Notwithstanding the fact that the Raja paid his monthly *kist* (instalment) regularly even after paying the war subsidy of Rs. 5 lakhs, Graham erroneously reported that he obtained the 4th *kist* with difficulty.[53] These reports of Graham must have been abused by Hastings to raise qualms on the probity of the Raja and portray him as a great menace for the Company in the eyes of Sir Coote so that the latter may staunchly support Hastings's every measure against the Raja. There was not a modicum of veracity as these reports were based on the information given by the Raja's enemies. Even Mill stated, "The Raja continued to pay his tribute with an exactness rarely exemplified in the history of the tributary princes of Hindustan."[54]

Even the Raja was aware of these collusions and had written to the Governor General unequivocally that he was to be considered as a loyal subject and the Governor General should not land his credence to fallacious reports of "mischief mongers".[55] When the Raja was encircled by enemies, Asaf-ud-daula also availed himself and sent a proposal to Hastings in June 1779, for giving the territories of Raja Chait Singh to him on annual revenue of Rs. 35 lakhs, but Hastings never accepted this proposal. In December 1779, he divulged to Coote, had the Nawab been competent he would have restored the territories to him.[56] On July 19, 1779, Hastings proposed for the next year war subsidy of 5 lakh *muchhlidar* rupees[57] that passed unanimously. The decision was communicated to the Resident with the direction to remit the amount soon.[58]

Hastings tried to maintain a very diplomatic relation with Raja Chait Singh after the demand was fulfilled. During this time he had a very amicable correspondence with the Raja assuring him of good will and favour, but he was obdurant in the exaction of second demand. Raja Chait Singh instantly resisted any such demand to the Resident. On 16th August, Graham forwarded Raja's representation to the Council, in which the Raja wrote to Hastings, "Last year, you directed Sheck Ally Nucky, that I should by any means, by disposing of my effects or by borrowing make this one payment and I shall not be called on in future". The Raja solicited that the repetition of demand was too much for his meagre income and "nothing may be demanded of me beyond the amount expressed in the Pottah which through your favour, I obtained from English Company."[59] Thus the Raja in a most humble and submissive language, brought to the notice of the Council that he was not accountable to any such unjust demands, but to no avail. Hastings soon replied to Raja Chait Singh expressing his surprise and called his action as most "objectionable". He obdurantly denied Raja's *arzee,* and directed to make the payments immediately or Graham with the assistance of force recover the amount by "whatever way he thinks fit" and he would be responsible for additional expenses incurred in the course of recovery.[60]

Without waiting, on August 26, 1779, a resolution was passed by Hastings, Coote and Barewell with harsh statement, "Commander-in-Chief be requested to give orders to Major Camac or officer in Command of his detachment for march of two Battalions of sepoys to Benares on requisition of Mr. Graham resident and to remain at that place for further orders." The resolution was passed within 38 days since the demand was made. Such a stringent action within a short span of time, without giving any response to the Raja's representation manifests itself that the Governor General was implacably opposed to the Raja where he had full support of Sir Eyre Coote and Barewell.

Though it was demurred by Francis and Wheeler, but being in minority all proved abortive. Francis opined, "I never approved the additional demand beyond his stipulated tribute I cannot therefore concur in the measure proposed I firmly believe it to be unnecessary, even for its avowed purpose and I am very much afraid that it will be attended with consequences ruinous to the Rajah and to his country; that country is one of the richest jewels that we possess. The great revenue we draw from that Country may be permanently secured under mild and equitable Treatment. Measures of a different nature may extort more for a moment, but they will ruin the future resource." Hastings retorted, "Benares is not a jewel in our possession if you leave the Rajah an option to obey or disobey the orders of his superior Government and to maintain himself in the independency of a tributary Prince as to the ruin portended from this order the terms of the Question itself put in his power to prevent even the execution of the orders..."[61]

On the same day, Hastings wrote to Graham that the Council cannot admit any plea from the Raja to exempt from its orders and it empowered him to call Major Carnac with two battalions of sepoys from Danapore, if the Raja persists in refusing payment.[62] On September 2, 1779, Graham informed to the Council, "I have used every agreement in my power to convince him that as a subject it was his duty inseparable from his allegiance to afford every assistance, it might require, whilst it was engaged in war and Denial under such circumstances was never admitted of."[63] Graham was of the considered opinion that he would not be required to exercise his discretionary power under any circumstance to compel the Raja for payment.[64] On September 17, 1779, the Raja informed the Governor General of his consent to make the payment in four months by installments by the end of the month of *zelhedge* i.e. mid of January.[65]

Graham showed his qualm on Raja's punctuality stating that the Raja would be dilatory upon disbursement of payments,[66] though the Raja had lucidly expressed, "I have for this time agreed to pay neither am I dilatory or inattentive in providing for its discharge but the amount considerable and can only be liquidated by degrees".[67] Despite the Raja's consent to pay, there were inexorable demands for the discharge of the amount. How much the Raja was being coerced and mortified can be known by the fact that from 12th September to 16th September within four days the Resident demanded for payment many a time. He even sent a person to attend the Raja's *durbar* for expeditions compliance, though the Raja, through his *vakeel*, had already solicited to be "indulged with time".[68] The Raja had even complained that the incessant applications were creating inconveniences and his endeavours were being interrupted.[69] Soon, Hastings obdurantly repudiated these requests and took an extreme measure of directing march of two battalions under Major Carnac at Dinapore to Benares and to remain there until the full subsidy was received from the Raja. Though the resolution of August 26, 1779, ordered the march of battalion on the requisition of Mr. Graham only, but on September 25, 1779, the Council directly ordered immediate march without any requisition from the Resident and the Raja was informed of the same.[70] On 29th September, Hastings wrote to Graham, "compulsory means should be immediately used to oblige him to discharge it."[71] This is axiomatic of the implacable attitude of the Council for the ruin of the Raja.

Hastings further directed the Resident to receive from the Raja the expenses of the march of detachment.[72] On 17th October, the Raja Chait Singh made a payment of Rs. 1 lakh.[73] The Dinapore regiment under the command of Captain Crabb arrived Benares on 19th October and encamped near the Raja's palace. This compelled the Raja to make the full payment by 22nd October, with one installment of Rs. 1, 90,000 on 20th October [74] and another installment of Rs. 60,000 on 22nd October.[75] Later, on October 26, 1779, Raja paid Rs. 20,000 more as the expenses of troops March.[76] This amount was based on the calculation of Officer-in-Command, Captain Crabb. He calculated the monthly expenses of two battalions which amounted Rs. 40,130 of which Rs. 20,000 was claimed based on the number of days of the detachment service from 29th September-22 October 1779, was 24 days.[77] The second demand of Rs. 5 lakh was paid by the Raja as follows:

12th October 1779	Rs. 1, 19,000
After 12th October	Rs. 31,000
18th October	Rs. 1, 00,000
20th October	Rs. 1, 90,000
22nd October	Rs. 60,000

The Council directed the Resident to remit to the Chief and Council at Patna.[78] The Council reported about the payments of the second subsidy to Court of Directors on January 14, 1780, which states: "We shall make but this short observation upon the conduct of the Rajah, that whether it proceeded from the Apprehension of establishing a Precedent for exceeding the sum of his Annual and stipulated Revenue, or from a sense of independency, it was equally unreasonable, and an ungrateful Return for the Benefits which he has been allowed to derive from the Company's protection."[79] It was nowhere indispensable for the Raja to pay any amount for enjoying the protection of the Company. In fact the Company was deriving much more benefit by taking Benares into its authority and what the Raja was getting from its protection that was only of name. Indeed, they had put the Raja, Benares and its people in a position where they needed to protect themselves from the Company itself. By implication, the very purpose of enlisting and accepting the support of the English Army—to ward of any attack from the internal enemies—was defeated when the protectors demand arbitrarily huge sums of money, that, too at short notice, which was beyond the means of the Raja and it might spell disaster to him, to the city and the people of Benares. This is analogous to killing the hen that lays the golden egg. The Company being a trading Company would never take any stride that may not return a whooping profit, which was the sole end and purpose behind every action. Benares because of its immense wealth, geo-political and religious reasons was returning much more through trade and commerce other than the revenue.

In December 1779, Sir Eyre Coote commenced his journey to Benares, which the Raja's enemies communicated that the object of the Commander-in-Chief's journey was to chastise him. Being precautionary the Raja sent his family and valuables to the fort of Lateefpur and Bijaygarh. He sent a deputation to welcome Sir Coote including his brother Sujan Singh, Bakhshi Sadanand, Brij Lal and other confidants. General, who was already feeded with misconcieved information and conspiracy plotted by Graham against the Raja, refused to meet the deputation. Mr. Vansittart Henry, the Persian interpreter of the Commander-in-Chief, however, persuaded him to meet the deputation. Sir Coote consented to meet Raja Chait Singh at Ghazipur where he was presented with many valuables. He also visited Ramnagar where he demanded a sum of Rs. 1 lakh, which the Raja's father had promised to give to Major Munro 15 years ago, but never paid. Graham and other enemies tried to exact money from the Raja on the pretext that they would persuade Sir Coote not to claim for Rs. 1 lakh, but the unfortunate days of the Raja had already started and he had to pay total Rs. 2 lakhs instead of the demanded sum. The Raja never received any letter from Major Munro or any receipt of the money paid.[80] It was like a blatant illegal act by the legal authorities themselves.

The Raja gave such a warm welcome, valuables, presents and sum more than what demanded just to please Sir Coote still the latter was not gratified and reported to Hastings that the Raja had no respect for the English authorities and had raised an army of 30,000 men and was fortifying all the strategic places within his jurisdiction.[81] Hastings replied on December 18, 1779, that he was apprehensive of an underhand alliance between Francis and the Raja and could even use his influence in England. He divulged, "He will do yet more mischief by exciting the spirit of discord there than by secret machinations or even open revolt here. He has more than one example to lead him into that road."[82] The fortification of strategic places and raising the strength of the army was Raja's right and in no way it can be construed as his infidelity to the Company. Hastings, with the support of Barewell and Coote, was incessantly giving reports to prove Raja's infidelity to the Company that later could be used to legalize any measures taken by the Board against the Raja.

Hastings evaded the appointment of Fowke since last two years as the Court of Directors through their letter of January 30, 1778, had demurred the appointment of Fowke. It states, "We must be of opinion that Mr. Fowke was removed without just Cause, to make room for Mr. Graham". It deplored the removal of Fowke instead of his "greatest punctuality and exactness" and directed Hastings to reinstate Fowke in the Office of Resident and Post Master, Benares.[83] Hastings complied with the order on February 27, 1780,[84] when it was impossible for him to shun it further. In May 1780, Raja Chait Singh deputed Sadanand, his *Bakshi*, with a representation to Hastings to assure his submission to the orders of the Government and solicit Governor General's forgiveness for the past conduct. Hastings articulated, "I accepted his excuses and promised him an oblivion of all that had passed exceptionable in his conduct, and my future protection and every good office in my power, so long as he adhered to his professions." The deputation paid Rs. 2 lakhs, which Hastings accepted.[85]

This conduct of Hastings was highly unconstitutional in two ways, withholding of this transaction from the knowledge of the Council, and acceptance of private presents from an Indian chief was a flagrant violation of one of the principal provisions of the Regulation Act of 1773. Hastings himself divulged this to his friend Sullivan in a letter dated 30 August, 1780, "The money was not my own; it was a peace offering from the Raja of Benares, which he had deputed his most confidential servant to Calcutta to make to me, and to solicit my pardon for all his past offences. I gave the man assurances of my forgiveness, but refused to accept the money, and he was on the point of returning when these debates in our Council began. It occurred to me to convert it to a public use; I gave him an opportunity of repeating the offer, and accepted it, directing it to be delivered to Mr. Crostes, our Sub-Treasurer, and him to receive it as a deposit in my name. It has since been re-coined, and turns out about two lakhs of sicca rupees. I believe I shall communicate this fact to the Court of Directors; but if I do not, I give you permission to make what use of the above relation of it you think proper, declaring upon my honour that I never will reclaim the money, and that I disclaim any title to it as I should not have taken it, but for and on the occasion which induced me to receive it, or one similar to it." He alluded this acceptance to Court of Directors after six months on November 29, 1780, "The money was not my own, I neither could, nor would have received it, but for your benefit."[86]

The Select Committee observes, "If presents which when they were given were unlawful, can afterwards be legalized by an application of them to the Company's service, no sufferer can ever resort to a remedial process at law for his own relief. The moment he attempts to sue, the money may be paid into the Company's treasury." Parliamentary Committee noted, "The acceptance of that gift by Mr. Hastings must have pledged a tacit faith for some degree of indulgence towards the donor."[87] Even the 11th report of the Select Committee of 1783 states, "The complication of cruelty and fraud in the transaction admits of few parallels. Mr. Hastings...displays himself as a zealous servant of the Company, bountifully giving from his own fortune... on the credit of supplies, derived from the gift of a man whom he treats with the utmost severity, and whom he accuses in this particular of disaffection to the Company's cause and interests. With L 23,000 of the Raja's money in his pocket, he persecutes him to his destruction."[88] Acceptance of money from the Raja gives an impression of his tacit support to the Raja of remission as Mill, too, opined, "This however included not the payment of the five lacs, of which the agent was instructed to use his utmost endeavours to obtain a remission. For the better accomplishment of this object, he was furnished with a secret compliment to the Governor General, of the amount of two lacs of rupees."[89]

Before putting forward the next demand, Hastings appointed Captain John Scott, one of his confidants, to the command of the sepoys stationed at Chunar.[90] Soon after being paid Rs. 2 lakhs on June 15, 1780, the question of further demand of subsidy was put forward in the Council for discussion. Though it was demurred by Francis and Wheeler on the grounds that the demanded sum was not being applied in war, but was being appropriated in the general estimate of the revenue.[91] Eventually, on 22nd June, it was resolved that the Raja should pay a subsidy of Rs. 5 lakhs as the war was still continuing [92] and Fowke, on the same day, was directed to demand the same as Raja's proportion of charge of current year.[93] It should be deprecated that this money was demanded for expense of war between Britain and France, but was being used in the establishment of the British Empire in India i.e. for the Maratha war. It is extremely lamentable that there is not only an impropriety in the system of accounting but also, the Representatives of the British Empire in India, committed a grave impropriety and extreme degree of ingratitude to the Indians by way of illicitly exacting from the Raja of Benares money to the tune of Rs. 5 lakhs, which sum was earmarked for launching war with Indians living an another side of India, namely, the Marathas. One of the letters states more explicitly, "It is impossible for me to start any new idea to you on this subject (the Mahratta war). The only difficulty we can possibly feel in the prosecution of the war will be from a want of money, and this difficulty may, I think, be easily obviated by your insisting upon Cheyt Sing's contributing his quota to the expenses of our advanced army, in lieu of being ordered to join it at the head of his own forces. Were he a zemindar, dependant on any other government than our own, this would be insisted upon; and as his ability to advance a large sum seems to be universally acknowledged, why should he alone be exempted from the expenses, as well as the devastations of war?"[94]

The Raja paid Rs. 1 lakh in July[95] and asked Banker Kashmiri Mal to make the rest payment, who showed his inability.[96] Subsequently, the Raja sent an *arzi* on 5th August to the Council that he may be allowed a period of three months for the payment of remaining four lakhs. In September two more installments were paid. On October 19, 1780, Fowke was instructed by the Council to demand instant payment of the balance and in case of delay, empowered to call the army stationed near to Benares for the collection of balance Rs. 1 lakh and also impose a fine of Rs. 1 lakh for his "past disobedience".[97] The same day the Council directed Brigadier General Stibbert to sent troops to Benares,[98] but before the compliance of this order, Raja Chait Singh had fortunately paid full subsidy by October 7, 1780, and so the orders were countermanded.[99] But Mill was of the view that Rs. 1 lakh was extorted from the Raja in spite of full payment before the order of the march. He opines, "The payment of this mulct is stated as doubtful, in Burkes Charges; but as it is passed without mention in the Answer, the silence must, in this as in other cases, be taken for confession."[100] Thus in 1780 the Raja paid the third demand in four installments on following dates.[101]

23rd July	Rs. 1, 00,000
19th September	Rs. 1, 70,000
26 September	Rs. 1, 30,000
7 October	Rs. 1, 00,000

If we exclude the last paid installment of the subsidy, the information of which Council may not have received, even then by the end of September Raja had paid Rs. 4 lakh of the subsidy within the time period of three months since 22nd June, the day when the demand was resolved in the Council and he had even assured of the full payment. The regularity with which the Raja was paying his revenue, any such assurance from his side should be taken seriously. Still such a stringent measure to direct the troops to march against him shows the avidity of Hastings to end up inviolable power, authority, prestige and rights of the Raja for which he was assured by the Governor General himself and the most important thing to be observed was that despite all these forceful payments, the Raja's revenue was being paid regularly to the Company for which *farighkhati* and *khil'at* was granted to the Raja.[102]

In July 1780, Captain Issac Eaton, the Commanding officer stationed at Buxar, had deputed some sepoys to procure grain from a village for provision of an English detachment, situated near the boundary of Raja Chait Singh's territory, but the *zamindar* of Narainpur denied to send *dukandars* with grain.[103] Coote wrote to the Resident on August 3, 1780, "The Merit or Demerit of the sepoys is a matter which is not now in point; admitting that they misbehaved, the conduct of the *foujdar* merits the severest punishment."[104]

Another matter was reported on November 14, 1780, where three English officers Irwin, Horne and Basset were insulted by a gang of robbers near the village of Barpur in the territory of Raja Chait Singh.[105] Three of their servants were killed, one officer wounded and a boat laden with goods was plundered at the instigation of the *jamadar* of the place.[106] Eaton wrote to the Council on November 16, 1780, "Outrages of this kind are perpetrated in almost every village of Rajah Cheyt Sing's country. This need be ended."[107] The Raja sent a *parwana* of censure to the *fauzdar*. The Bengal Government on December 14, 1780, directed the Raja to exercise his authority in seizing the *faujdar* of Ballia and the *jamadar* of Narainpore and to institute a strict enquiry into their conduct in the presence of the Resident.[108] The Raja was told specifically that if the offenders were not punished, he would be held responsible.[109] This incident clearly manifests the discontent among the people of Benares against the English power and the action taken by the Council was a clear interference into the judicial matters of the Raja, of which they had no right in conformity with to the agreement.

Hastings received information through an anonymous letter dated October 18, 1780, about the alluring wealth of the Raja in his coffers. The letter states, " The shock which public credit has received, and the failure of almost all the capital bankers at Benares, is attributed, and I think very justly, to his withdrawing all the money which he had in their hands from them, and lodging it in his fort. I have taken all the pains in my power to procure information as to the quantity of specie he is possessed of, and no person rates it at less than a crore and a half, most people at two crores, of rupees."[110] This increased the Governor General's insatiable greed. On November 2, 1780, the Governor General was requested to write to the Raja to furnish a part of his cavalry in the service of the Company and to inform what number he could supply. He was also to be assured that the force provided would not be a permanent imposition on him and would be returned as the war ends.[111] The Governor General wrote a letter to the Raja to the same effect.[112] The basic reason behind this demand was the appearance of the Maratha force of 30,000 under Chimnaji Appa, son of Madhoji Bhonsle of Berar and need for imperative military aid.[113] The stationing of such large force on their southern borders compelled Fort William to prepare against the impending invasion. Sir Coote in his minute of September 26, 1780, recorded the proposed plan for defence of Bengal and Oudh. "The two regiments of Cavalry to be ordered down there, to be joined by four battalion of sepoys, the third Company of Artillery from the field, and 1000 Horse, if they can be procured, from the Rajah of Benares: Boggeh Battalions to make on of the four Benares for this service."[114] The demand of thousand horses by Coote was on the basis of intelligence report of Raja's army given by Graham while he was the Resident.[115]

Total horsemen	2100
The Companies of sepoys each consisting armed and disciplined after English manner	1250
Matchlockmen	2000
Peons with swords and targets	500

Total foot	3750
Horsemen in service of Raja's relations	325
Matchlockmen and peons in service of relatives	4300
Peons employed in different places	1050

Before the demand was made, Fowke was asked to enquire into the army of Raja Chait Singh to which he responded on August 10, 1780, that the Raja was assembling his forces and industriously concealing the strength from him.[116] This must have nettled Hastings who already had information of the army given by Graham, but waited for the Raja's response. On January 7, 1781, the Raja informed that he could provide 250 horses only.[117] Instantly after this, Fowke was replaced by Markham as the Resident of Benares. Hastings expressed in his minute, "he stands a screen between the Raja and Government instead of an instrument of control and that the Raja himself and every Chief in Hindostan with whom we are in connection will regard it as the pledge and foundation of his independence." He stated that the office of Benares Resident being a "representative station" could not be under charge of a man "not preferably chosen" by the members of actual Government. He expressed in his minute, "Mr Francis Fowke is not my agent that I cannot give him any confidence that while he continues..."

This minute was fully approved by Mr. Wheeler. Markham was also appointed as agent for the provision of all boats to be employed for the military services of this establishment, with an allowance of commission of 15% upon all disbursements in this office. John Benn was appointed Assistant to the Resident. Since Fowke's new appointment was to take effect after three months, he was permitted to draw his salary for the time as Resident of Benares. Thus, at a time when Company was in dire need of finance, it was taking a burden of salary of two residents at the same posts for three months.[118] Markham was appointed at this juncture on ad hoc basis that the later events would explain.

The new Resident arrived at Benares on February 1, 1781, for which Hastings asked the Raja to station two companies to attend the Resident and to grant a *tankhwah* for disbursement of their pay and this was complied with by the Raja. Markham wrote to Hastings on February 10, 1781, "If you think proper, an officer may be appointed to command them as they may be useful at some future period, if taught the European discipline." After joining as Resident, within few days Markham put forward the demand of 2,000 cavalry which was reduced to 1500 on the plea of the Raja for his inability to supply such numbers. The Raja informed that he had total 1,300 horses in his service and could provide 500 horses and 500 *barqandazes,*[119] but Hastings did not respond to the Raja as by then he had already made up his mind to make this situation propitious for the Company that was under grave financial stringency. He admits, "I do not know but it may be true. He had received positive orders, and those had been repeated. It was his duty to obey them, not to waste my time with letters of excuse."[120] The annual cost of 1,000 horses at the rate of Rs. 20 per trooper per mensem would be Rs. 2, 40,000. However, the king at Delhi paid at the rate of Rs. 30 per horseman of his cavalry.[121] Adding to this Officers and contingencies the amount would be whooping Rs. 5 lacs. After paying the third demand of Rs. 5 lakh, this demand within a short time period, was a heavy burden on the Raja. Annual establishment of charge of 1,000 horse [122]

Pay of 1 *jamadar* of 1000 horse	Rs. 25,000
Pay of 100 *Ahshamdars* @ Rs. 1500	Rs. 1,50,000
Pay of 5 *Imtiazis* @ Rs. 5000	Rs. 25,000
Pay of 5000 *Qaravals* @ Rs. 500	Rs. 2,50,000
Pay of 400 *Rahli* drivers @ Rs. 400	Rs. 1,60,000
Pay of 5 *Karkuns* @ Rs. 1000	Rs. 5,000
Total	Rs. 6,15,000

Hastings planned to meet the Nawab and Dewagur Pandit, *dewan* of Raja of Berar. This plan was in his mind since last year as he had expressed it in one of his letter to Laurence Sulivan in November 1780. Though Hastings had expressly stated in his letter to Scott in April 1781, that the ruling motive for his expedition was to meet Dewagur Pandit, but the same letter expresses, "Something too will be required at Benares, and something more than I shall dare to attempt; for if it were left to my option, I would restore that zemindarry to the Nabob of Oude. Either that ought to be done, or the Rajah reduced to the condition of a zemindar."[123] Hastings was a man of great farsightedness and had always shown that there was no real purpose to visit Benares other than meeting Dewagur Pandit.

On May 21st the Council passed a minute for this purpose. On July 3, 1781, Hastings was invested with full power and authority to form an "arrangement with the Rajah of Benares for the better Government of his *zamindary* and to perform such acts for the improvement of the interest which Honourable Company possess in it, as he shall think fit, and consonant to the mutual relation and actual engagement subsisting between Company and Rajah." The Council declared that any act or engagements or Treaties made by the Governor General will be binding upon Governor General and Council and as effective as had been passed by "the special and immediate concurrence and actual sanction of Governor General and in Council assembled."[124]

The Council also vested military power in the hands of Governor General as it mentions, "It is ordered that all such orders as he shall from this time and think it proper issue to the troops stationed beyond the provinces as well as in the dominions of the Nabob Vizier as those which are situated beyond them, shall be obeyed, and that his single authority shall be considered and received as of the same force as that of the Governor General and Council collectively, until this order shall be revoked." This order was signed by Hastings and Wheeler and passed to Colonel Morgan, Colonel Muir, Colonel Cumming, Major Popham, Mr. Middleton and Mr. Mackham. It is to be observed during this time Hastings was holding the post of Commander-in-Chief also and Wheeler was the only member of the Council other than the Governor General.[125]

Hastings had adroitly and with great sagacity choosen an opportune time to pass this resolution, as Wheeler was the only Councillor. Even if he had demurred the resolution then also Hastings would have effortlessly passed it using his casting vote.

The statement given in the minute was highly ambitious, regarding which Mill wrote, "The aptness of the expression consisted in its having sufficient laxity to stretch around all that the actor had in view, while its more obvious signification led not the mind of the hearer to any but ordinary transactions."[126] Even before departure Hastings had made up his mind to impose a substantial pecuniary mulct of Rs. 50 lakhs as he divulged this to Wheeler on the eve of departure, but these were not mentioned in the minute.

Wheeler himself admitted that on the eve of departure there was a confidential discourse between them where Raja Chait Singh was the principal subject. He divulged in his letter, "The Rajah's offences were declared to require early punishment, and as his wealth was great and the Company's exigencies pressing, it was thought a measure of policy and justice, to exact from him a large pecuniary mulct for their relief. The sum to which the Governor, declared his resolution to extend this fine, was 40 or 50 lacks. His ability to pay it was stated as a fact that could not admit of doubt, and the two alternatives on which the Governor declared himself to have resolved, if Chait Singh refused to comply with the requisition, were, to the best of my remembrance, either a removal from his zemindary entirely, or by taking possession of his forts, to obtain out of treasure deposited in it the above sum for Company."[127] Raja Chait Singh received the intelligence of Hastings's visit to Benares and feeling the premonition signs he offered a whooping sum of Rs. 20 lakhs before Hastings departure from Calcutta, which was brusquely refused by the Governor as he had some ulterior motives in his mind.[128]

The last demand of cavalry was unjudicial. Firstly, the Government had committed itself in 1775, that the Raja was not bound to maintain any cavalry although they recommended maintaining 2000 horsemen. Secondly, the Company should pay a gratuity of Rs. 15 p.m. per *sawar* to the Raja's cavalry if the Company requires them for their service. After exaction of Rs. 15 lakh, another substantial demand within a short span of time and then also expecting him to pay his monthly *kist* was extreme oppression and humiliation of the Raja. When in 1775, the Nawab having no means of discharging payments from him due to the Company he imposed a *Tunkaw* of Rs. 5 lakh two times on Raja Chait Singh, it was the Company that supported the Raja's cause, "Rajah had been induced to pay the first *Tuncaw* of five lakhs with great difficulty and did it solely to avoid altercation. That he would not now by a repetition establishes a precedent so disadvantageous to himself and contrary to the terms of the Treaty." The Nawab was at that time clearly explained "Honourable Board would never suffer the rights of their dependents to be in fringed. Raja Chait Singh was to be considered in this light and he must expect to see him protected for that he was not to be put upon a footing with his other zamindars."[129] How can a measure taken by the Nawab, which was unjudicial in the eyes of the Company, be held judicial when taken by the Governor General himself?

The Raja was continuously paying subsidy for three years. The method of exaction of these demands could not be called judicious. Even in payment of tribute the Raja could get 51 days grace by paying the amount in bills and in case of further delay only a fine of 4% was to be imposed as the Company previously mentioned it. But in case of subsidy, a slightest delay was met with a measure as harsh as march of troops against the Raja. Even after making all the payments, Hastings charged him for dilatory methods and contumacy. Francis in his minute of September 28, 1778 supported the cause of Raja Chait Singh stating, "If such demands can be increased upon him at the discretion of the Superior Power, he has no Rights; he has no Property, or at least, he has no Security for either. Instead of Five Lacs, let us demand fifty; and whether he refuses, or is unable to pay the Money, the Forfeiture of his Zemindary may be the immediate Consequence of it, unless he can find Means to redeem himself by a New Treaty."[130]

Hastings's visit for Benares with Durgbijay Singh, father of Mahipnarain, one of the strongest claimants of Benares was the final phase of Hastings's plan. All these events shows that the ulterior motive of Hastings was to take harsh steps against the Raja, hammer his prestige and provoke him to raise against the English authorities so that he may prove every action judicial in the eyes of Court and Council, remove the Raja and put Mahipnarain in his place with an increasing amount of the stipulated revenue. How long the Raja being a novice, misinformed and encircled by enemies could shun the inevitable.

References

1. FPD, 23 December 1776, No. 10.
2. FPD, Sec Pr., 11 November-30 December 1776, Vol. 45, Minutes of Governor General dated December 23, 1776, pp. 3857-58.
3. DR, BCO, Basta 1, Vol. 2, December 1776, letter from Council to Graham, 9 January, 1777, p. 3.
4. PD, letter from Court, 30 January, 1778, para 66.
5. FPD, June 12, 1775, No. 3, Governor General's minute.
6. BM, Add.Mss No. 45422, Graham to Anderson, April 5, 1777, NAI.
7. FPD, 13 January, 1777, No. 8, letter from Commander-in-Chief to Dow, Commanding Garrison at Chunar, 2 January, 1777.
8. FPD, 13 January, 1777, No. 9, letter to Colonel Dow, 13 January 1777.
9. Davies, C.C., *Warren Hastings and Oudh*, Oxford University Press, London, 1939, p. 134.
10. PD, letter from Court, 23 December 1778, para. 31 and 33.
11. DR, BCO, Basta 1, Vol. 2, December 1776, letter from Court of Directors to Hastings and Council, 20 June, 1777, p. 24.
12. PD, letter from Court, 23 December, 1778, para. 36, 37 and 38.
13. DR, BCO, Basta 1, Vol. 2, December, 1776, letter from Court of Directors to Council, 24 June, 1777, pp.38-40.
14. Hastings, Warren, *A Narrative of The Late Transactions At Benares*, London, 1782.
15. FPD, 2 June, 1777, No. 1, letter from Graham to Council, 23 May, 1777.
16. FPD, 2 June, 1777, No. 2, letter from Council to Graham, June 2, 1777.
17. DR, BCO, Basta 1, Vol. 2, December 1776, letter from Hastings to Ausan Singh and Raja Chait Singh, pp.47-48.
18. Letter from Hastings to Raja Chait Singh, October 5, 1774, No. 1317, CPC, IV.
19. DR, BCO, Basta 1, Vol. 2, December 1776, letter from Hastings to Raja Chait Singh and Graham, pp. 46-47.

20. Letter from Babu Ausan Singh to Governor General, No. 834, March 10, 1778, CPC, V,.
21. Letter from Sambhunath to Maharaj Misar, No. 854, March 31, 1778, CPC, V.
22. Letter from Babu Ausan Singh to Governor General, No. 834, March 10, 1778, CPC, V.
23. FPD, 29 September, 1777, No. 2, letter from Graham to Council, September 17, 1777.
24. FPD, 29 September, 1777, No. 4, letter from Council to Graham, September 29, 1777.
25. FPD, December 1, 1777, No. 6, Council to Graham, 1 December 1777.
26. Letter from Raja Chait Singh to Hastings, No. 825, March 2, 1778, CPC, V.
27. DR, BCO, Basta 1, Vol. 2, December 1776, letter from Council to Graham, 12 December, 1777, p.68.
28. Letter from Sambhunath to Maharaj Misar, No. 854, March 31, 1778, CPC, V.
29. BM, Add.Mss 29141, letter from Graham to Hastings, 23 July, 1778, held at Private Section, NAI.
30. FPD, 9 July, 1778, No. 2; letter from Hastings to Raja Chait Singh, July 11, 1778, No. 1008, CPC, V.
31. News from Benares, No. 1067, September 1, 1778, CPC, V.
32. FPD, 17 August, 1778, No. 7, letter from Raja to Governor General.
33. News from Benares, No. 1067, September 1, 1778, CPC, V.
34. Mill, James, *History of British India,* Vol. 2, Associated Publishing House, New Delhi, 2nd reprint, 1978, p.821.
35. News from Benares, No. 1067, September 1, 1778, CPC, V.
36. FPD, 17 August, 1778, No. 6.
37. PD, letter to Court, 17 August, 1778, para. 12.
38. Letter from Hastings to Sullivan dated August 18, 1778, Gleig, *op.cit.*, Vol. II, p.204,
39. Letter from Raja Chait Singh to Hastings, No. 1106, September, 28, 1778, CPC, V,
40. HPC, 28 September, 1778, No. 4, Council to Graham, 28 September, 1778.
41. HPC, 5 October, 1778, No. 22, Graham to Council, 22 September, 1778.
42. HPC, 12 October, 1778, No. 6, Council to Graham, 12 October, 1778.

43. Hastings, *op.cit.*, p.4.
44. Letter from Nawab Asaf-ud-Dowla to Hastings, No. 1117, October, 1, 1778, CPC, V.
45. Letter dated October, 12, 1778, No. 1146, CPC, V.
46. Letters from Raja Chait Singh to Hastings, No. 1194 and No. 1196, November, 13, 1778, CPC, V.
47. News from Ramnagar, January 28, 1779, No. 1336, CPC, V.
48. Letter from Sambhunath to Raja Benares, January 31, 1779, No. 1338, CPC, V,
49. Letter from Ali Naqi to Raja Benares, February 11, 1779, No. 1356, CPC, V.
50. Letter from Ali Naqi to Raja Benares, February 15, 1779, No. 1362, CPC, V.
51. Gleig, *op.cit.*, Vol. II, p. 260-61.
52. Fort William-India House Correspondence, Vol. 8, p. 601, notes.
53. HPC, 28 June, 1779, No. 17, Graham to Council, 25 May, 1778.
54. Mill, *op.cit.*, Vol. II, p. 820.
55. Letter from Raja Chait Singh, July 18, 1779, No. 1546, CPC, V.
56. BM. Add. Mss. No. 29155, letter from Hastings to Coote, December 18, 1779.
57. FPD, 19 July, 1779, No. 1, Governor General's order.
58. FPD, 19 July, 1779, No. 2, letter from Council to Graham.
59. FPD, Sec Pr., 3 July-23 December, 1779, Vol. 57, letter from Raja Chait Singh to Hastings enclosed with Graham's letter to Hastings dated 16 August 1779, 26 August 1779, pp. 1149-1151.
60. Letter from Hastings to Raja Chait Singh, No. 1569, August 27, 1779, CPC, V.
61. FPD, Sec Pr., 3 July-23 December, 1779, Vol. 57, 26 August, 1779, Minutes of Council Members, pp.1151-52.
62. FPD, Sec Pr., 3 July-23 December, 1779, Vol. 57, 26 August, 1779, letter from Governor General to the Resident dated August 26, 1779, p. 1154.
63. HPC, 13 September, 1779, No. 20, Graham to Council, 2 September, 1779.
64. FPD, 29 September, 1779, No. 1, letter from Graham to Hastings.
65. FPD, 29 September, 1779, No. 4, letter from Graham to Council with enclosure translation of Raja Chait Singh's letter dated September, 17, 1779.
66. FPD, 29 September, 1779, No. 4, letter from Graham to Council dated September, 12, 1779.

67. FPD, 29 September, 1779, No. 4, letter from Graham to Council with enclosure translation of Raja Chait Singh's letter dated September, 17, 1779.
68. FPD, 29 September, 1779, No. 3, letter from Graham to Hastings dated September, 16, 1779.
69. FPD, 29 September, 1779, No. 4, letter from Graham to Council with enclosure translation of Raja Chait Singh's letter dated September, 17, 1779.
70. Hastings, *op.cit.*, p. 3; also see letter from Hastings to Raja Chait Singh, September, 25, 1779, No. 1618, CPC, V.
71. FPD, 29 October, 1779, No. 5, letter from Council to Graham, 29 September, 1779.
72. FPD, 1 November, 1779, No. 9, letter from Council to Graham.
73. FPD, 28 October, 1779, No. 1, letter from Graham to Council, 19 October 1779.
74. FPD, 1 November, 1779, No. 4, letter from Graham to Council, October, 20, 1779.
75. FPD, 1 November, 1779, No. 5, letter from Graham to Council, October 22, 1779.
76. FPD, 12 November, 1779, No. 2, letter from Graham to Hastings dated October 27, 1779.
77. Roberts, P. E., *Cambridge History of India*, Vol. V, p. 295.
78. FPD, 1 November, 1779, No. 9, letter from Governor General to Resident dated November 1, 1779.
79. PD, letter to Court, 14 January, 1780, para 41 and 42.
80. Balwantnama, pp. 284-85 vide Sanyal, *Benares and the English East India Company*, World Press Pvt. Ltd., 1979, pp. 96-97
81. BM. Add.Mss. No. 29144, letter from Coote to Hastings, December 2, 1779.
82. BM. Add.Mss. No. 29115, letter from Hastings to Coote, December 18, 1779.
83. PD, letter from Court, 30 January, 1778, para No. 66 and 67; also see letter from Court 27 May 1779.
84. Letter from Hastings to Sullivan, March 4, 1780, vide Gleig, *op.cit.*, pp. 251-53
85. Hastings, *op.cit.*, p. 5.
86. Letter from Hastings to Sullivan, 30 August, 1780, vide Forrest, G.W., *Administration of Warren Hastings*, *op.cit.*, pp.164-65.
87. Report from Committees of House of Commons, 11th report, VI, p. 586, vide Roberts, *Journal of Indian History*, III, Madras, Hastings

and His Accusers, p. 99-100.

88. 11th Report of the Select Committee, 1783, vide Roberts, *The History of British India Under the Company and the Crown*, Oxford University Press, London, first ed. 1921, 1st Indian ed. 1976.)
89. Mill, *op.cit.*, p. 822.
90. Letter to Raja Chait Singh, April 18, 1780, No. 1831, CPC, V.
91. BM. Add.Mss. No. 29199, Accession No. 270, Roll No. 270, Minute of Wheeler and France, 15 June, 1780.
92. FPD, 22 June, 1780, No. 1; also see letter from Hastings to Raja Chait Singh, June 22, 1780, No. 1920, CPC, V.
93. FPD, 22 June, 1780, No. 6, letter from Council to Fowke dated 22 June 1780.
94. Gleig, *op.cit.*, Vol. II, p. 399, letter dated 25 June, 1780.
95. Hastings, *op.cit.*, p. 6.
96. Letter from Kashmiri Mal, August 1780, No. 1980, CPC, V.
97. HPC, 26 October, 1780, No. 21, Council to Fowke, 19 October, 1780.
98. HPC, 26 October, 1780, No. 22, Council to Stibbert, 19 October, 1780.
99. FPD, 2 November, 1780, No. 1, letter from Council to the Resident dated November 2, 1780.
100. Mill, *op.cit.*, p. 848.
101. Letter from Raja Chait Singh to Warren Hastings, No. 207, August, 15, 1781, CPC, VI.
102. CPC, V, No. 1156, No. 1178, No. 1230.
103. BCO, DR, Basta 1, Vol. 3 (1777-1780), a petition from the deceased *subadar's* son, enclosure to Coote's letter, 3 August, 1780, pp. 49-50, RAA; also see letter to Raja Chait Singh, December 15, 1780, No. 2064, CPC, V.
104. BCO, DR, Basta 1, Vol. 3 (1777-1780), Coote to Fowke, 3 August, 1780, pp. 47, RAA.
105. HPC, 14 December, 1780, No. 46, Eaton to Council, 16 November, 1780.
106. Letter to Raja Chait Singh, 15 December, 1780, No. 2064, CPC, V.
107. HPC, 14 December, 1780, No. 46, Eaton to Council, 16 November, 1780.
108. HPC, 14 December, 1780, No. 48, Council to Fowke, 14 December, 1780; also see letter to Raja Chait Singh, December 15, 1780, No. 2064, CPC, V.

109. CPC, V, No. 2064, letter to Raja Chait Singh, 15 December, 1780, pp. 503-04.
110. Letter dated 18 October, 1780, Gleig, Vol. II, *op.cit.*, p. 400.
111. FPD, 2 November, 1780, No. 1, letter from Council to the Resident dated November 2, 1780.
112. CPC, V, No. 2059, letter to Raja Chait Singh, November 25, 1780, p. 501.
113. Forrest, Selections from State Papers of Warren Hastings, Vol. II, pp.714-715.
114. Forrest, *Administration of Warren Hastings*, Calcutta, 1892, p. 190.
115. BM, Add Mss 29205, Accession No. 273, Roll No. 273, Report from Graham, 30 July 1778 or 1779 (year not legible).
116. Davies, C.C., *op.cit.*, p. 134.
117. Marshall, *Impeachment of Hastings*, p. 100.
118. FPD, 4-19 January, 1781, Vol. 62, No. 12, 14 January, 1781, Minute of Governor General, pp. 144-149.
119. Letter from Raja Chait Singh, August 15, 1781, No. 207, CPC, VI.
120. Hastings, *op.cit.*
121. CPC, IV, No. 913, p. 163.
122. Letter of Rajaram Pundit to Beniram Pundit, No. 2069, December 29, 1780, CPC, V, This is the most authentic letter for the estimate of contingent of 1,000 horse at that time.
123. Gleig, *op.cit.*, II, p. 335.
124. FPD, SC, 3 July, 1781, No. 7, Credential given to Governor General dated 3 July, 1781.
125. FPD, SC, 3 July, 1781, No. 8 dated 3 July, 1781.
126. Mill, *op.cit.*, p. 824.
127. Hastings, *op.cit.*, pp.18-19.
128. Gleig, *op.cit.*, Vol. II, p. 408.
129. FPD, Secret Committee, 27 April, 1775, No. 5, letter to Hastings.
130. FPD, 28 September, 1778, No. 2, Francis' Minute.

Chapter 6

The People's Rising in Benares Against the English Power

After a long period of interference and diplomacy, the change of the Resident and Hastings's plan to march towards Benares for an "arrangement" wielding full military power in a single hand, were ominous signs for the Raja. Hastings became more voracious with the information about Raja's treasury, of which he wanted to make optimum use by channelizing it in the establishment of the British Empire in India, as they were in war with two powers-Marathas and the Mysore. Regarding his motive of Benares visit, he remarked: "Let my motive be consulted. I left Calcutta, impressed with the belief that extraordinary means were necessary, and those exerted with a strong hand to preserve the Company's interests from sinking under accumulated weight which oppressed them. I saw a political necessity for curbing the overgrown power of great member of their dominion, and for making it contribute to the relief of their pressing exigencies."[1] He left Calcutta on July 7, 1781,[2] accompanied by his wife and retinue of friends including Sulivan, Private Secretary; Major Palmea, Military Secretary and Mr. Coolbrooke, Persian Secretary. The other *aides-de-camp* were Captain Hogan, Lieutenant James Anderson and

Governor General's cousin Lt. Jurner David Anderson.[3]

From Danapur Durgbijay Singh, father of Mahipnarain Singh, accompanied him. Raja Chait Singh was at Buxar with a large contingent of 2,000 armed men to pay his customary respect to the Governor General. Hastings called this act a deviation from the established rules of decorum.[4] Rejection of an enormous amount of Rs. 20 lakhs offer by a man who had earlier accepted an offer of Rs. 2 lakhs and that, too, at a time when the Company was going through great pecuniary stringencies, made the Raja's mind full of apprehensions and trepidation, which impelled him to come prepared for the worst that may happen and the huge centourage of security in various ranks was nowhere to insult the Governor General but for his own security.

The Governor General though received the Raja with civility and without any expression of displeasure, but denied to have any meeting with him and left Buxar. The Raja was able to meet him and have conversation with him during their second meet in a boat, where he assured his loyalty to the Government and expressed his fear for Ausan Singh who was incessantly colluding against him, but Hastings adroitly evaded to record this meet and conversations between them in minutes stating that the meet was accidental and was not included in his plans.[5] Even if it were so, then also, since one of the purposes of visiting Benares was to charge the Raja for his previous conduct, each and every word transpired between the Raja and Hastings should be recorded notwithstanding whether it was planned or accidental.

When Hastings reached Benares on 14th August, 1781,[6] he denied to have any meeting with the Raja and even asked him to defer any future visits, as he had to settle some matter with him for which he would depute the Resident next morning.[7] Though the Raja was so solicitous to have an interview with the Governor General and to settle all the contentious matters between them to the full gratification of the Governor General, yet he was not permitted. Through Markham, Hastings sent a letter to Raja Chait Singh charging him directly for "disaffection and infidelity to the Government" on which he depends. Hastings charged the Raja in following instances saying that these happened at a time when it was his duty to exert himself in support of its interest.[8]

1. "Either consulting temper of the Times or conforming to a premeditated design," the Raja withheld the remittance of the remaining amount of the demand of Rs. 5 lakhs to the army under the command of Carnac, which was set to march towards Malwa. Since no other provision was made for it, this led to great distress of the army and as many as 100 deserted.
2. Though the demand of a Body of Horse was reduced from 2,000 to 1,000, the Raja gave evasive answers and did not contribute even a single horseman.
3. The Raja, through his secret agents, had endeavoured to excite disorders in Government on which he depend.
4. Neglect of his duty towards the Government and his subjects leading to increasing number of robbery and murder cases in Benares city. He demurred these were "in violation of the conditions on which you received the confirmation of this zamindary."

Raja Chait Singh denied all these charges on the same day in a most submissive manner.[9]

1. For the first charge, he stated that he paid the first installment of Rs. 1, 70,000 to the Resident and solicited time for further payment, but being rebuked by the Governor General he paid the remaining. Since the remitting of this sum to the army does not depend on him, he categorically disowned any responsibility for any delay in payment.
2. He informed the Government that he had 1300 horse in his service and had informed the authorities that 500 horses and 500 *Burkandazzes* were ready for the Government service, but no response was given to this information. He stated that he instantly stationed two companies of sepoy and also *tunkhawah* was issued for payment on the Government orders.
3. He summarily denied the third charge stating, except Abdullah Beg and his attendants, none of his men had been to Calcutta and, as a matter of fact, his enemies had made

false representation to him.

4. Regarding robberies, he stated that he had given injunctions to his *Ameens* and taken a penalty bond from them, and had been very careful in punishing the culprit.

Hastings judged his answer "not only unsatisfactory in substance, but offensive in stile, and less a vindication of himself than recrimination upon me", and further considered it "as a strong indication of that spirit of Independency which the Rajah had for some years past assumed."[10] Speaking candidly, it was not an explanation that Hastings was waiting for the accusations made out against the Raja as Hastings had already prejudged the issue expartie without sufficient and requisite evidence available at his (Hastings) disposal; and he had already decided the measures to be taken against the Raja. Hastings directed Markham at 10 p.m. to arrest the Raja next morning, "It is my order that you proceed early tomorrow morning to the House of Rajah Cheit Sing with your usual guard and put him in arrest, you will require his immediate submission informing him that you act under orders given you by me and in case of his refusal you will wait the arrival of two companies of sepoys belonging to Major Popham's detachment who are directed to follow and assist you in execution of this service. Having secured the Rajah, you will keep him in your custody until further orders."[11]

In compliance with the order, Markham accompanied by Lt. Stalker and few orderlies, went to *Shivala ghat* early morning on 16th August, where Raja quietly submitted to the arrest. Markham wrote to Hastings, "He assured me that whatever your orders he was ready implicitly to obey. He hoped that you would allow him a subsistence; but as for his zamindary his forts and treasures he was ready to lay them at your feet, and his life if required." Hastings, very adroitly selected early hours of day for arrest the Raja to pre-emt any endowment. Lieutenant Scott arrived with two grenadier companies of Major Popham's regiment after a quarter of an hour. Markham before leaving the command under Scott, Lieutenant Stalker, Symes, instructed to disarm every servant of the Raja and allow only 8-10 persons for the Raja's attendance as he may approve and these men should be shown to the sepoys to obviate any possibility of deceit.[12] The guards were stationed in an enclosed square, which surrounded the Raja's apartment and the Resident guard returned with him.[13]

Markham returned to Hastings with a letter from the Raja written in a most submissive language calling himself servant of the Government.[14] Raja Chait Singh sent another *arzee*[15] in reply to which Hastings asked him not to conceive any terror or apprehensions and that Markham would explain him the particulars in the evening.[16] The letters manifest that the Raja was completely submissive to the Governor General and ready to comply with all his orders whether it be surrender of forts or treasures, still he had to go through humiliation and insolence. On the other side, the news of the Raja's arrest by the British Resident spread like a wild fire and large number of armed men crossed the river from Ramnagar and proceeded to rescue the Raja.[17] Chait Ram, a dismissed mace-bearer and *Chobdar* of Markham was sent to Raja Chait Singh to convey a message of Governor General,[18] "your people want to quarrel and fight, it will be better if you forbid them, for every sepoy is as an European, and every European is as a (or the) Company; If a drop of their blood is shed you shall be plundered and destroyed".[19] Chait Ram's insolent behaviour with the Raja made the crowd uncontrollable.

Hastings had candidly expressed his opinion on this incident in a letter to Major Scott, "you will observe in the Rajah's letter a repeated allusion to the insolent language of a chubdar of Markham's named Cheitram. I have no doubt of the fellow's insolence, but I have taken no notice of it in the narrative, because it had no necessary relation to it. The chubdar did not arrive at Shawalla till the tumult had almost begun. This I know, because he accompanied a Vackeel of the Rajah's, whom I ordered to go to the Rajah, and to tell him that if any blood was spilt, his should answer for it. I had then heard of the forces that had crossed and landed at Shawalla. I addressed this message both to the Vackeel and the Chubdar. The latter delivered it in his own fashion, and added some impertinence. He lost his life for it, and he deserved it; for he had been, as I have since learned, guilty of frequent instances of ill behaviour."[20] At 10 a.m. Hastings was informed that large number of people had crossed Ramnagar and surrounded Shivala palace in Raja's support. At the same time Lt. Stalker solicited for an immediate supply of ammunition as the troops in Shivala were without ammunition. Regarding non-availability of ammunition, Hodges remarked, "It was now found that such delicacy had been observed towards inorder to prevent any suspicion being entertained of an intention to carry the punishment rather than was really proposed, that the sepoys muskets were not loaded, nor had they (as no serious opposition was expected) any ammunition."[21] Glieg attributed this to some "uncountable negligence".[22]

Instantly on orders, Major Popham sent another Company of sepoy with ammunition to reinforce the first party. When the company arrived at Shivala Ghat, they found it surrounded and all avenues blockaded by multitude of armed men, who opposed their entry to the fort.[23] There is no evidence as to which side fired first, but according to Hastings it was Raja's men that first fired upon the sepoys and regarded this as a "concerted signal" and immediately after that the whole multitude made a fierce attack on the sepoys. The English Company made a feeble resistance and almost every man of this "unfortunate party" were hacked to pieces with officers being the first victim.[24]

On the first intelligence of this incident, Hastings directed Major Popham to march instantly with remainder of his detachment to support the Company in Shivala, but Major Popham's camp was at a distance of two miles from the Resident and Rajah's house, and by the time he arrived it was too late. Hastings stated though Major Popham executed as expeditiously as possible, but arrived too late "to be a spectator of the effects of a massacre which he could neither prevent nor revenge." In the midst of this confusion, Raja escaped through a wicket window, which opened to the river, and got down with the help of a turban tied together into a boat, which was already waiting for him. He went to the opposite shore followed by his people.[25] Had the Raja shown enough courage to attack Hastings in Madhodas garden, who was indubitably unable to resist any attack with the feeble security, the history of India and British Empire would have been something else.

Hastings divulged his trepidation in his Narrative, "If Chait Sing's people, after they had effected his rescue, had proceeded to my quarters at Mahdoodass's garden, instead of crowding after him in a tumultuous manner, as they did, in his passage over the river, it is most probable that my blood, and that of about 30 English gentlemen of my party would have been added to recent carnage, for they were above 2000 in number, furious and daring from easy success of their last attempt nor could I assemble more than 50 regular and armed sepoys for my whole defence. Let it not be thought that I attribute too much consequence to my own person when I suppose fate of the British empire in India connected with it."[26] Even Gleig, too, expressed his surprise, "Happily for the interests of British India, however, Cheyt Sing either did not perceive or was too much agitated to avail himself of the opportunity."[27]

The Shivala Palace was completely evacuated by the Raja's men who were landed on the opposite side of the river. Very few remained alive of the two Grenadier Company commanded by Lt. Stalker and majority were severely wounded. Major Popham reported to Hastings, "the bodies of Lt. Stalker, Scott and Symes were lying within a small distance of each others shockingly mangled and without any signs of life." For Burrell and his Company he reported, "the Burrell was dispatched with one Company of sepoys upon first rumor of Rajah's intentions but the fate of the Company's which proceeded him was decided prior to his being able to enter the Palace."[28] About 205 persons of different denominations were killed and wounded in Shivala.[29]

Raja Chait Singh along with his family and effects left Ramnagar in midnight and went to Latifpur, 10 miles from Chunar. He was accompanied by his brother, Sujan Singh, and Maniyar Singh, adopted son of Raja Balwant Singh; Rani Golab Kunwar, widow of Raja Balwant Singh; Durgbijay Singh, son-in-law of Raja Balwant Singh, accompanied by his two sons. Hastings at this juncture opined that Raja Chait Singh possesses every member of his family who could make plea to dispute with him the right of inheritance from his father Raja Balwant Singh, if that question ever arises.[30] Rani Golab Kunwar, instead of following Raja Chait Singh to Latifpur, remained in Benares along with her son-in-law Durgbijay Singh and his two sons. Durgbijay Singh and Mahipnarain also visited Hastings on the morning of 17th August.[31] Major Popham left a company with a subaltern in the palace and returned to Madhodas garden to submit his report to the Governor General.[32]

Hastings, without squandering any time, thought about the revenue collection, which was his utmost priority and for this purpose no other person suited better than Babu Ausan Singh, who not only possessed ample experience of the administration but was also an archenemy of the Raja. He was appointed as *Naib* for the time being by a proclamation and *parwanas* were issued to all the *Zamindars* and *Aumils* for the execution, of which Hastings ordered a battalion of sepoys from Chunar, the remainder of Popham's detachment from Mirzapur, and a regiment of sepoys from Danapore, to march immediately to Benares.[33]

On August 19, 1781, a large contingent of force arrived at Benares from Mirzapur under the command of Captain Mayaffre. Blair, with his Battalion and Mayaffre, with the remainder of Popham's detachment were ordered to assemble for march to Ramnagar and Major Popham was to join and conduct the operations according to a concerted plan. After the joining of Blair, Mayaffre, who was a senior officer, without waiting for Popham, marched precipitatedly towards Ramnagar on the morning of the 20th August in conformity with the order of the Governor General. The army under the command of Mayaffre was intercepted in the narrow streets of town and was butchered. Captain Mayaffre, Captain Doxatt and all sepoys of Captain Blair battalion that entered with him, were killed. The rest of the detachment retreated to Chunar with loss of two guns, howitzer, innumerable arms and ammunitions, and 103 men of all denomination killed. Blair somehow managed to flee to Chunar.[34] Captain Mayaffre was furiously assaulted and his head was carried in procession on a spear through Benares as "trophy". A company of 100 Frenchmen that Eyre Coote brought from Madras was also miserably hacked to pieces and only 14 of them managed to escape.[35] Popham's detachment, which consisted his own regiment, and detachment of artillery under Captain Mayaffre was now reduced to a Company.[36]

On 21st August, while Hastings was still at Madhodas, the Raja sent messages for overtures and that whatever happened was due to the insolent behaviour of Chait Ram and eventual resentment of his own people. He even professed his obedience and submission to the will of the Governor General as he may dictate. Hastings ignored them considering it "filled with expressions of slight concern for what had passed, and professions, but indefinite and unapplied of fidelity."[37]

Meanwhile, Hastings was at Madhadas Bagh with 400 men of Major Popham's first party, which was incapable to provide firm defence. Hastings had already ordered battalion from Chunar to reinforce his defence army and waited for them till evening at 7 p.m., but receiving repeated intelligence that Raja's boats were in motion he thought it prudent to move to Chunar, for which a resolution was passed for the march and was instantly executed.[38] Very few English men were present at that time in Benares along with Hastings.[39] The Governor General divulged his fear of attack, "The reports of an intended assault, which was fixed for that night, grew stronger as the day advanced. The boats on the other side of the river were seen to be in motion, and besides the moral certainty of real existence of such a design, the obvious advantages which it presented to enemy, who had nothing left to fear, and nothing else to do, precluded all hesitation, but on choice of expedients for defeating it."[40]

Before moving for Chunar, Hastings left the wounded sepoys under the protection and charge of Nawab Saadat Ali Khan, brother of Nawab of Oudh, who offered his support with a thousand men.[41] The communication through *dawk* had been completely cut off between Company's territories and Benares, and not a snippet of intelligence could be received from Benares to Patna. The bank of *Ganges* through Raja's country was completely lined up with armed men who fired upon all the boats indiscriminately.[42] Many Englishmen were tied together in a bundle of 5-6 and were chucked into the river and many were cut down to pieces.[43] New *dawk* were established from Chunar to Benares station for securing speedy conveyance of intelligence.[44]

On the bank of *Karamnassa*, Bechut Ray commanding 2,000 horsemen, 4,000 peons and six companies of sepoys with four guns were prepared to oppose any one crossing the river. At Ghazipur Bullub Ram was ready to assist Buchut Ray with 2,000 horsemen, 4-5,000 peons and two guns. In Ballia Meer Sheriff Ally, Aumil of Ballia with 400 horsemen, two Companies of sepoy and 2500 peons prepared to march on any intelligence of Major Crowford's Regiment advance beyond *Karamnassa*. The trepidation and apprehensions in the mind of English people could be felt in the letter of Grome, Collector of Sircar Sarun, Bihar to Wheeler, "...the above force which will find in difficulty in forming junction if necessary may be the mains of harefiring and impeding (if nothing worse happens) march of Major Crawford's regiment at Dinapore... there are not more than nine Company's of what are unserviceable it will therefore be in vain to expect assistance from that quarter should any misfortune befall Major Crawford's regiment not to mention the inevitable destruction which these districts will be exposed to in case of such an event with other bad consequences too dreadful to think of."[45]

Hastings fled to Chunar in the midnight of 21st and reached Chunar on 22nd at daybreak. They reached the bank of the river opposite to Chunar without any opposition and on 23rd morning, crossed the river. Hastings was also joined by Babu Ausan Singh, Mahipnarain and Durgbijay Singh. During this time Popham was encamped on Plain East of Bijaygur fort. Governor General was soon expected to be joined by Regiment from Kanpur for his guard. While on the other hand, Raja's fixed establishment exceeds 10,000 men and his recruits were armed. His forces were divided between Ramnagar and Lateefpur.[46] A popular saying of Benares displaying the confusion during the fleeing of Hastings and his men on the night of 21st August, 1781.

> *"Ghore par Hauda, Hati par Jin,*
> *Bhago bhago Warren Hastings."*

"With *Haudah* on the Horse and saddle on the elephant, Run Run Warren Hastings."

The English army left at Benares followed the suit on August 23, 1781, vacating the city at the hands of Raja Chait Singh's supporters.[47] When Hastings reached Chunar substantial loss of credit was observed and failed to raise money even for ordinary needs. Lieutenant Col. Blair somehow managed to arrange a small sum of Rs. 2,500 only by extortion from Chunar *shroff* "and that, too, with great difficulty besides imposing a degree of violence."[48] Hastings, under these constraints, accepted the offer of Rs. 1 lakh made by Beniram Pundit, *vakil* of Madhoji Bhonsle, which was in possession of his family, then residing at Benares; but Hastings failed to procure it as the Raja's men apprehended Gopal Dass (Banker), through whom the money was to be transported.[49]

Truely speaking Hastings was virtually isolated from the eastern provinces. As Captain Noakes, Commander of a battalion in Major Crawford's regiment at Buxar, on his way to Benares, wrote to Captain Hawkesely Hall at Danapore on August 25, 1781, "I fear greatly that there no assistance can arrive at Chun Ghur from any other place, but Futteh Gur assistance which and Cawnpore."[50] There were people stationed in every part of the *zamindary* to keep a close vigil and intercept any letter of Governor General. The Governor General was greatly apprehensive of these interceptions by *Dandees* that the letters of events were purposely abbreviated and codified for safer means of conveyance.[51]

The uprising in Benares spread wildly to Faizabad and the extensive territory north of river *Dewa* as far as Gorakhpur and Behraich. In Faizabad, Nawab Allia and Junaby Allea, mother and grandmother of Nawab overtly espoused Chait Singh by encouraging people to list for his service. Their people even raised arms against the English. Two battalions under the command of Lieutenant Colonel Hannay were attacked and many were hacked to piece. Colonel Hannay, somehow, narrowly escaped from same fate. Hulteh Shaw attacked Sircar Sarun of Bihar at the encouragement and financial assistance from Raja Chait Singh. Many *zamindars* of Bihar who had discontentment against the English supported the Raja. The uprising of Benares had its far-reaching consequences even in Nepal where people seized some villages by force, which they had been claiming for years. Hastings apprehensions can be judged by his articulation, "I dreaded that every packet would bring a fresh accumulation to our distresses, and the news of commotion on every quarter."[52] Though Hastings was throughout very confident of suppressing this rebeliion as he was expecting two regiments of sepoys, 40 artillery, and two companies of European Infantry within an hour from Kanpur, another regiment from Lucknow and Major Crawford too, was about to join him.[53]

The first reinforcement to arrive for relief of Governor General was the detachment of six companies of sepoys of Nawab *Vazir's* bodyguard stationed at Allahabad under the command of Lt. Polhill, which arrived at Chunar on August 27, 1781,[54] and freed the lines of communication with the opposite shore. At a time when the greatest distress was want of money and provision due to total cut off of supply line, seizure of 5,000 maunds grain by Lt. Polhill on August 30, 1781, from a village 3 miles from Chunar came as a respite. Polhill was resisted by 150 horses, two companies of sepoys and more than 2,000 matchlockmen and *Gawarras* or armed villagers. First Raja's army dispersed, but soon they reassembled to reinforce for further attack. The English army suffered no loss in this skirmish,[55] and procured grain from the fort and town of Seekar by defeating Sahabut Khan, the principal commandant of the place.[56] It was only after the seizure of money and grains, and arrival of army from different quarters that Hastings, who had fled from Benares to Chunar under great trepidation, was quite confident for the success of his army as he expressed in his letter to Wheeler on August 31, 1781, "I can assure you that my situation is actually such as the reservation of that influence which under every circumstance must be allowed to fortune in the events attendant on a state of Warfare will warrant expectation of an easy and compulsory success."[57]

On September 3, 1781, Major Popham sent Blair with his battalion and two companies of grenadiers and two guns (6 pounders) to attack the Raja's forces concentrated at Pateeta, which according to Hastings numbered 8-9,000 while Captain

Blair judges it to be 3-4,000. Though the Raja's forces made a very "spirited resistance", but were routed completely, in which the English army lost 105 men and many were wounded. Hastings himself admitted in his letter to Wheeler, "It is remarkable that the enemy's artillery and carriages made at Ramnagar are almost equal to ours. Their cartridges and Post fires compounded with equal skill and their powder much better."[58] Appreciating the weapons, Hastings articulated, "Their guns were well-served, and it was from their execution that we principally suffered."[59] Blair's bold but well-judged manoeuvre turned the scale in favour of the English forces, which earned a "dear but decisive" victory. The soldiers of the Raja were routed; their (4) guns, tumboils (4), and "unmeasurable" ammunitions were seized. Two big guns on the flank were silenced.[60]

As per Hastings, the strength of the English army was 550 men while that of the Raja's above 4,000. During this time, Raja made repeated overtures for peace, but were rejected by Hastings stating such actions should be checked to deter any repetitions in future.[61] He contented that it was not sincere on the plea and when the Raja was soliciting an accommodation his people persisted in acts of violence against the English.

A detachment from Kanpur under the command of Major Crabb, which consisted of 100 European Infantry, 30 Artillery with Captain Hill and two regiment of sepoys arrived on 10th September.[62] During this time Asaf-ud-daula, who had already set out for Benares with few companies of sepoy and 100 horses[63] to receive the Governor General offered his assistance. Hastings himself accepted that his rabble troops would be of invaluable services by its influence on the Company's credit by keeping the region in awe at this exigent moment and by diverting the attention of Raja's troops; but he denied his help as this would "give him a superiority in their proposed meeting, which would defeat the purpose of it" and would not be "conssitent with the dignity of the Company's government to employ a foreign aid for the suppression of a rebellion of its own subject."[64] Asaf-ud-daula sent his second minister Hyder Beg Khan to join Hastings, but was prevented from reaching Chunar by destruction of a bridge over *Varuna* and so he encamped on the bank and later because of the inundated trubulent river[65] Hyder Beg Khan could join Hastings only on 11th September, at the same time as Nawab himself arrived and encamped on the shore opposite to Chunar.[66]

Major Roberts with his regiment and Rs. 1 ½ lakhs in silver reached from Lucknow on 13th September. Though Ramnagar was to be attacked first, but on the basis of intelligence about the escalating strength, Hastings thought it prudent to first reduce the forts of Lateefpur and Pateeta.[67] The force thus mobilized in Benares by 15th September consisted of following strength:

1 company of European grenadiers, commanded by Captain Grant.
1 company of light infantry, commanded by Captain Harrison.
1 company of French Rangers, commanded by Lieutenant Wade.
30 European artillerymen, commanded by Captain Hill.
1 regiment of sepoys the 7th, commanded by Major Crabb
1 regiment of sepoys the 19th, commanded by Major Balfour.
1 regiment of sepoys the 30th, commanded by Major Roberts
1 regiment of sepoys the 35th, commanded by Major Popham
1 battalion, the 1st of 6th regiment, commanded by Captain Blair
6 companies of Nawab's bodyguards commamnded by Lt. Polhill.

List of established forces in service of Chait Singh:

Cavalry	Rs. 1700
Select troops of bodyguards, horse and foot	Rs. 700
Sepoys	Rs. 1150
Matchlockmen	Rs. 1,800
Attached to Bullum Dass, horse 300, foot 500	Rs. 800
With Sujan Sing, cavalry and infantry, 500	
With two guns, sepoys and artillery men, 340	Rs. 840
With Muniyar Sing, cavalry and infantry	Rs. 700
Total established troops	Rs. 7,690

Troops entertained after arrival of Chait Singh at Lateefpur

1st entertained at Lateefpur matchlock and sword men	Rs. 2,000
2nd Nujjeb sword men from Lucknow	Rs. 1,000
Total	Rs. 3,000
Troops assembled from different places horse and foot, Juggardev Singh	Rs. 500
Matchlockmen arrived with Bukht Singh by order from Raja	Rs. 1,200
With Gomaun Singh, sent for Raja, Matchlockmen	Rs. 500
From Fauzdar of Biddevi arrived, matchlockmen	Rs. 1,000
Rajpoots of tribe of Raghubansi from Kerakat	Rs. 3,000
Arrived with Dullum Singh, fauzdar of Mukurun Badshahpur Matchlockmens	Rs. 1,500
Cavalry and infantry, arrived with Ruzza Cooli Khan from Mirzapur	Rs. 300
Rajputs collected from Agoree and Purwa, by Dia Lutchoo	Rs. 500
Of the tribe or cast of Kammaur, collected by Sujan Singh	Rs. 1,000
Sword and Matchlockmen with Ranjjeewam	Rs. 2,000
Total troops in service of Chait Singh	Rs. 22,190

Other than this husbandmen and adventurers raised arms voluntarily escalating the number near to 40,000.[68]

Earlier, the plan of Hastings was first to recover Benares followed by Ramnagar as "it had been the scene of our first disgrace, and principally because the repossession of the capital, which would follow the capture of Ramnagar, would, it was thought, redeem our credit with the public and he deemed equivalent in distant reports of it to the complete recovery of our, authority over the country, as existence of a fugitive chief in wilds and mountains would be little regarded, when he was expelled from capital of his government, and seat of his collections." Bandhu Khan, a native of Chunar, divulged that the Raja's force was mainly concentrated in Lateefpur and Pateeta and was daily accumulating. Any further delay in the attack on both the forts would give them time to increase their strength making it exceedingly difficult to dislodge. He advised that since both the forts were unassailable and firmly guarded, the only way to reach there was through Sukreet pass and it would be expedient to execute two attacks simultaneously one on Pateeta fort and the other on Sukreet pass leading to fort.[69] The leakage of Lateefpur secret information by Nanda Lal and Bandhu Khan and their readiness to usher the English army in Surkeet pass made tremendous harm to the Raja and his army. Hastings, trusting the information—clandestinely supplied by Nanda Lal and Bandhu Khan—now planned to attack simultaneously on both the forts-Pateeta under Major Popham and Lateefpur under the command of Major Crabb.[70]

Major Popham commenced his march for Patteta on 16th September with 19th, 30th and 35th regiments, two companies of European infantry, the corps of rangers and 30 artillery with six 6-pounder, two 8 ½ inch howitzers and 8 inch mortar. The fort was surrounded by high rampart and deep ditches and the town surrounded by entrenchments. Moreover, because of being cloaked with thick bushes, Major Popham thought it prudent not to attempt an immediate attack without regular approach and battering cannon.[71] He ordered erection of a battery of 18 pounders. There were 5,000 foot and 1,000 horsemen stationed at Pateeta under Raja's principal *sardars*. On 19th morning breaches were made and on 20th the place was attacked by grenadiers under Major Roberts with great success.[72] A large body of the Raja's army posted on the hills to the left rear of Popham's army retaliated, but were routed by European Grenadiers and Lieutenant infantry that Popham had kept as corps reverse. The Raja's men evacuated in utter confusion leaving all cannons behind and the fort was occupied on 20th September, 6 a.m.[73]

On the other hand, in the night of 15th September, army was marched against Lateefpur under the command of Major Crabb, which consisted of first battalion of the 6th Regiment, the 7th Regiment, Battalion of the Nawab's bodyguard under Lt. Polhill with 6 six-pounders and one 5 ½ inch howitzer. The mountainous tracts were so circuitous and impracticable that the guns could not be driven by bullocks and was to be carried by soldiers. On 20th September morning the army arrived at Losa, a place that commands the pass to the fort of Lateefpur. This expedition did not meet any opposition in their route because of the secrecy otherwise it would have been impossible for the English army to cross such a difficult route.[74] The tract was so difficult that it took three days to pass instead of one as expected. This pass was a repository of all Nawabs' ammunition.[75]

The Raja's troops were advantageously deployed to intercept the progress of English army further. They made a firm resistance but were routed with great loss and fled through the pass to Lateefpur. Major Crabb lost 12 men and 22 wounded of all denomination. The detachment followed to the head of the pass of Sukreet and encamped there for a day.[76] The Raja's 2,000 strong force suffered a crushing defeat with loss of 200 men, guns and ammunitions and had to disperse in different directions. At the same time, the Raja also received the information of capture of Pateeta fort. Alarmed by double defeat, the Raja fled away from Lateefpur towards Bijaygarh. In the morning of 21st September, Major Crabb took possession of the pass and the fort of Lateefpur, which was by then evacuated.[77] All these reports of success made easy for Major Balfour to capture Ramnagar next day i.e. 22nd September at 2 p.m.[78]

This plan of simultaneous attack proved to be a great success. Hastings writes, "No design could be more judiciously planned, or more happily executed. Even the impediments and disappointments which attended to it served but to promote the coincidence of the final movements of its operation".[79] About the fort of Lateefpur, Hastings wrote to his wife in a letter 24th September, "He (Major Crabb) describes Lutteefpoor as a Place of great Strength and Extent, and the Pass behind it absolutely impracticable (sic) against any Defence but from above. Our Plan has proved an excellent one, its Effects beyond Hope and equal to one of your best Moves at Chess."[80] So complete was the annihilation of the people's confidence in the Raja's success by this overwhelming disaster that Ramnagar palace and the fort of Suttessgur, 7-8 miles north of Lateefpur, were evacuated on the same evening. Hastings further wrote, "the allegiance of the whole country restored as completely in the course of a few hours, from a state of universal revolt, to its proper channel, as if it had never departed from it."[81]

Raja Chait Singh reached Bijaygurh on 21st September morning but giving instructions to the *killadar* and leaving his whole family in the fort he moved to Agoree, a fort on *Soan* river close to the border of the territory with plethora of treasure on elephants and camels. Though Major Crawford with his Corps and one battalion was in pursuit of Raja but it proved futile as he moved towards Bundelkhund for protection. Major Crawford placed a garrison in Agoree, which was evacuated when he arrived.[82] Chait Singh fled from Bijeygurh with as much treasure as could be carried on his elephants and camels. According to Hastings, it included 1 lakh gold mohurs, 15-16 lakhs silver and unknown amounts of precious jewels.[83] According to Khairuddin, Raja Chait Singh departed with all jewels and money loaded on 25 elephants, 50 camels, 1,500 bullocks, 1000 *coolies* and 200 *bungy bardars*.[84] On 25th September afternoon, Nawab Asaf-ud-daula returned to Lucknow and in the evening, Hastings left Chunar and reached Ramnagar on 26th September from where he returned to Benares on the morning of 28th September as it was represented to him that his presence in the city "would be a means of quieting the minds of its inhabitants."[85] On September 29, 1781, a proclamation was issued, by which Raja Chait Singh, Sujan Singh and their dependents had no further right or interest in the *zamindary* of Benares. All those *zamindars* and *Aumils* who would submit to the Governor General or Major Popham within a month would be pardoned except the Raja and Sujan Singh and the inhabitants of Gopiganj were to be punished for their ardent support to the Raja.[86]

Hastings thought that the English army would face no resistance in the occupation of Bijaygurh fort as the Raja, leaving his family and principal dependents, had escaped with few followers.[87] An economic aid of Rs. 1 lakh by Beniram Pundit to Hastings on 30th September and 1st October was of great importance,[88] as preparations were afoot for the conquest of Bijaygarh. On October 16, two batteries were opened at the fort from a distance of 500 yards. One of the four 6-pounders, two 5 ½ inch howitzers, an 8-inch mortar and 8-inch howitzers were also fixed and the English army began to fire, but the loss could not be perceived as spies were unable to get way into the fort. It was very difficult to storm the fort, as the rock was exceedingly steep making it difficult to ascend. Popham himself reported that, "If the assailed would act resolutely, next to impossible would be endeavours to capture the fort." At that time, the Raja's mother, wife, all women and principal dependent were inside the fort. Raja's mother tried to negotiate with Popham but he calling "unreasoned" rejected her proposals. By the time an epidemic of fever broke out inside the fort making the situation exceedingly difficult for them.[89] Two 18 pounders were stormed on the fort, but the walls were impregnable and no breach could be effected. Eventually, a mine was opened to blow up the wall. Three Hill Rangers from Rani's side attacked the English batteries, but it was a futile attempt.[90]

Rani decided to surrender the fort on the condition that she might get the possession of the wealth in the fort and *pargana* of Hulak, but the Governor General rebuked to accept so gross conditions. Regarding wealth he wrote to Popham, "that is rather your consideration than mine. I should be very sorry that your officers and soldiers lost any part of the reward to which they are so well entitled; but I cannot make any objection, as you must be the best judge." This letter was written to encourage the army to break the resolute resistance of the Raja's men and capture the fort but was highly misinterpreted.[91] Despite utmost endeavours of the English army, no substantial breaches could be made in the walls of the fort.[92] Eventually, Popham started negotiations with Rani for the surrender of the fort of Bijaygarh, which were finally settled in the night of the 9th November. The Rani was permitted to hold 15% of the property of the fort and a residence agreeable to the Governor General's wishes in this Province unless she prefers going to her son, in which case she would be escorted to the frontiers, and delivered over to a person as Chait Singh may send to receive her.[93] With the occupation of Bijaygarh, peace and tranquility was restored and Benares now became a part of the expanding British dominion in India.

As soon as the fort came under the possession of Major Popham, he captured all the treasures and distributed the amount as prize money to the troops. Gleig articulated, "They appropriated, without reserve, every coin that fell into their hands, and left the Government which they served not only as embarrassed as it was here the expedition began, but loaded with fresh debts, contracted in order to equips and put the troops in motion."[94] Hastings was highly annoyed at this incident as his avowed object was to exact money from the Raja's coffers. He expressed his annoyance to Major Scott, "... the distribution of plunder was begun before I knew that the place was in possession, and finished before I knew that it was begun."[95] The treasure in the fort amounted to Rs. 23 lakhs and in distribution even the subalterns received Rs. 20,000 each.[96]

Upon receiving the views of plunder of the contry's treasures and distribution even to the lowest ranks of British Army by its officers, for gratification it caused great uprising which spread like wildfire, throughout the whole kingdom of Oudh. It raged more violently in the *mahals* of Sultanpur, Khairabad, Koonry and Sylack, *mahuls* from Fyzabad to Benares, and those on the eastern side of the *Ghaghra*. Hastings himself aptly remarked, "This town (Fyzabad) has more appearance of belonging to Chait Singh than Vizier." The Begums had also placed guards to prevent Englishmen from entering the town. Forts of Gorakhpur, Ballia and Dumriagunj (presently in Siddharthnagar) were captured by the *zamindars* from the *Aumils* of Nawab. A detachment of thousand horse and foot men was raised under Shaak Chaan within four days, which marched to Benares to conjoin the army of Raja. To the west of *Ghaghra* between Faizabad and Khyrabad, Raja like Fateh Shah, Ghinu Roy, Ajeetmul, Zalim Singh raised troops of 5,000 men with the financial assistance of Chait Singh to consolidate his forces. Jawahar Ali Khan and Bahar Ali Khan, the eunuchs of Begums of Oudh were charged by the Resident with formenting disturbances.[97] Fateh Shah, chief of Hathwa, collected about 1,500 men and espoused the cause of the Raja of Benares.[98] The spirit of defiance to the English authority received a crushing blow when Naylor inflicted a severe defeat upon 10,000 rebels at Sakrora on the morning of October 8, 1781.[99] In spite direct of this challenge, Ross issued necessary orders to Major Hardy, the commander of a militia, to collect as many people as possible.[100] Hussain Ali Khan, the renter of Arwal-Musauree was arrested on the charge of propagating the cause of Raja Chait Singh.[101]

In October, Hastings sent Colonel Muir empowered with full powers and authority as Public Minister of Governor General and Council for direct negotiations with Mahadaji Sindia,[102] as Hastings received an intelligence that there was a general plan of attack by the Marathas from three sides. Numerous army of horses were deployed to attack English sircars, another under Bhosle and other Maratha Chiefs was to attack Bengal by way of Cuttack and the third army under Sindhia was to proceed from Malwa to support Chait Singh in Benares.[103] These plans were never fruitful and the events turned out to be damp squible and favourable for the English. On 13th October treaty was concluded between English and Sindhia. To confirm this treaty Hastings deputed Anderson to Sindhia.[104] In December 1781, Chait Singh deputed his *vakeel* to Sindhia, who solicited on behalf of his master for assistance to invade Benares. In return to this assistance the Raja offered to pay the arrears of Sindhia's army and defray monthly expenses of the army that would attack for his cause. There were intelligence that all the Nagas in Sindhia's army had withdrawn themselves and joined Chait Singh.[105]

Sindhia also had an interview with Chait Singh while he was near Dattia, but the English regarded the relations mainly because of alluring wealth of Chait Singh. The English had hopes that the Marathas were kind and positive because of the pecuniary exigencies due to recent war and would not carry the relation much long violating the alliance entered with the English.[106] Hastings immediately directed Anderson that if Sindhia refuse to meet his deputation or shall retain Chait Singh in his camp or provide him ostensible protection his commission would be instantly declared void. He stated, "your Commission is from that instant void, unless he shall change his purpose and recall you with reservation of Chait Singh's dismission before you shall have passed the Caramnassa in which case you may return and proceed to him and with that view I wish you to make as little expedition as you chose in your journey this way." After Chait Singh's coming under the aegis of Marathas, Hastings grew so suspicious that he even ordered Colonel Muir to be prepared with his detachment for prompt service and also directed Colonel Morgan to be ready to join Colonel Muir in any exigent circumstances. He also directed to suspend the order for reductions of the army. In case of Sindhia's faithful adherence with the English, the deputation would become active and would work under the instructions given previously.[107]

Then, Company's authority was reestablished by the end of December 1781,[108] but Hastings was still full of apprehensions regarding Chait Singh's relation with the Marathas. Chait Singh also contacted Rana and offered his assistance to encounter the Marathas.[109] In February 1782, Hastings received a formal assurance from Sindhia that he would neither accept any solicitations of Chait Singh nor would render any assitance to him in any way and would also prohibit him and his attendants from attending *durbar* and *Cutcherry*.[110] In March 1782, Madhoji Bhonsle put forth some articles for peace with Maratha State, in which he demanded Benares be given to him in exchange of some other Country and assured that he would pay the same amount of revenue as was being paid by Chait Singh till this exchange finally implemented. He also demanded that all resentment and displeasure against Chait Singh "must be laid aside."[111] These were never fruitful with the signing of the treaty of Salbai in 1782 between the Poona Government and the English Company.

Chait Singh's family was residing in town of Jhansi. Though the Marathas later did not overtly espouse the cause of Chait Singh, on account of the former's equivocal stand and decided vacillation, he (the Raja of Benares) still had considerable resources at his disposal.[112] A *jageer* of Rs. 10 lakhs annually was conferred upon Chait Singh including Bhind and part of Cutchwagar.[113] On 28th March 1811, he died in Gwalior.[114]

After the restoration of peace Hastings awarded many local

inhabitants for their zeal and support during the rising in Benares that included Raja Govind Jeet, Raja Adal Singh, Babu Bhagat Singh, Ausan Singh, Ali Azeem Khan etc. The fact to be observed is that most of these were *zamindars* dispossessed by Balwant Singh during the time of Safdar Jang. In 1781 Hastings acknowledged their claims and restored their zamindaries. Even the Council, too, disregarded these claims stating that no claims in the possession of zamindaries in Benares should be recognized in cases where dispossession had occurred prior to July 1, 1775, the day when Benares was transferred to the Company. This bears ample testimony to the fact that Hastings was colluding with other frustrated and disgruntled elements against the Raja and supported every individual who had least hostility against the Raja.[115]

Hastings was well aware that the charges that claimed against the Raja were not enough to divest him of his *zamindary*. In search of that single strong reason, he ordered Markham to arrest the Raja within his own fort perceiving that the Raja revolt against this action and take a step which can be easily dubbed as an act against the Government on which he depends. Otherwise Hastings had no cogent reasons to take such a stringent measure to apprehend the Raja within his own fort in the city, notwithstanding the fact that the Raja was ready to surrender all his forts and treasures. He thought that it would be easier for him to prove the Raja's open misconduct against the Government in the city since the Raja was encircled by his own enemies. This becomes more evident with the time chosen for the arrest of Raja. The mind of Hastings before giving the order of the arrest can be clearly read in his letter to Wheeler, "To have left him in full exercise of power which he had notoriously abused and which it was to be apprehended he would employ to the most dangerous purposes was totally inconsistent with the maxims of justice and prudence. To divest him entirely of the zemindary though justifiable on grounds stated above would be attended with an appearance of severity and might have furnished ground for constructions unfavourable to the credit of our government and to my own reputation."[116]

Though Hastings was alone taking decision on behalf of the Council, but still Wheeler, too, shared the responsibility, as he supported Hastings decision of Raja's arrest. He stated in a minute, "...stricker degree of Restraint would not only have been justifiable but necessary for whilst the Rajah was professing deepest contradiction for his former Conduct, he appears to have been concerting a plan to assert his independency against that Government which raised him to his present situation."[117] Hastings had the motive of extending the Company's sway as he wrote to Wheeler, "I have every reason to expect happiest termination of it in the extension of powers and influence of Company and that past example may contribute to permanency of both by prompting us to guard against secret growth of like evil which has produced it."[118] When Hastings got to know about the multitude of armymen in Shivala Ghat, he should have never sent his message through dismissed mace bearers unless there were armed Englishmen to control the situation. A mere *Chubdar* could not dare to bring the Raja so insolently unless he was sure of the English support. The Raja had no plans to create any disturbance. Had it been so, he would have never waited for the intelligence to reach the Governor General and armed Englishmen of Popham's army to reach Shivala.

References

1. Hastings, Warren, *A Narrative of The Late Transactions at Benares*, London, 1782, p. 16.
2. *Ibid*, p. 2.
3. Grier, C., *Letter of Warren Hastings To His Wife*, London, MCMV, p. 120.
4. Hastings, *op.cit.*, p. 2.
5. *Ibid*, pp.2-3.
6. FPD, 18 October, 1781, No. 2, letter from Warren Hastings to Wheeler, August 27, 1781.
7. Hastings, *op.cit.*, p. 20.
8. FPD, Sec Pr., 4 September-22 October, 1781, Vol. 68, No. 4, letter from Warren Hastings to Raja Chait Singh, September 4, 1781, p.

1999-2003.

9. FPD, Sec Pr., 4 September-22 October, 1781, Vol. 68, No. 4, letter from Raja Chait Singh to Warren Hastings, September 4, 1781, pp.2004-2008.
10. FPD, Sec Pr., Vol. 68, 4 September-22 October, 1781, letter from Hastings to Wheeler, p. 2010.
11. FPD, Sec Pr., 4 September-22 October, 1781, Vol. 68, No. 4, letter from Hastings to Markham, 4 September, 1781, pp.2012-2013.
12. FPD, Sec Pr., 4 September-22 October, 1781, Vol. 68, No. 4, letter from Markham to Hastings, September, 4, 1781, pp. 2015-2017.
13. FPD, Sec Pr., 4 September-22 October, 1781, Vol. 68, No. 4, letter from Hastings to Wheeler, September, 4, 1781, p. 2020.
14. FPD, Sec Pr., 4 September-22 October, 1781, Vol. 68, No. 4, letter from Raja to Hastings, September, 4, 1781, p. 2014.
15. *Ibid*, p. 2018.
16. FPD, Sec Pr., 4 September-22 October, 1781, Vol. 68, No. 4, letter from Hastings to Raja, September 4, 1781, p. 2019.
17. FPD, Sec Pr., 4 September-22 October, 1781, Vol. 68, No. 4, letter from Hastings to Wheeler, September 4, 1781, p. 2020.
18. FPD, SC, 4 September, 1781, No. 4, Hastings to Wheeler, 24 August 1781.
19. Hastings, *op.cit.*
20. Glieg, II, *op.cit.*, p. 425.
21. Hodges, William, *Travels in India*, 2nd edition, London, 1794, p. 50.
22. Glieg, II, *op.cit.*, p. 410.
23. FPD, Sec Pr., 4 September-22 October, 1781, Vol. 68, No. 4, letter from Hastings to Wheeler, September, 4, 1781, pp.2021-2022.
24. FPD, Sec Pr., 4 September-22 October, 1781, Vol. 68, No. 4, letter from Hastings to Wheeler, September, 4, 1781, p. 2022.
25. FPD, Sec Pr., 4 September-22 October, 1781, Vol. 68, No. 4, letter from Hastings to Wheeler, September, 4, 1781, pp.2023-2024.
26. Hastings, *op.cit.*, pp.39-40.
27. Glieg, II, *op.cit.*, p. 411.
28. FPD, Sec Pr., 4 September-22 October, 1781, Vol. 68, Report of Major Popham to Governor General, August 16, 1781, pp.2024-2025.
29. Hastings, *op.cit.*, p. 39.
30. FPD, Sec Pr., 4 September-22 October, 1781, Vol. 68, No. 4, letter from Hastings to Wheeler, September, 4, 1781, pp.2026-2027.

31. FPD, Sec Pr., 4 September-22 October, 1781, Vol. 68, No. 4, letter from Hastings to Wheeler, September, 4, 1781, p. 2029.
32. FPD, Sec Pr., 4 September-22 October, 1781, Vol. 68, Report of Major Popham, August 16, 1781, pp.2024-2026.
33. FPD, Sec Pr., 4 September-22 October, 1781, Vol. 68, No. 4, letter from Hastings to Wheeler, September, 4, 1781, pp.2028-2029.
34. FPD, Sec Pr., 4 September-22 October, 1781, Vol. 68, 18 October 1781, No. 2, letter from Hastings to Wheeler, 27 August 1781, pp.2422-2423.
35. FPD, Sec Pr., 4 September-22 October, 1781, Vol. 68, September 7, 1781, No. 11, letter from Captain Noke, Commanding Battalion in Major Crawford's Regiment at Buxar, August 25, 1781, pp.2090-2091.
36. FPD, Sec Pr., 4 September-22 October, 1781, Vol. 68, September 11, 1781, No. 14, letter from Grome, Collector of Sircar Sarun, Bihar to Wheeler, August 28, 1781, pp.2101.
37. Hastings, *op.cit.*, p. 48.
38. FPD, 18 October, 1781, No. 2, letter from Hastings to Wheeler, 27 August 1781.
39. FPD, 18 October, 1781, No. 7, list of Englishmen at Benares on August 21st, 1781.
40. Hastings, *op.cit.*, p. 43.
41. Grier, *op.cit.*, p. 130.
42. FPD, Sec Pr., 4 September-22 October, 1781, Vol. 68, 7 September 1781, No. 11, letter from Ross to Council, 28 August, 1781, pp.2086-2088.
43. FPD, Sec Pr., 4 September-22 October, 1781, Vol. 68, 7 September, 1781, No. 11, letter from Ross, Acting Chief of Revenue to Council, p. 2093.
44. FPD, Secret, September 7, 1781, No. 15, letter from Colonel of Sircar Sarun to Governor General, August 22, 1781.
45. FPD, Sec Pr., 4 September-22 October 1781, Vol. 68, 11 September, 1781, No. 14, letter from Grome, Collector, Sircar Sarun, Bihar to Wheeler, August 28, 1781, pp.2103-2105.
46. FPD, Sec Pr., 4 September-22 October, 1781, Vol. 68, 7 September, 1781, No. 11, 18 October, 1781, No. 2, letter from Hastings to Wheeler, 27 August, 1781, p. 2424; also see CPC, VI, No. 207.
47. FPD, SC, 18 October, 1781, No. 2, letter from Hastings to Wheeler, 27 August 1781.

48. Hastings, *op.cit.*, pp.46-47.
49. FPD, SC, October 29, 1781, No. 3, letter from Hastings to Wheeler.
50. FPD, SC, 7 September, 1781, No. 11, Noakes to Hawkesley, 25 August, 1781.
51. FPD, SC, 18 October, 1781, No. 3, letter from Hastings to Wheeler, August 31, 1781.
52. Hastings, *op.cit.*, pp.51-54.
53. Grier, *op.cit.*, p. 142.
54. FPD, Sec Pr., 4 September-22 October, 1781, Vol. 68, 18 October, 1781, No. 2, letter from Hastings to Wheeler, 27 August, 1781, p. 2425.
55. FPD, 4 September-22 October, 1781, Vol. 68, 18 October, 1781, No. 3, letter from Hastings to Wheeler, 31 August, 1781, pp.2426-2427.
56. Hastings, *op.cit.*, p. 55.
57. FPD, 4 September-22 October, 1781, Vol. 68, letter from Hastings to Wheeler, August 31, 1781, pp.2428-2429.
58. FPD, October 18, 1781, No. 8, letter from Hastings, September, 4, 1781.
59. Hastings, *op.cit.*, p. 56.
60. FPD, SC 18 October, 1781, No. 11, letter from Hastings to Wheeler, 11 September, 1781.
61. FPD, SC, October 18, 1781, No. 9, letter from Hastings to Wheeler, September 11, 1781.
62. FPD, SC, October 18, 1781, No. 9, letter from Hastings, September, 11, 1781.
63. FPD, SC, October 18, 1781, No. 12, letter from Hastings to Wheeler, September 29, 1781.
64. Hastings, *op.cit.*, p. 50.
65. FPD, Sec Pr., 4 September-22 October, 1781, Vol. 68, 18 October, 1781, No. 3, letter from Governor General to Wheeler, August 31, 1781, p. 2430.
66. Hastings, *op.cit.*, p. 59.
67. FPD, SC, October 18, 1781, No. 12, letter from Hastings to Wheeler, September 29, 1781.
68. Hastings, *op.cit.*, pp.60-62.
69. *Ibid*, pp.65-66.
70. FPD, SC, 18 October, 1781, No. 10, letter from Hastings to Wheeler, September 20, 1781.

71. FPD, SC, 18 October, 1781, No. 12, letter from Hastings to Wheeler, 29 September, 1781.
72. FPD, SC, October 29, 1781, No. 7, letter from Popham to Hastings.
73. FPD, SC, October 18, 1781, No. 10, enclosed letter from Popham to Hastings, September 20, 1781.
74. FPD, SC, 18 October, 1781, No. 12, letter from Hastings to Wheeler, 29 September, 1781.
75. FPD, SC, 18 October, 1781, No. 10, letter from Hastings to Wheeler September 20, 1781.
76. Hastings, *op.cit.*, p. 68.
77. FPD, SC, 18 October, 1781, No. 12, letter from Hastings to Wheeler, 29 September, 1781; also see FPD, SC, October 18, 1781, No. 11, letter from Hastings to Wheeler, September 22, 1781.
78. FPD, SC, 18 October, 1781, No. 11, letter from Hastings to Wheeler, September 22, 1781.
79. Hastings, *op.cit.*, p. 69.
80. Leter No. X from Hastings to his wife dated 24 September, 1781 vide Grier, *op.cit.*, p. 160.
81. Hastings, *op.cit.*, p. 69.
82. FPD, SC, October 29, 1781, No. 7, letter from Popham to Hastings.
83. Hastings, *op.cit.*, p. 73.
84. Saletore, G.N., *Banaras Affairs*, Vol. II, Central Record Office, Allahabad, 1959, p. vi
85. FPD, SC, October 18, 1781, No. 12, letter from Hastings to Wheeler, September 29, 1781.
86. FPD, SC, October 29, 1781, No. 5, Proclamation made public at Benares on September 29, 1781.
87. FPD, SC, 11 October, 1781, No. 4, letter from Fort William to Lieutenant General Sir Coote, October 11, 1781.
88. FPD, SC, October 29, 1781, No. 3, letter from Hastings to Wheeler, October 13, 1781.
89. FPD, SC, November 5, 1781, No. 2, letter from Popham to Hastings, October 10, 1781; also see CPC, VI, No. 262.
90. FPD, SC, November 19, 1781, No. 2, letter from Popham to Hastings, November 4, 1781.
91. Gleig, II, *op.cit.*, pp.415-416.
92. FPD, SC, 19 November, 1781, No. 2, letter from Popham to Council, 6 November, 1781.

93. FPD, SC, 19 November, 1781, No. 4, letter from Major Popham to Governor General, 10 November, 1781.
94. Gleig, II, *op.cit.*, p. 417.
95. Letter from Hastings to Major Scott, 21 February, 1782 vide Gleig, *op.cit.*, p. 428.
96. Grier, *op.cit*, 157.
97. Letter from Middleton to Governor General and Council, 17 October 1781 vide Hastings, *op.cit.*, pp.95-101.
98. FPD, SC, 7 September, 1781, No. 12, letter from Grome to Ross, 27 August, 1781.
99. FPD, SC, 29 October, 1781, No. 2, letter from Middleton to Hastings, 9 October, 1781.
100. FPD, SC, 28 September, 1781, No. 11, letter from Ross to Council, 28 August, 1781.
101. FPD, SC, 28 September, 1781, No. 1, letter from Ross to Council, 2 September, 1781.
102. FPD, SC, 5 November, 1781, No. 1, Credentials from Governor General to Col. Muir.
103. FPD, SC, 29 October, 1781, No. 10, letter from John Hollond to Hastings, 8 October, 1781.
104. Hastings, *op.cit.*, p. 72.
105. FPD, Sec Pr., 2 January-18 February, 1782, Vol. 70, 2 January, 1782, No. 13, letter from Col. Muir to Governor General, 5 December, 1781, pp. 130-131.
106. FPD, Sec Pr., 2 January-18 February, 1782, Vol. 70, 2 January, 1782, No. 15, letter from Anderson to Hastings, 6 December, 1781, pp. 141-142.
107. FPD, Sec Pr., 2 January-18 February, 1782, Vol. 70, 2 January, 1782, No. 16, letter from Hastings to Anderson, 12 December, 1781, pp. 145-46.
108. FPD, Sec Pr., 2 January-18 February, 1782, Vol. 70, 2 January, 1782, No. 6, p. 70.
109. FPD, SC, 18 March, 1782, No. 4, letter from Anderson to Hastings, 25 January, 1782.
110. FPD, SC, 5 February, 1782, No. 1-B, letter from Hastings to Board.
111. FPD, SC, 18 March, No. 2.
112. FPD, SC, 21 April, 1783, No. 10.
113. FPD, SC, 16 June, 1783, No. 11.
114. Saletore, G.N., *Banaras Affairs*, Vol. II, *op.cit.*, p. vii.
115. BCO, DR, Vol. 4, 1782-1788, Basta 1, Proceedings of Governor

General in Council, 11 April, 1788, RAA.

116. FPD, Sec Pr., Vol. 68, 4 September-22 October, 1781, letter from Hastings to Wheeler, No. 4, 4 September, 1781, pp. 2010-2011.
117. FPD, SC, 4 September, 1781, No. 5, minute of Wheeler.
118. FPD, SC, 18 October, 1781, No. 3 letter from Hastings to Wheeler, August 31, 1781.

Chapter 7

Benares from Raja Maheep Narain to the Merger into the Dominion of India

The rising of 1781 by Raja Chait Singh raised the pertinent and crucial question of succession of *Zamindary*, which was then being administered by Ausan Singh by the order of the Governor General. On September 30, 1781, Mahip Narain, the grandson of the late Raja Balwant Singh, was placed as the Raja of Benares.[1] Hastings wanted to bring Benares under the direct administration of the Company "precluding the possibility of a renewal of the like scenes."[2] He wrote to Wheeler, "I had very early apprised the Rajah (Mahip Narain Singh) that I should not allow him the exercise of any privilege or authority on which an opinion of independency could be founded."[3]

Sunnud dated September 14, 1781, was granted to the new Raja by which Benares, Ghazipur and Chunar was given to him in return for fixed annual revenue of Rs. 40 lakhs that was to be paid in monthly installments of Benares *Sicca* Rs. 2, 90,000 for first eleven months starting from *Aswin* and *Benares Sicca* Rs. 8,10,000 for the last month of *Bhadon* with a deduction of *Benares Sicca* Rs. 6,66,666..10..10 from the revenue of *fasli* year 1189 on account of the disturbance. Thus the amount payable to the

Company in 1189 *fasli* was *Benares Sicca* Rs33,33,333.5. By new *sunnud* Hastings not only doubled the amount to be paid as revenue but also curtailed all those powers of the Raja that allowed him to use his authority in uncontrolled manner within his territory. He was not given the *adalat* and *fauzdary* of Benares town. Within the town, his powers were extended only to the collection of revenues and appointment of officers acting under his authority for that purpose. He was neither permitted to erect forts or any sort of defences nor he was to employ any troop, horse or foot, for any purpose without the order or permission of the Governor General and Council or their successors. In case of requirement of troops for revenue collection or maintaining order such troops was of the Company, furnished by the orders of their representatives. The places, which were granted to him, mentioned in the *Zimmun* are following:

"The office of the zamindari of Sircar Benares, Ghazipur and Chunar, the kotwali of Jaunpur, the duties and the aumini and faujdari within the limits of the said zamindari in the Subah of Allahabad, excepting the adalat and faujdari of the town of Benrares have been conferred upon the great Chief, Raja Mahip Narain Singh, Bahadur, Sircar Benares, Sircar Chunar, Sircar Ghazipore, the mahals of Sircar Jaunpur, comprehending both mal and sayer, Haveli Mohemedabad, Benares, the mahals of the Mulbus Khas, the pargana Bhadohi, the taluka Sungra Mow dependent on the pargana of Chandali, Saktisghur, Cantit, otherwise called Bijepore, Secunderpore, Kherid, Shadiabad, Tuppe Serencha, the Mokkem of Benares. The Yettismab of officer-Muttussui of Benares, the Sungwazini or weighing of Benares and the other mahals."[4]

The Raja also accepted to pay whatever balance of the former Raja's administration for the *fasli* year 1188 [5] and 1% of the annual *jumma* to Hay and Coolebrooke for preparing the *sunnud.*[6] He was given the possession of the fort of Agoree on the condition that he would deliver it to the troops of Governor General and Council without delay, whenever asked to do so in future.[7]

As the Raja was a novice in the field of administration, his father Durgbijay Singh, was appointed as the *Naib*.[8] "To deprive the new Raja of every prerogative which denoted either sovereignty or independence" the right over Mint and administration of justice was taken away from him and the Mint was given to the Resident. The administration of justice, civil and criminal, in the Benares city and internal police was entrusted to Ally Ibrahim Khan, the Chief Magistrate and the Resident was strictly instructed not to interfere into his administration.[9] Regarding this new settlement Governor General expressed his gratification stating, "I lost the Zemindary with a rent of twenty two lacs. I recovered it with revenue of forty. The Company possessed only its stipulated rent under Cheit Sing. It is now as much a member of their Government as the Zemindary of Burdwan and more effectively theirs than many parts of Bihar."[10]

There was also a supplement to the agreement containing Raja's proposals in form of six articles, which were mostly accepted by the Governor General.[11] The Governor General after fulfilling his interests was now displeased with Ausan Singh, directed him to leave Benares and also directed the *Naib* to dismiss and all persons appointed by Ausan Singh and appoint his own men in their place.[12] The *Naib* demanded deductions on some articles from *Malguzary* of Benares for the *fasli* year 1189 amounting to about Rs. 2, 57,359.6.3 out of which articles amounting to Rs. 1,12,277.3.3 were granted to him.[13] On account of being found guilty of "gross mismanagement and peculation of the revenues",[14] Governor General directed Markham to dismiss Babu Durgbijay Singh and authorized him to nominate a new *Naib*.[15] Durgbijay Singh was dismissed and Babu Jagger Deo Singh, who was from the family of Raja Balwant Singh, was appointed as the new *Naib*. Governor General also ordered the Resident to establish an office, which "might not only be a reciprocal check upon each other but might also prevent any collusion on part of Naib." In compliance with these orders, a *Dewan* was appointed for receipts of revenue into the treasury. According to Markham, Babu Durgbijay Singh had sufficient amount to pay the arrears of the last month and so recommended the Board to confine him for the payment of the amount collected by him.[16]

On the Board's instructions, Babu Durgbijay Singh was

deprived of his *jagir*, which was reunited to the *Malguzzary*[17] and apprehended on November 13, 1782. Since new year commenced on September 21, 1782, so from 21st September to 13th November (his last day to hold the office of *Naib*) nearly two *kists* were due from him to the Government. He gave a written engagement to the Resident that he would pay the remaining amount. The new *Naib* made the full payment of revenue of the whole year independent of the previous collections made by Babu Durgbijay Singh in spite of severe drought in the whole Oudh region. Fowke, the new Resident expressed his surprise, "It may appear extraordinary or at least doubtful, how present Naib has been enabled to discharge the whole amount due from this Country to Government independent of Collections made at the beginning of the year by his predecessor and not brought to Public account."[18]

On June 13, 1784, Hastings submitted a temporary plan for the administration in Benares claiming that he had proposed nothing that encroaches upon the rights of the Raja under the agreement of 1781. These points of the plan are enumerated below:[19]

1. The Raja was to be declared "principal in all official acts of the province" and all official documents shall be authentic only after his signature and seal, but neither he can interfere into the official matters nor can he refuse or delay authentication of any document.
2. Babu Ajaib Singh, brother of Rani Golab Kunwar, was to be appointed as New *Naib*.
3. *Ameen* or Inspector shall be appointed by Chief Magistrate to assist *Naib* but he was not to command. In case of complaints, the *Naib* can make an inquiry through two persons, one appointed by him on behalf of the Raja and other by *Ameen*, but the final judgment shall rest in the hands of the *Naib*.
4. The *Qanungoes*, appointed in every *pargana*, were to represent complaints made by *Ryots* and refer them to *Aumil*. In case of *Aumil's* indifference, he shall transmit it to *Ameen* and then to *Naib*.

5. The Resident shall receive the monthly payment of revenue. The Raja and *Naib* shall appoint *Aumils*. He shall refer whatever complaints made to the Resident to the *Naib* who shall inquire into the matter in a manner as mentioned in article three.
6. The Raja and the *Naib* shall establish a *Kutcherry* or office of treasury for receipt of revenue. *Mutasaddi* shall be appointed in *Kutcherry* by the Resident and *Ameen* jointly to keep the accounts of receipts and disbursements.
7. The surplus of the revenue shall be appropriated for the private expenses of the Raja and for extraordinary expenses of the adminnistration.

The Council considered the plan on June 30, 1784, and accepted it as interim expediency excluding part of article 1, by which the Raja was not given the power to delay or refuse authentication of any document; and as "such a regulation should neither be declared or enforced with reference to rights and privileges and dignity of Rajah".[20] In September 1784, during Hastings visit to Benares, the possession of Kara Mungroor was given to the Raja.[21] He also procured the *pargana* of Bhadohi producing prodigious revenue of Rs. 1,50,000 annually as personal *jagir*.[22]

The interference and the increasing power of the Resident can be envisaged by the letter of Governor General dated May 14, 1787, addressed to the President, Board of Control, London, "The Resident, although not regularly vested with any power, enjoyed almost absolute government of the country without control. His emoluments, besides the Rs. 1000/- per month allowed him by Company, certainly amounted to little less than four lac a year, exclusive the complete monopoly of whole commerce of the country, with power of granting purwannahs." In August 1787, Jonathan Duncan, then Secretary of Public Revenue Department was appointed as Resident Benares.[23] Duncan proposed a new plan including five articles to stop the irregularities in the system of Public collections, but was demurred by the Raja claiming that the proposed new *Pottah* would materially affect and prejudice the collections for the current year.

How obdurately and implacably the Raja demurred the plan can be envisaged by the statement of Resident, "... the Raja's aversion... was expressed even in terms of a degree of violence and asperity unusual with the Raja."[24] Still no consideration of his objections were taken, in fact his dignity was greatly hampered, as it was decided that if the Raja does not agree to the plan, Resident would use his sway on the farmers of Sheopoor and Kutehar *pargana* to cajole them to issue new form of *Pottah* throughout the *pargana*.[25] These intimatory tactics compelled the Raja to give his assent to the execution of the plan and pay the balances of the current year also.[26] The actions taken by the Resident had full approbation of the Secretary to the Governor General "not only as relation to the past but as a foundation for the future system of regularity."[27]

Duncan was instructed to form a new settlement for the improvement of management. Though he was asked to include the Raja in the Executive management, but was also authorized to act as he may deem expedient and carry out his arrangement without interference of the Raja. The Resident was also asked to calculate the surplus amount of revenue, which the Raja receives annually.[28] Accordingly, Duncan sent a report on the surplus revenue to the Board calculating it to be more than Rs. 1,40,000 after defraying all the charges of collection with his recommendation that Rs. 1 lakh of the surplus be appropriated to the Raja "otherwise his annual income may become unreasonably large to the prejudice of the country", and the remaining should be utilized by the Government for the public work.[29] There were also plans to introduce Permanent Settlement of Bihar in Benares and instructed the Resident to explain to the Raja the principles.

After prolonged discussions an agreement dated October 27, 1794 entered into between the Raja of Benares and the Resident of Benares, on behalf of the Government, was sent for approval to the Government by which a new permanent system was introduced in Benares. From the beginning of 1202 *fasli* the administration of justice, which was in the hands of the natives, was to be conducted by Englishmen. A Collector should be appointed (a British subject) for the realization of the revenue. The Court of Appeals was to be conducted under similar regulations as in Bengal. The agreement included three articles.[30]

1. Out of the surplus revenue, other than Rs. 40 lakhs revenue, Rs. 1 lakh annually shall be given to the Raja for his private expenses, exclusive of the *jagirs* and *altumghas* that were in his possession, and the remaining surplus shall be earmarked for defraying the expense of civil and judicial establishments, Hindu College, repair of roads, construction of bridges, promotion of cultivation etc. under the authority of the Government.
2. The *pottahs*, receipts and *farigh-khutties* will continue to pass under the seal and signature of the Raja to the *aumils*, *zamindars*, farmers and treasurers.
3. Any revenue complaints were to be settled through the channel of the Raja or the officers of his *kutcherry* and in case of discontent on part of the aggrieved, the Collector would have the onus to settle the matter in conjunction with the Raja. It shall be incumbent upon the Collector who—in the course of discharging his duties—must keep in view the honour and dignity of the Raja, which is of paramount importance. If in case, the matter remained unsettled between the two, the decision accorded by the Governor General in Council shall be final.

This agreement highly hampered the dignity and honour of the Raja. The Raja firmly demurred the introduction of any *mofussil* or interior settlement within his own domain i.e. Gangapur, Bhadohi and Kara Mungroor. The domains of the Raja were excluded and rules regarding their administration of revenue were mentioned in Regulation II, V, XV of 1795. Section 3 of Regulation XV mentions, "...the complaints are not to be taken cognizance of in the courts of justice, but the parties are to be desired to make an application to the Rajah or to his Dewan; and in case of their not obtaining justice, they are to have recourse to the Collector, who will proceed to bring such causes to a just and equitable termination, in the manner stated in the under-specified article of an agreement concluded by the Resident with Rajah Muheep Narain, under date the of October 27, 1794. An option, however, is reserved ro the persons deeming themselves injured, to prefer their applications for redress in the first instance to the Collector, who in all cases, by reference to, and communication with, the Rajah and his officers, is to cause substantial justice to be rendered to the parties."[31]

In September 1795, Raja Maheepnarain Singh died due to severe illness[32] and was succeeded by Raja Udit Narain Singh *Bahadur* who was granted the *sunnud* along with *jagir*, *mahals* and *altumgha* etc. with same privileges and rights as enjoyed by his father. The Raja was bound to comply with the stipulation specified in the agreement of 1794 and "to exert himself in accordance with those terms in the management of his zamindary."[33] In 1805, Raja Udit Narain Singh presented a memorandum asking for the annulment of the agreement of 1794, and to restore him full powers of the Government of four *sarkars* (Benares, Ghazipur, Mirzapur and Jaunpur) and in his family *jagir*. The Raja contended that the above agreement was a temporary arrangement and was not meant for posterity, but the Government brusquely reprimanded his plea,[34] and the system continued to work in the same manner till 1828.

In consequence of many a grievance by the inhabitants of Bhadohi regarding administration in Family Domain, Governor General Lord Amherst appointed W.W. Bird as Special Commissioner on November 16, 1826, to enquire into the matter and to suggest measures, accordingly.[35] On May 25, 1826, Bird submitted his Report to the Government stating that the Regulation XV of 1795, serves only to enable the Raja to oppress his tenants with impunity and he was surrounded by agents who were "notoriously corrupt and unprincipled". He recommended that instead of the Collector some other intermediate authority may be employed who would be "less exposed to the intrigues of the Raja and more accessible to the tenantry" in whom both the sides could confide, the Raja for maintenance of his honour and tenants for protection against injustice.[36]

Basically, this Report was used as a weapon to curb the

powers of the Raja and a British attempt to enter into the administration of the Family Domains of the Raja. Firstly, their lone purpose was to establish an authority by "whom the control required may be exercised in direct communication with the Government" and to fulfil this, the report firmly recommended the establishment of an office of Superintendent. Secondly, the Raja had issued a Proclamation on March 21, 1826, to revise the settlement by the end of the present year and even assured that rent free land would be resumed without full enquiry and approbation of the Government still they did not want to give serious consideration to his assurances as stated by Bird himself, "I have no doubt that the Raja was perfectly sincere in all those assurances, but surrounded as he is by men on whom no dependence can be placed, and being himself indolent, careless and unable to exercise that personal control necessary to carry out his good intentions into effect those assurances will, I am fully economical be overlooked or disregarded, unless the affairs of the Pergunnah are placed under the sort of Superintendence." He was of the view that, however, serious may be the intentions of the Raja, but nothing would be fruitful without the Superintendent.

Thirdly, even the Raja complained that all the grievances are merely effect of the collusions among certain vested interests and disappointed individuals aided by the authorities of the Mirzapur for the purposes of undermining his rights and interests. Fourthly, most of the managing village occupants were either descendants or derived their title from *Moones*, to whom the *pargana* of Bhadhoi was given by the Emperor in 929 *fasli* (near about 1521). They exercise privilege of assigning rent free lands for charitable purpose, which was resumed by Udit Narain Singh. It was all these circumstances, which created discontent among the tenants and the English availed themselves.[37] Bird was directed by the Government to keep vigilant eye over the circumstances and to interpose his influence and authority, as he may deem expedient till further actions were taken in this regard.[38]

Though Governor General and Council regarded the indispensability of new Regulation to be introduced in concert with the Raja, but it also stated, "the Government will be prepared in case a reform of the kind desired cannot be made reconcilable to his feeling, to assert and act upon the principle of authoritatively interfering for the preservation of the rights of those subjects to his authority, and with which he has been permitted too long to trifle."[39] Regulation VII of 1828, declared the regulations of 1795 subject to modification contained in it and introduced English system of administration in the Domains, which it was excluded by the agreement of 1794. The Regulation laid down rules in detail regarding the settlement in the Domains and provision for revenue management and judicial administration.

1. A Superintendent of the Domains shall be appointed by the Governor General and Council.
2. The Raja, as regards the collections of arrears of his rent or revenue, to exercise the powers of a Collector.
3. A Native Commissioner was to be nominated and maintained by the Raja in each of the three parganas subject to the approval of the Superintendent for the trial of suits related to land within the Domains. They can be removed by the same procedure i.e. by the Raja subject to Superintendent's approval.
4. The Courts of the Native Commissioner were to follow the rules of Regulation XXII of 1814.
5. These Courts can execute their own decrees subject to an appeal to the Superintendent.
6. In the sale of land where the Raja vested the powers of a Collector, the Superintendent shall exercise the power of Board of Revenue.
7. Appeals from the orders of Native Commissioner shall be made to the Superintendent, subject to limitation of six months.
8. Complaints against the Raja and his officers to be cognizable by the Superintendent.
9. Appeal against the orders of the Superintendent was to be made to the Governor General in Council.

This Regulation not only commenced English administration but also made the Raja's decision subject to Superintendent's approbation. The Raja made his objections to Governor General Bentick during his visit to Benares appealing for the repeal of the "obnoxious regulation" but all in vain.[40] The Commissioner reported that the Raja would never give his "willing assent", but impede it as far as he may be able[41] and the Raja was asked to immediately commence the settlement of *pargana* Bhadoi, Kera, Mungroor and Kuswar.[42] The Raja's objections were—[43]

Section VI- No one should have the right of disposing of the property of the soil, but only such rights in perpetuity or for period as they derive from their engagements with him.

Section VII- It shall not be necessary for the Raja to send all settlements to the Superintendent but only in cases where there are grievances.

Section XIV- Superintendent should not possess powers exercise over Collectors with respect to the Raja but rather the powers vested in Collector by Regulation XV of 1795.

Section XIV- By this Superintendent was authorized to make over criminal matters to the Magistrate but as the criminal regulation were previously in force in these *parganas* and particularized in section XV of new regulation there seems no necessity for this section.

Section XVI-XXIII – The Raja demanded that he should be given exclusive powers to appoint or dismiss Commissioner on the basis of their fitness.

Section XXIV- If any person can appeal against the Commissioner's decision to the Raja within one month and if there be no justice from the Raja's side within two three months, then he shall send petition to the Superintendent on the subject.

A Commission was formed to enquire into the allegations made by the Raja, which reported that new law had undoubtedly infringed Raja's rights, as it recognized rights independent of Raja that had no existence previously and were opposed to the pledge of the Government under treaty and agreement of 1794.[44] Consequently, in 1831 it was decided that an European Officer was to be appointed by Sudder Board of Revenue to co-operate with the Raja in settling the lands specified in Regulation VII of 1828 and to superintend the realization of revenue. Further, it laid down that the Board would now exercise the control vested in the hands of the Government by the Regulation VII of 1828. In October 1831, the Board nominated an officer as the Deputy Superintendent.[45] The changes which were introduced as consequence of the objections raised by the Raja, exacerbated the situation and was entirely subversive of his rights and privileges in a more severe manner than before as now Sudder Board was in the position of the Governor General in Council i.e. now the Raja was to make his appeals not to the Governor General in Council, but to the Board that was completely violating the agreement of 1794 and Regulation of 1828. Raja Udit Narain Singh, till his death in April 1835, had remained unremitting in his opposition to the provisions of the repugnant regulation and proceedings taken under it.

He was succeeded by his nephew and adopted son Raja Ishwari Prasad Narain Singh Bahadur who was granted *sunnud* along with *jagir, mahals* and *altumgha* etc. with same privileges and rights on August 18, 1835.[46] With the succession of new Raja, the British again made endeavours to interfere in the matters of the Raja. They considered to introduce General Regulations into the Family Domains of Raja Benares, which was excluded by the Regulation VII of 1828 and to avow the estate of the Raja subject to the laws and regulations in force in Benares.[47] Raja Ishwari Prasad Narain obdurately demurred this measure through his letter to Officiating Agent to Governor at Benares articulating, inter lia, "Permit me to observe that, in consideration of the conditions of the treaty which had been concluded between the Government and my grandfather, I cannot accede to the introduction of the regulations which are promulgated for the community in general into my zemindaree. As the British Government is more disposed to maintain stipulations than former kings, I entertain a sanguine hope that no order will be passed contrary to that agreement; but I readily concede to whatever my father the late Maharajah had represented by a petition presented to His Honor the Governor of Agra, on the 28th February 1835."[48]

By the end of 1836, with the completion of settlement, the office of Deputy Superintendent was abolished and his duties were passed over to the Collector of Benares; and Sudder Board of Revenue was supposed to act as the Superintendent. In 1839, Captain Stewart was appointed as Separate Superintendent to correspond directly to the Sudder Board of Revenue and the cost of his office was to be defrayed by the Government. On April 6, 1843, by order of Governor General, Lord Ellenborough, the office of the Superintendent was abolished due to unnecessary expense and his duties were transmitted to Collectors of Benares and Mirzapur; but, neverthless, it was soon re-established in 1844.[49] According to the original arrangement of 1845-46, the Superintendent was to receive a salary of Rs. 12,000 per annum and expense on establishment was fixed at Rs. 3000. Half of the expense of the officer was to be defrayed by the Raja and the other half by the people.[50]

Raja Ishwari Prasad expressed his utter discontent over this arrangement of expense of the Superintendent's office, "It would occasion a disparagement of my ancestral honour and dignity, by being put on terms of equality with my tenantry from my copartnership with them in the payment of fees and charges of the Superintendent's office; and the other, that the very tenor of the order is calculated to affect the treaty entered into by the Hon'ble Company and my ancestors, which is the groundwork of all my rights." He proposed that either the Government impose any charge on suits instituted by his *ryots* or fix similar tax as in force in the rest of the province of Benares and therefrom pay all the expense of the Superintendent's office. In consideration of his ancestors' and in conformity with his own and dignity, he was even ready to defray all the expense of the Superintendent's establishment provided it should be limited to Rs. 15,000 per annum.[51] Later by the order of the Secretary to Government in November 1853, the distribution of the expenses of the Deputy Superintendent's office was fixed in the following manner:[52]

	Covenanted Assistant	Establishment	Total
Government's moiety	4800	2700	7,500
Raja's moiety	3600	3900	7,500
	8400	6600	15000

During the period elapsing between December 1845 and January 1846 the following changes were incorporated in the administration:[53]

1. The Raja will henceforth exercise the powers entrusted to him by Regulation VII of 1828 under the control and direction of the Superintendent. The Board will continue to exercise supervising and appellate authority in matters connected with the Domains.
2. The Raja will appoint a *Naib* to assist him in revenue administration and appeals of his acts will be made to the Superintendent.
3. All summary suits for rent or possession of land will be cognizable by the Raja or his Deputy.
4. The three Native Commissioners were to be replaced by one judicial officer with jurisdiction over all the three *parganas*.
5. The Raja will pay half expense of the Superintendent's office i.e. Rs. 7, 500 annually in Collector's office along with the revenue installments and rest charges was to be defrayed by the Government who will manage this amount by introducing stamp laws in the Family Domains, which will be enforced in all suits and petitions. The Raja was exempted from the operation of stamp laws.
6. Whatever general changes might be introduced from time to time into the system of Government for the rest of Benares province, should be followed in the Raja's domains, too.

By 1853 the situation went to its extreme when the use of Raja's signature and seal on the revenue documents was also abolished. He now only enjoyed the privilege of taking copies of revenue documents without the payment of fees and receiving the cost of the Treasury as an annual grant. The administration continued to work in the same manner. During the revolt of 1857, Raja Benares came forward with all his military and financial resources in assistance of the British government. For his staunch support and eminent service, he received thanks from Governor General and was conferred with the title of Maharaja in 1859. After the restoration of peace, Lord Canning himself visited Benares and held a *Durbar* where Maharaja was permitted a salute of 13 guns.[54]

The existing courts of civil and revenue jurisdiction during that time was as follows:[55]

Civil

Court of First Instance,	Principal Sudder Ameen
Court of Appeal	Deputy Superintendent
Court of Special Appeal	Sudder Board of Revenue

Revenue

District Courts	The Maharaja Principal Revenue Officer Deputy Principal Revenue Officer
Commissioner	Deputy Superintendent
Sudder Board of Revenue	Sudder Board of Revenue

The Government's encroachments upon Maharaja's rights were inexorable. In 1867-68 there was a proposal to bring the Domains to the subjection within the jurisdiction of High Court and enforcements of current legislation and Act I of 1845. The Maharaja resolutely objected to introduction of any new laws without his consent, "for if this is done, the wall of distinction which has been erected for the preservation of the honour and dignity of my family will remain no more." He also refused any change in stamp laws and office of Principal *Sudder Ameen.*[56] Things remained same and no further changes were introduced. In March 1862, he was granted adoption *sunnud*.[57]

Maharaja Ishwari Prasad Narain presented a Memorandum to Lord Northbrook, Viceroy and Governor-General of India regarding his status in response, to which a memorandum of the statement was made by the Viceroy dated November 23, 1875, which coherently states, "The Government of India do not consider that His Highness is simply an influential zamindar, to whom certain concessions have been made, and have not and do not designate him as such His Highness does not, indeed possess sovereign rights but His Highness does possess exceptional jurisdiction within the limits of his Family Domains in revenue and other matters set forth in Regulation 1828. His Excellency observed that he was averse from attempting to define the Maharaja's status by any single term such as "feudatory, "tributary" or "dependent" as no single term correctly describes His Highness position."[58]

In 1877, Imperial Assembly was held where Lord Lytton, the Viceroy, presented a gold medal and awarded a Royal salute of 13 guns to the Maharaja.[59] He also presented a banner that was later used as the flag of the State.[60] Though there were incessant endeavours to lower the dignity of the Maharaja, which the British assured to his ancestors in 1781 and reiterated in 1794; but all the same, the Maharaja enjoyed great honour among his subjects of which the British were well aware. Contemporary writer M.A. Sherring wrote, "This nobleman is the recognized head of the native community of the city and district of Benares, and in virtue of such position, exerts a great influence upon all classes of the people. In ordinary times, this influence operates calmly and secretly, yet its incidence is felt in every direction. Its recognition and acknowledgment have become part of the instinctive consciousness of the Hindus of the city and neighbourhood; they have never question its weight and authority... The people look to the Maharaja as to their natural leader, and place themselves at his disposal. His word comes to them with far greater force than the command of any other person, be he who or what he may."[61]

In 1889 he died and was succeeded by Maharaja Prabhu Narain Singh *Bahadur* and with his succession, Benares entered into a new phase. His Installation *Durbar* was held on December 21, 1889, where he was presented a *khil'at*, an elephant, a horse and a palanquin.[62] By the order of the Government a privilege was conferred upon him by which about 700 of his Retainers were exempted in North Western Provinces and Oudh under section 27 of the Arms Act (XI of 1878) by the Governor General in Council from operation of all prohibitions and directions under sections 13, 14, 15 and 16 of the act, other than those related to canon, war rockets etc. The numbers of retainers exempted were the highest for the Maharaja of Benares in the Province.[63] The Maharaja submitted a Memorial on March 18, 1905, asking to give him and his successors a defined and permanent status among the Ruling Chiefs. On the basis of the agreement of 1794 and *sunnuds* granted in 1796 and 1835, the Maharaja presented three claims in his memorandum:—

1. That until the agreement of 1794 Benares had been a native State and the Raja a Ruling Chief.
2. That the surrender of the administration by the Raja in the agreement of 1794 was only meant interim measure.
3. That the position of the Raja in the Family Domains since 1784 was of Ruling Chief.

Though the first claim of the Raja was conceded as Lord Northbrook opined, "The Maharaja of Benares both before and after the cession of the province by the Government of Oudh and both before and after the agreement of prince possessed of a limited sovereignty" but he denied the other two claims stating that 1794 agreement was permanent agreement. Regarding third claim the Raja contended that the agreement of 1794 referred only to the *zila* of Benares and does not affect two *parganas* of Domain-Bhadohi and Kara Mangroor. It was reprimanded by the British Government stating that half revenue of Bhadohi was included in the annual revenue of Rs. 40 lakhs and both the *parganas* were being administered in accordance of the agreement of 1794 since the day of its execution i.e. the agreement included whole of the Domains.[64]

Making the position of the Raja distinct and unambiguous, it stated four seminal points that make the Raja's position quite different from that of a *zamindar* since the agreement of 1794.

1. Payment of Rs. 1 lakh of the surplus revenue.

2. "Honorific Connection" with the administration of the Province by article 2 of 1794 agreement under which *sunnud* was granted to Raja Udit Narain Singh in 1796 and Maharaja Ishwari Prasad Narain Singh in 1835 confirming them.
3. Grant of adoption *sunnud* similar to those granted to Ruling Chiefs.
4. He enjoys special jurisdiction and authority in the Family Domain by virtue of article 3. The Raja, subject to superintendence of the Local Government, still holds revenue administration of the Domains, and civil justice in matters relating to land, was administered by his Courts. His concurrence was necessary under section 9 of Regulation VII of 1828 for the extension of legislation in the Domains regarding realization of revenue and his opinion was to be considered, under section 22, in framing rules regarding procedure of rent courts and administration of the Domains.

The Raja's position differed from other Ruling Chiefs as the territory was the integral part of the British India and Bengal Regulation XV of 1795, Regulation VII of 1828 and Act XIV of 1881 conferred special jurisdiction of the Raja. The administration of the Domains was exactly same as implemented in Allahabad and Bihar, in which they were included (Bhadohi in Allahabad and Kara Mangroor in Bihar) and British government was the taxing authority in the Domains. The Raja was considered as a British subject who pays revenue of Rs. 2 lakhs on property outside the Domain in Benares district. The Government accepted that inspite of these differences the Maharaja exercises some of the functions of "internal sovereignty" and a ruling to a "limited extent".[65]

In 1907, Maharaja Prabhu Narain Singh owned 1,758 ½ *bighas* in Ramnagar and 5,980 *bighas* in immediate suburbs. Moreover, he owned total 860 villages in the districts of Mirzapur, Benares, Ghazipur, Jaunpur, Ballia, Allahabad and Shahabad.[66] A proposal was forwarded by Lieutenant Governor for the consideration of Government of India, which recommended that Bhadohi and Kara Mangroor should be transferred to the Raja's administration and Gangapur should be brought under the same system of administration as the rest of Benares district. Regarding this proposal, Chief Secretary to Government, United Provinces submitted a draft of Instrument of Transfer in the foreign department, by which the above mentioned areas was to be termed as the State of Benares[67] with a map illustration the proposals made by this Government on Maharaja's memorandum.[68] Eventually, on 1 April, 1911 an Instrument of Transfer was signed by Viceroy and Governor General Lord Harding that states Bhadohi and Kara Mangroor, and Fort of Ramnagar and its appurtenances would constitute a State of Benares and the Maharaja was to be the Ruling Chief with full powers in these territories subject to the suzerainty of His Majesty. It included following terms:[69]

1. His Highness Maharaja shall be the Ruling Chief of Benares from April 1, 1911 in the mentioned territories, which will be termed as the State of Benares and remain faithful in allegiance and subordination to the King of U.K. of Great Britain and Ireland.
2. He shall enjoy the same salute and honours and receive annual payment of Rs. 1 lakh from Lieutenant Governor of U.P. of Agra and Oudh.
3. Maharaja and his successors shall be entitled to administer the State of Benares and the succession to the Chiefship shall devolve on the lineal descendents of the Maharaja by blood or adoption, but the succession shall be valid only after being recognized by the Governor General of India in Council
4. A sum of Rs. 1,90,000 shall be payable annually by the Ruling Chief of Benares as tribute due from his State of the British Government.
5. The Maharaja without the permission of Lieutenant Governor shall neither build any new fort nor repair the defences of existing ones nor he shall import into the State arms, ammunitions or military stores and allow their manufacture.
6. The military force employed within the State for maintenance

of internal order shall not exceed the strength fixed by the Governor General of India in Council.

7. He shall neither have any communication with any other State or Power nor employ any person who is not a native of India without the previous approbation and through the medium of Lieutenant Governor of U.P. of Agra and Oudh.
8. The coins of the Government of India shall be the legal tender in the State and no separate coinage shall be permitted.
9. The Maharaja shall grant all land that may be required by the Lieutenant Governor of U.P. of Agra and Oudh for any public purposes for which he would receive compensation as may seem proper by Lieutenant Governor.
10. He shall cause to arrest or surrender any person within the State to the officers of British Government accused of committed an offence in British India and shall afford assistance for the trial of such persons.
11. He shall permit to execute in his State all warrant, summon, or other processes, civil, criminal or revenue issued by the authority in British territory as if the State had continued to be a British territory.
12. No change shall be made in the system of administration as established when His Highness Maharaja will take the possession of the State.
13. The Ruling Chief shall conform to such advice as Governor General of India in Council may offer him for management of his finances, revenue, justice etc.
14. The Commissioner of Benares shall be Political Agent to the Lieutenant Governor for the State.
15. Death sentence shall be subject to confirmation by the Lieutenant Governor of United Provinces of Agra and Oudh.
16. The right to repeal or amend Bengal Regulation VII of 1828 by which the Raja of Benares enjoys privileges in Kaswar Raja within his Family Domains, but excluded from Benares State will be expressly reserved to the Lieutenant Governor of U.P. of Agra and Oudh.
17. The Maharaja shall have the status of landholder within

his estates outside the State.

18. In case of breach or non-observance by the Ruling Chief the Governor General of India in Council may resume possession of the State of Benares and assume direct administration.
19. Should any question arises as to whether any of the above conditions have been faithfully performed, or as to whether any person is entitled to succeed, or is fit to succeed, to the administration of the State of Benares, the decision by Governor General of India in Council shall be final.

Total area given to the Maharaja Benares constitutes:

Bhadohi Pargana	391.6 sq miles.
Kara Mangroor	area 473.9 sq miles
Ramnagar Fort and its appurtenances	233 acres.

In September 1911, the Government of India permitted the Maharaja to enter British territory with armed retainers less than 100 and Maharani, *Kunwar Shahib* and his consorts could enter with armed retainers, less than 50.[70] *Pargana* Kaswar Raja i.e. Gangapur, which was within the Family Domain of Maharaja Benares was transferred to British Government after the creation of the State.[71] The State flag is of yellow colour in triangular shape with following description:

Arms	Azure, a plate between two fish argent counter embowed arc.
Crest	A Trident
Supporters	Bulls

The fish was borrowed from or granted by Oudh, the Trident and bulls referred to Benares, the spot of the earth most sacred in the eyes of a devotee of Shiva, and said to rest on the point of his Trident. The motto of the State was *Satya Nasti Prodharmah* meaning, "There is no virtue greater than truth".[72]

On July 9, 1913, an assurance was given by the British Government that other than Rs. 1 lakh the Maharaja would get Rs. 14,856 for *Mulki* treasuries, Rs. 4,562-8 as compensation for abolition of *Kamachha abkari* and Rs. 1000 for surrendering the

Government his right as hereditary revenue collector of Karnadandi. The Maharaja gave valuable assistance to the British Government during the first World War, for which he was conferred the title of Maharaja as hereditary distinction on January 1, 1918. On August 6, 1919, a supplementary Instrument of Transfer was signed by Chelmsford, Viceroy and Governor General of India by which the administration of additional territories was made over to the Maharaja and the revenue villages included were of Ramnagar, Bazidpur, Kodupur, Kutlupur, Ralhupur Khas, Tengra, Bhiti and Sultanpur with total area of 3, 198.02 acres (including 233 acres of Ramnagar fort and its appurtenance given in 1911). For the administration of these territories included in the State of Benares the terms would be same as declared by the Instrument of Transfer in 1911 and the annual tribute payable to the British Government would be raised from Rs. 1,90,000 to Rs. 2,19,000.[73]

During the World War of 1914-1918, the Maharaja generously contributed to the Government. Total 1005 men from the State went to the Great War, out of these 82 men sacrificed their lives, in memory of which Lord Reading established a historical *Shaheed Samaruk*, on December 1, 1921 in Ramnagar with five tablets intact. The material supplied by the State were:

Horses	173
Tent	16

Motor, Ambulance, aeroplane and number not clear.
Other particulars
Contribution in money amounting to Rs. 1,25,585

The State supplied material amounting to Rs. 7,43,305 and purchased war bonds totaling to Rs. 8,55,163. Other than this two sections of ambulance corps were raised. One section served in Mesopotamia under the command of Cap. Murli Sing and another served at Aden, commanded by Lt. Suraj Narain Rai. Each section consisted of one commanding officer, one second-in-command, three non-commissioned officers, 50 drivers and camp followers and 52 ponies. There were total 352 men and 4 officers on the two fronts, out of which three lost their lives and

7 disabled. Total expenditure of the State on these two sections was Rs. 2,98, 563. Lady Chelmsford War Hospital was inaugurated on July 10, 1916, for the treatment of wounded soldiers and was closed after the termination of the War. About 1395 patients were received in it from different seats of War—France, Salonika, Palestine, Mesopotamia, Aden, Egypt and East Africa. The number of staff in the hospital, besides three officers, was 72 and total expenditure was to the tune of Rs. 2,02,920. During these services of the State Maharaja Kumar Anant Narain Singh was the Commander-in-Chief with Cap. Girja Prasad Singh as the Chief of the Staff of Commander-in-Chief and incharge of the war activities.[74]

It was the standing order of the Government of India that the Ruling Chiefs were not allowed to acquire land in British India without permission. So with the creation of Benares State, there was a moot question of Maharaja's position regarding property, which he then possessed in British India, but were not included in the State. Government of India directed that the Maharaja should be allowed to acquire the remainder of any village, in which he allegedly owns a share amounting to 8 *annas* or more and that he should sell his rights in any village or *mahal* in which his share does not reach that amount within a reasonable period.[75] Maharaja Prabhu Narain Singh was a great philanthropist and lover of Indian architecture and Hindu sculpture. He erected many Hindu temples in Benares and its adjoining areas like the *Shivmandir* at Gowdowlia, Ramnagar, Shivala building, a two story temple of *Bal Roop* Ram in Dev Kali campus of Faizabad city. He made great contributions in the field of education. He donated a magnificent building with its surrounding lands to the Central Hindu school and was described as "the first patron of the Institution"[76] and played a cardinal role in the establishment of Banaras Hindu University. The scheme to establish the University was first discussed in a meeting held at Mint House, Benares in 1904 under Maharaja's Presidentship.[77] He also donated land to the University.

On August 4, 1931, Maharaja Prabhu Narain Singh died and was succeeded by Maharaja Aditya Narain Singh *Bahadur*.

His Coronation *Durbar* was held on February 17, 1932, in Nadesar House where Sir Malcolm Hailey, Governor of U.P. of Agra and Oudh presented him *Kharita* of Viceroy Lord Willington dated September 19, 1931.[78] Substantial amount of Rs. 1,86,000 was expended in the Coronation and February 12,15,16 and 17 were declared holidays in the State.[79] He declared to give priority to the development in the field of education and health in Benares State. He also declared exemption of revenue and canal rate, other than 25%, that was declared by the late Maharaja and this exemption was extended to the *tehsils* of Gangapur, Jaunpur Mirzapur, Allahabad, Benares, Pindara for two *fasli* years 1339 and 1340 (1931-1932). He always emphasized democratic principle with village as the pivot of administration.[80] He died on April 4, 1939 for which condolence was declared for one week from 5th to 11th April.[81]

His adopted son Vibhuti Narain Singh succeeded him in the *Kharita Durbar* held on December 8, 1939.[82] In 1947 the Maharaja passed his minority and took the administration in his hands, which was till now in the hands of Mr. C.R. Peter as his Regent. In the Investiture *Durbar* held on July 11, 1947, Lieutenant Colonel Russell invested His Highness Maharaja Vibhuti Narain Singh Bahadur with the Ruling powers.[83] On October 27, 1947 it was proclaimed that the Maharaja instituted a responsible Government in the State as *Praja Mandal* Government with Defence, Chief Judiciary, External Affairs and Finance under his own charge and other powers were given to *Praja Mandal.* The Government of Banaras State Act 1949 was enacted in which the members of *Praja Mandal*, the State Legislature was to be elected directly by the people of not less than 21 years of age.[84]

After independence of India in August 1947, an agreement was signed between Governor General of India and His Highness Maharaja Benares by which the State of Benares was merged into the Dominion of India as part of United Provinces. His Highness Maharaja Prabhu Narain Singh signed this on September 5, 1949 on behalf of himself, his heirs and successors and V.P. Menon, Advisor to Government of India in the Ministry of States on behalf of Governor General of India, which included following clauses:[85]

1. "The Maharaja of Benares hereby cedes to the Dominion Government full and exclusive authority jurisdiction and powers for and in relation to the governance of the State and agrees to transfer the administration of the State to the dominion Government on 15 day of October 1949, (hereinafter referred to as "the said day")."
   "As from the said day, the Dominion Government will be competent to exercise the said powers, authority and jurisdiction in such manner and through such agency as it may think fit."
2. "The Maharaja, his heir and successors shall with effect from the said day be entitled to receive from the revenues of the State annually for his privy purse the sum of Rs. 2,80,000/- free of taxes. This amount is intended to cover all the expenses of the Ruler and his family, including expenses on account of his personal staff, maintenance of his residences, marriages and other ceremonies, etc. and will neither be increased nor reduced for any reason whatsoever."
   "The said sum may be drawn by the Maharaja in four equal installments in advance at the beginning of each quarter by presenting bills at the State Treasury or at such other Treasury as may be specified by the Dominion Government."
3. The Maharaja shall be entitled to the full ownership. Use and enjoyment of all private properties (as distinct from State properties) belonging to him on the date of this agreement. The Maharaja will furnish to the dominion Government before 5 September 1949, an inventory of all the immovable property, securities and cash balance held by him as such private property. If any dispute arises as to whatever any item of property is the private property of the Maharaja or State property, it shall be referred to such offer with judicial experience as the Dominion Government may nominate and the decision of that officer shall be final and binding on both parties.

4. The Maharaja and his family shall be entitled to all personal privileges enjoyed by them whether within or outside the territories of the State, immediately before the 15 day of August, 1947.
5. The Dominion Government guarantees the succession, according to law and customs, to the *gaddi* of the State and to the Maharaja's personal rights, privileges, dignities and titles.
6. No enquiry shall be made by or under the authority of the Government of India and no proceedings shall lie in any court against the Maharaja whether in a personal capacity or otherwise in respect of anything done or omitted to be done by him or under authority during the period of his administration of that State.
7. The Government of India hereby guarantees either the continuance in services of Benares on conditions, which will be not less advantageous than those on which they were serving on the 1st day of August, 1949, or the payment of reasonable compensation. The Government of India further guarantees the continuance of pensions and leave salaries sanctioned by the Maharaja to members of the public services of the State and of the Benares State forces who have retired or proceeded on leave preparatory to retirement and also guarantees grant of pensions, gratuities and leave earned by and due to the members of the aforesaid public services of the State and of the Benares State forces.
8. Except with the previous sanction of the Government of India no proceedings, civil or criminal shall be instituted against any person in respect of any act done or purporting to be done in the execution of his duties as a servant of the State before the said day.

Along with the agreement, a collateral letter was also issued to His Highness Maharaja Benares on the same date by which assurances were given on behalf of the Government of India. Some important points are enumerated below:[86]

1. His Highness will be accorded the same precedence in and outside the State as he was enjoying as the Maharaja of

Benares. There will be no question of Commissioner, Benares Division or any other officer of the District taking precedence over His Highness in Benares district at official functions.

2. The *Gaddi* of the Maharaja shall continue at Fort Ramnagar and the Fort and its appurtenances and His Highness private palace as *Nadesar Palace* shall not be liable to attachment or sale and shall descend to the successors of His Highness. This will be exempted from all property or other municipal taxation.
3. Adequate police arrangements will be made during His Highness visit to Benares for *Darshan* and in connection with the *Ramlila* held at Ramnagar and His Highness dignities will be maintained on these occasions.
4. His Highness expressed desire to set apart a sum of Rs. 5,00,000 from the balances of the State for creating a Trust known as *All India Kashi Rajya Trust* for the promotion of Hindu culture and Sanskrit learning to which the Government of India agree to the creation of the Trust.
5. His Highness will enjoy exclusive rights in some of the forest blocks.
6. The Government will pay annually to His Highness Rs. 1 lakh for expenditure in connection with the *Ramlila*, the management of the temples within the State and other charitable institutions maintained by the State.
7. The allowance sanctioned to relatives and *sardars* of His Highness shall continue for their lifetime.
8. The annual payment of Rs. 1 lakhs which was payable to His Highness under the agreement of 1794 shall be paid to His Highness and his successors by the Government of India in perpetuity in addition to the privy purse amount fixed under the Agreement.
9. No private property of His Highness shall be requisitioned or acquired without his consent and payment of full compensation.
10. The facilities enjoyed by His Highness in respect of attachment of his saloon to trains will be continued.

A Memorandum was issued by the Government of India including personal privileges that were to be enjoyed by the Rulers of States merged into Provinces or Union of States.[87] As per the agreement, Government of India shall create a trust with His Highness Maharaja Benares and his successors as Chairman, and members nominated by the Maharaja, Government of India and U.P. Government for which Rs. 5 lakhs would be kept from State funds and U.P. Government will make a grant of Rs. 2 lakhs per year to this trust. All the temples, *dharmshalas* and other institutions conducted by His Highness would be considered as Trust properties. The objects of the trust mentioned are as following:[88]

1. Promotion of Sanskrit learning and Indian culture generally.
2. Maintenance of temples.
3. Holding of annual All-India conference of scholars connected with Sanskrit learning.
4. Management of other charitable institutions that may be taken over by the Trust.
5. Translation and publication of literature of ancient Indian culture into other languages and books of culture of other languages in Indian language.
6. Repairs of *ghats* and other properties in Kashi.
7. To arrange for and look after the pilgrims and visitors of Kashi.

A Notification was issued by the Ministry of States by which Central Government delegated its extra-provincial jurisdiction to the Provincial Government of U.P. for and in relation to the governance of the State of Benares.[89] The Provincial Government issued a notification for taking over the administration of Banaras State on October 15, 1949 published in U.P. Gazette Extraordinary. This was called Banaras State (Administration) Order 1949 and was to come in force on October 15, 1949. It was decided that the territories of Banaras State would be incharge of District Magistrate, Banaras, assisted by Additional District Magistrate who will be responsible for the work relating to these territories and the Commissioner, Banaras-Gorakhpur division will exercise general supervision over their work. Sri. B. Seth, former Additional District Magistrate Banaras was appointed as Additional District Magistrate for new territories. The Official of the State in service immediately before the merger would continue to exercise their function subject to general supervision and control of District Magistrate, Banaras. However, the Ministers of the State and State legislature would cease to function. All the powers exercised by the Ruler of the State under any law or in his prerogative immediately before the merger shall be exercisable by the Provincial Government or any authority as authorized on behalf of Government. The laws in force prior to the merger would continue until repealed or amended. All taxes, levies fees, duties under the State shall also continue to be levied. The Government may appoint Judges, Magistrates and other officers as may deem prudent for administration of the State.[90]

Regarding the integration of three areas of the State i.e. Chakia or Kara Mangroor, Bhadohi and Ramnagar, the Commissioner of Banaras division in consultation with other authorities recommended that it should be amalgated with Banaras as they were connected by *pucca* road and easily accessible from Banaras and historical tradition justifies the amalgation. Further, as compared to other contiguous districts Mirzapur and Jaunpur, Banaras had least number of *tehsils*, villages and areas in square miles, though its population was denser mainly due to Banaras city.[91] Maharaja before integration in the Province also expressed his desire to fulfill his promise to donate Rs. 6 lakhs for B.H.U. from the assets of the State, which was estimated to be about Rs. 34-35 lakhs at that time. It got the approbation of the Government of India.[92]

On the day of merger i.e. October 15, 1949, programmes were organized in Ramnagar, Chakia and Gyanpur.[93] On that occasion Sardar Patel sent his message assuring His Highness Maharaja that the Government and U.P. Government both will give him "no cause of regret". He articulated, "Today they mark the end of a State, but it can never obliterate the existence of an institution, the roots of which go back to the remote past. Kashi Raj is our ancient heritage; the holy city of Kashi receives the homage and devotion of millions throughout the country. The name of Kashi will live as long as humanity takes pride in its heritage, its religion and the very essence of culture and civilization. I can assure the Ruler and the people of Banaras State that the sanctity and name of Kashi will be preserved by us in the best manner possible."[94]

All the officials of the State were absorbed by the U.P. Government into their equivalent post. The State had three Collectors out of two were absorbed in P. C.S. and one retired.[95] The departments of the State were merged to the corresponding departments of the Provincial Government. By the Notification issued on October 15, 1949 *Praja Mandal* was dissolved and its staff was temporarily taken by the Secretariat.[96] After independence there was no exodus of minority in the district of Bhadohi, Ramnagar and Chakia as it happened in other parts of India.[97]Maharaja Prabhu Narain Singh was a highly revered prominent scholar and was Chancellor of Banaras Hindu University from 1992 till his demise in 2000 at the age of 73 years. At present his son Kunwar Anant Narain Singh continues the historic traditions of the Royal family.

References

1. FPD, 29 October, 1781, No. 4, Hastings to Wheeler, October 18, 1781.
2. Dodwell, *Letters of Hastings*, p. 82.
3. FPD, 3 December, 1781, No. 1, Hastings to Wheeler, November 21,1781.
4. Aitchison, C.U., *A Collection of Treaties, Engagements and Sanads relating to India and Neighbouring Countries*, BCO, DRII, Mittal Publications, Delhi, 1983, pp.77-83.P
5. FPD, 14 January, 1782, No. 11.
6. FPD, 27 December, 1783, No. 42, letter from Hastings.
7. FPD, Sec. Pr., 5 August, 1782, No. 5, letter from Markham, July 20, 1782, p. 2573.
8. Gleig, *op.cit*, II, p. 414.
9. FPD, 24 March, 1783, No. 2, letter to Francis Fowke, March 24, 1783.

10. Gleig, *op.cit.*, p. 421.
11. Aitchison, C.U., *op.cit.*, pp.81-82.
12. CPC, VI, No. 296, November, 17, 1781; No. 297.
13. FPD, 16-31 December, 1783, BCO, DR 92, No. 40 and 41, pp. 6800-01.
14. FPD, 24 March, 1783, No. 2, letter to Francis Fowke, March 24, 1783.
15. FPD, 4 December, 1782, No. 2, letter from Governor General to Markham, September 29, 1782.
16. FPD, Sec. Pr., 11 November-31 December, 1782, BCO, DR77, No. 3, letter from Markham, November 12, 1782, pp.3532-34.
17. FPD, 24 March, 1783, No. 2, letter to Francis Fowke, March 24, 1783.
18. FPD, Sec. Pr., 16-31 December, 1783, BCO, DR92, No. 35, 27 December 1783, letter from Fowke, June 5, 1783, pp.6793-95.
19. B.M.Add. Mss., No. 29121, Hastings to Council, June 13, 1784.
20. FPD, Sec. Pr., 30 June, 1784; Secret letter from Bengal to Court, July 5, 1784.
21. CPC, VI, No. 1442.
22. *Ibid.*
23. *History of the Province of Benares*, Carruther and Sons, Inverness, Medical Hall Press, 1882, Benares, p. 138.
24. BCO, DR, Basta No. 2, Vol. 10, June, 1788, Resident's Proceedings dated June 25, 1788, RAA.
25. *Ibid*, Residents Proceedings, June 29, 1788.
26. *Ibid*, letter from the Raja to the Resident, Proceedings dated June 30, 1788.
27. BCO, DR, Basta No. 3, Vol. 18, October, 1788, letter from Secretary to Resident, October 3, 1788, RAA.
28. BCO, DR, Basta No. 3, Vol. 18, October, 1788, Instructions from Secretary to Resident, October 3, 1788, RAA.
29. BCO, DR, Basta No. 40, Vol. 85, Resident's Proceedings 13 October, 1794, letter from the Resident to the Board.
30. BCO, DR 1788-99, Vol. 1, Basta No. 1, list B, index No. 819, letter of Resident to Sub. Secretary to the Government dated October 27, 1794.
31. *Report upon proposed Amendment of Regulation VII, 1828* by Duthoit, Allahabad, 1870, File No. 7, 1882, Administration of Family Domain of Maharaja Benares, RAV, pp.2-3.
32. *Ibid.*
33. Aitchison, *op.cit.*, p. 87.

34. Correspondence of the Agent to the Governor General at Benares, letters received, October 19, 1805, p. 45.
35. Pre Mutiny Records relate to Family Domains of Maharaja Benares (henceforth FDMB), Basta No. 97 A, Vol. 190 (iii), letter received from October 1848-1863, letter from Bird to Magistrate of Mirzapur dated December 13, 1826.
36. Pre- Mutiny Records related to FDMB, Miscellaneous letters issued from November 25, 1826, Basta No. 97(B), Vol. 190(iv), Report submitted by Bird to H.T. Princep, Acting Secretary to Government in the Territorial Department dated May 25, 1827, RAA.
37. *Ibid.*
38. *Ibid,* letter from Bird to Princep, Acting Secretary to Government, Territorial Department dated October 18, 1827, RAA.
39. *Report upon proposed Amendment of Regulation VII, 1828* by Duthoit, Allahabad, 1870, File No. 7, 1882, Administration of FDMB, RAV, pp.5-6
40. *Ibid*, pp.9-10.
41. Pre- Mutiny Records related to FDMB, Miscellaneous letters issued from November 25, 1826, Basta No. 97(B), Vol. 190(iv), letter from Officiating Commissioner Hutchinson to Secretary to Government, Territorial Department, November 14, 1827, RAA
42. *Ibid*, letter from Macnabb to the Raja, October 3, 1829.
43. *Ibid*, letter from the Raja to Macnabb, October 26, 1829.
44. *History of the Province of Benares, op.cit.*, p. 165.
45. Letter form Deputy Secretary to the Government to the Sudder Board of Revenue dated, July 26, 1831, file No. 7, Box No. 29, RAV, p. 10.
46. Aitchison, *op.cit.*, p. 87.
47. Letter from Secretary to he Government of Agra, Revenue Department to Officiating Agent to the Governor General, Benares, dated June 11, 1835, File No. 7, Box No. 29, RAV.
48. Letter from Raja Ishwari Prasad to Officiating Agent to Governor, Benares, November 17,1835, File No. 7, Box No. 29, RAV.
49. Report upon the Proposed Amendment of Regulation VII of 1828 by Duthoit, Deputy Superintendent, Administration of Family Domains, File No. 7, Box No. 29, RAV.
50. Letter from Roberts, Superintendent, FDMB, to Secretary to Sudder Board of Revenue, NWP, April 25, 1854, Department Board of Revenue, list-19 II, Box No. 3, File No. 8, UPSA.
51. Letter from Raja Ishwari Prasad to Agent to Lieutenant Governor,

NWP, Benares, August 16,1844, File No. 7, Box No. 29, RAV.

52. Letter from Secretary to Government to Secretary to Sudder Board of Revenue, NWP, No. 163A dated November 30, 1853, File No. 8, Box No. 3, List-19 II, Department Board of Revenue, UPSA.
53. Letter from Secretary to Government, NWP to Secretary, Sudder Board of Revenue, NWP, Agra, No. 45A, December 18, 1845 and No. 117A, January 23, 1846, File No. 7, Box No. 29, RAV.
54. Post Mutiny Agency Records, Basta No. 73, Department- Family Domains, File No. 2, list-8, letter from Secretary to Government, NWP to Secretary to Government of India, August 31, 1859, RAA.
55. *Report upon proposed Amendment of Regulation VII, 1828* by Duthoit, Allahabad, 1870, File No. 7, 1882, Administration of Family Domain of Maharaja Benares, RAV, p. 16.
56. Translation of the Proceedings of Maharaja of Benares, January 30, 1868, File No. 7, Box No. 29, RAV.
57. Aitchison, *op.cit.*, p. 88.
58. Memorandum of Statement made by Lord Northbrook, Viceroy and Governor General of India, November 23, 1875, File No. 697A, Box No. 62, list-2, Political, 1899, UPSA.
59. Foreign and Political Consultation, December 1877, Political A 286-496, NAI.
60. Sherring, M.A., *Hindu Tribes and Castes*, I, Trubner and Co., 1872, London, p. 44.
61. Collectorate Record Varanasi, list-8 Benares State, File No. 137, Department IV, Box No. 4A, year 1945-46, a replica of the flag is kept in this file, RAV.
62. D.O. letter no 654/PIV-89 to Col. Rusell, Resident at Gwalior and for States of Benares and Rampur, May 13, 1947, Collectorate Record Varanasi, list 8, Benares State, File No. 43, Box No. 6A, RAV.
63. Letter from Secretary to Government, NWP to Commissioner of all Divisions, October 21, 1899, list 3, File No. 37, Box-19, Department XVIII, RAV.
64. Letter No. 886 from Chief Secretary to Government, United Provinces to Secretary to the Government of India, Foreign Department, November 2, 1905, Political Department, File No. 24, Box-47, list No. 1, RAV.
65. *Ibid.*
66. Letter from Maharaja of Benares to the Commissioner, Benares, May 10, 1907, list –1, File-24, Box-47, RAV.

67. Letter No. 886 from Chief Secretary to Government, United Provinces to Secretary to the Government of India, Foreign Department, November 2, 1905, Political Department, File No. 24, Box-47, list No. 1, RAV, Outline of the Instrument of Transfer.
68. Letter no 2467/XII-27 from Commissioner, Benares Division to Chief Secretary to Government, United Provinces dated April 24, 1906, Political Department, File No. 24, Box-47, list No. 1, *Status of the Maharaja of Benares*, RAV.
69. *Instrument of Transfer*, 1911, list-4, File No. 67, Box-37, 1913-1917, RAV.
70. Government Order No. 811-14/I-20A, September 6, 1911, list-5, File-112, Box-3, Department-XVIII, RAV.
71. Letter No. 131/XVI-85 from Benares Division Commissioner to Collector Benares, November 27, 1919, list-5, File-95, Department-XVI, RAV.
72. Letter from Dewan, Benares State to Neubecker No. 10907/IV-1378, October 10, 1947, List-8, File-137, Box-4A, RAV.
73. Aitchison, *op.cit.*, pp. 95-97.
74. *Shaheed Smarak* established by Lord Reading on December 1, 1921 in Ramnagar. There are total 5 tablets intact with details of all contributions made by the Highness Maharaja and the Officials of the State. Another *Smarak* of the Maharaja is in Varanasi Cantonment with 3 tablets intact giving information regarding Lady Chelmsford War Hospital and the patients admitted.
75. Instructions from Commissioner, Benares to District Officer, Benares, April 3, 1919, list-5, File-54, Box-19, Department XVI, RAV.
76. The Central Hindu College Magazine, October 1905, Vol. V, No. 10, p. 243, The Theosophical Society, Indian Section, Varanasi.
77. *Prajna*, Journal of BHU, Vol. 54, year 2008-09, Article by Dr. Pandey, PRO, BHU, p. 259.
78. Letter from Viceroy Wellington to Maharaja Anant Narain Singh, September 19, 1939, list-8, File-13, Box No. - 3B, Department IV, RAV.
79. List-8, Collectorate Record Varanasi, File-163, Box No. -6, year 1931-32, Department IV, RAV.
80. *Sansar Saptahik, Kashi Raj Ank*, November 1949, Public Declaration of Maharaja Aditya Narain Singh, pp.81-82.
81. Benares State Gazette Extraordinary, April 6, 1937, Vol. XXXI, No. 17, list-7, Department IV, File No. 3, Box No. 6, RAV.
82. D.O. letter No. 654/PIV-89 to Col. Rusell, Resident at Gwalior

and for States of Benares and Rampur, May 13, 1947, list-8, File-48, Box-6A, RAV.

83. Collectorate Record Varanasi, Benares State, list-8, File-43, Box-6A, RAV.
84. The Government of Banaras State Act 1949, list-8, File-574, Box-4A, RAV.
85. General Administration Department (henceforth GAD), list 85A, File No. 517/1949, Box- 718, *Agreement for the Merger of Benares State*, UPSA.
86. *Ibid*, Collateral letter issued to His Highness Maharaja Benares dated September 5, 1949 by V.P. Menon, Advisor to Government of India from Ministry of States.
87. GAD, list No. 98B, File No. 521(5)/1949, Box- 966, UPSA.
88. GAD, listNo. 86A, File No. 517/1949, Box-718, *Merger of Benares State*, Appendix A, UPSA.
89. GAD, list-86A, File No. 517/1949, Box-718, UPSA.
90. GAD, list-86A, File No. 517/1949, Box-718, Gazette Extraordinary Notification to be issued on October 15, 1949, UPSA.
91. GAD, list-86A, File No. 517/1949, Box-718, Note For the Cabinet by Chief Secretary, U.P., September 22, 1949, UPSA.
92. GAD, list-86A, File No. 517/1949, Box-718, D.O.F-172-P/49 from V.P. Menon to Shri G.B. Pant, Premier. U.P. dated September 8, 1949, UPSA.
93. GAD, list-86A, File No. 517/1949, Box-718, D.O. No. 58-ST/III-49, from Civil Secretariat to Dr. Hafazat, October 7, 1949, UPSA.
94. GAD, list-86A, File No. 517/1949, Box-718, Message of Hon'ble Sardar Patel on the occasion of the merger of the Banaras State on October 15, 1949, UPSA.
95. GAD, list-86A, File No. 517(8)/1949, Box-, Integration of Banaras Consequent on Merger, *Reorganization Report by Commissioner, Banaras*, November 27, 1949, No. 282/5/BS, UPSA.
96. GAD, list-86A, File No. 517(19)/1949, Box-719, *Interim Preliminary Report showing Process of Integration* by DM, Banaras to Chief Secretary to Government, U.P. dated November 3, 1949, No. 8597/III, UPSA.
97. List-8, Box-6, File-17, Department IV, year 1948-49, letter from the Collector of three districts of Banaras State.

Conclusions

From the times immemorial, Benares has been a scintillating diamond in the eyes of people and no city of *Hindustan* enjoys so much antiquity and venerance by its people. It enjoyed being the capital city during the reign of Gharwal dynasty but later during the Sultanate and Mughal rule, Benares and its inhabitants had to weep for being the holiest and the most prosperous city in *Hindustan*. All along, the city was plundered many a time, temples were wrecked and mosques were constructed on the same place using the same material. Benares witnessed many revolts and disturbances during this period. Even Mughal Emperor Akbar, who was famous for his religious tolerance policy and had established his authority firmly throughout his dominions, had to stay in the region for 37 days to establish peace, and he, too, passed orders to plunder the city, which should be extremely deprecated. Though it was countermanded, yet by then it was too late. All this eventuated in great discontent among the people of Benares, who in retaliation refused to pay the revenue willfully to the Imperial treasury and on several occasions Imperial army was required for the collections.

The feeling of insecurity and discontentment prevailing among the people developed a strong and intense desire to have their own ruler who could save them from religious intolerance and plunders. During the third decade of 18th century, Mansaram, a *bhumihar Brahmin*, came into prominence as the *dewan* of Rustum Ali. Rustum Ali was entrusted with the management of four *sarkar* Benares, Jaunpur, Chunar and Ghazipur in 1728, by Saadat Khan. The administration of the region was totally dependent on Mansaram, as Rustum Ali was too indolent to manage the affairs. Mansaram and his son Balwant Singh, were conferred with the title of *Rajabahadur* by the Emperor Mohammad Shah himself in 1730. As in retrospect, revenue collection in Benares was an onerous task and Rustum Ali failed to pay it regularly. In 1738, Safdar Jang marched to Jaunpur, but Rustum Ali being so scared sent Mansaram to negotiate with Safdar Jang. With the frequent change of circumstances, Mansaram proffered annual revenue of Rs. 13 lakhs for the grant of *sunnud* of three sarkars Benares, Jaunpur and Chunar while Ghazipur was given to Sheikh Abdullah on payment of Rs. 3 lakhs annually. With the grant of *sunnud* and installation of Mansaram as the Raja of Benares a new dynasty emerged. Benares was strategically very important, first, because of being a border region of Oudh Suba and secondly, trade route, both land and sea, passes through it. At a time when the Imperial authority was ebbing, they were not in a position to take risk of further revolts and anarchy as this would not only mean revenue loss but even could be a door left ajar for the Marathas who had always manifested their interests in the holy city. All these factors forced the rulers to attune themselves in the direction of establishing a separate ruling dynasty.

Despite the fact that there was a Muslim ruler—both on the Imperial throne and in Oudh, emergence of a Hindu dynasty in Benares is a question of great consideration. Safdar Jang was cognizant that only a Hindu ruler would be acceptable to the people and Mansaram was the only person who could collect the revenue from the people otherwise he would have never promptly offered an increase of Rs. 5 lakhs in revenue, in spite of the fact that Ghazipur was taken away. The regular payment of revenue first by him and later by his son Balwant Singh itself corroborates this fact. Moreover, Mansaram had a good experience of administration of the region and was the head of the ancient and powerful clan of *Trikarma Brahmins*, a caste that shared a big chunk of the population of Benares due to which he enjoyed great influence within the province.

After the death of Mansaram in 1740, his son Balwant Singh succeeded him and sought the recognition directly from the Emperor Mohammad Shah. Imperial *sunnud* was granted to him declaring him as the only beneficiary of his father and bestowed upon him the title of Raja. Till 1748, the Raja regularly paid the revenue, but he soon endeavoured to make himself practically independent of the Nawab and by 1750 he became so powerful that he defeated the army of none other than Ali Quli Khan, Deputy Governor of Allahabad. Though both the Nawab Safdar Jang and his successor Shuja-ud-Daula wanted to punish the Raja for his extensions, but could take no stringent actions against him firstly, because of their engagements in Delhi politics due to attack by Bangash Pathans in 1750-51 and then Abdali's invasion; secondly, whenever they marched to Benares the Raja never appeared before the Nawab and always fled to steep hill forts covered by dense forests where it was difficult to chase him; and thirdly there was no viable alternative to the Raja who commanded enough support of the people and army and who could pay the demanded revenue regularly. So every time the Nawab allowed him to continue his possessions on the condition of increase in the revenue by few lakhs. Thus by his political determination and diplomacy, the Raja extended his possessions from inherited 18 *parganas* to 96 *parganas*.

In the sixth decade of the 18th century with the emergence of English East India Company from a trade to political power, Benares entered into a new phase, as it was contiguous to both the power—Muslim power in the west and Christian power in the east. This strategic location and economic and military power of the Raja made it conspicuous during the battle of Buxar. During this time Raja Balwant Singh was in a situation in which one finds himself seized by unavoidable danger and perform something imprudent, as on one side the English had deployed army on the banks of *Karamnassa* and on the other side, Mir Qasim had entered Benares with an army of 15,000 strength.

Turning against any power meant direct confrontation and he would be the first to suffer. The English knew that since Raja Balwant Singh's relation was overt hostile with the Nawab so any agreement with him would be a proper measure for the defence of the Bengal Province.

In pursuing their policy to protect and maintain the independence of Raja Balwant Singh, the English and Nawab of Bengal entered into a treaty with him on March 18, 1764, according to which the territory which he held under Shuja-ud-dowla would be granted to him. By then on March 26, 1764, the joint army of *Vizier*, Emperor and Mir Qasim also reached Benares. It was a time when Raja Balwant Singh was highly impelled by the circumstances. Though he entered into an agreement with the English, but the joint army on the bank of *Ganges* and the Nawab's call impelled him to appear. Even the Emperor had divulged to the English that he was not in favour of Mir Qasim, but unable to evade it. It can be envisaged that how difficult it was for the Raja to save himself from being sandwiched between two opposing powers on both sides of his territory along with the armed forces when the Emperor himself was impelled to march. Though Raja Balwant Singh joined the Nawab's side along with the army, but remained inactive throughout the Buxar battle on October 23, 1764.

There has always been an allegation that the Raja has cheated on both the sides, but the Raja's aim was to maintain his authority and to save the people of Benares from further being plundered and the ensuing events apparently proves his sagacity. If he had joined the English army openly, then before the battle of Buxar, the *Vizier*'s army would have completely ruined the Dynasty and plundered the city, the immense riches of which have always been an enticement for the sepoys. On the other hand, if he had joined the Nawab's army actively and entered into no agreement with the English, then after the battle the English army would have ruined the city and the Hindu Dynasty would have come to an end and so the aspirations of the people of Benares. It was his prudence and successful walking on the tightrope that he saved the Hindu Dynasty and Benares from being ruined by both the Muslim and the Christian power.

The role of Raja Balwant Singh during and after the battle of Buxar has always been belittled. Though he remained inactive, but his role cannot be denied as Benares strategic position between both the powers had automatically placed him in a position where he could break the supply line and communication of both the parties. Had the *Vizier* maintained affable relation with the Raja and had he not created trepidation among the people, and its Raja, Benares would have stood out to be a strong barrier for the defense of Oudh. When the English came out to be victorious, Raja Balwant Singh demanded to hold all his possession on same on the payment of Rs. 24 lakhs as revenue. The Fort William authorities had strictly instructed Major Munro, Commander of the English army, to have no confidence on the Raja for the double part he had played and to deprive him of his possessions, still he acquiesced in to grant *sunnud* to the Raja.

The moot question is what prompted Major Munro to be so impetuous to accept the demands of the Raja against the instructions of the upper echelon. He himself had accepted that there was no viable alternative to Raja Balwant Singh and giving command to any other person would mean deploying army in Benares for an indefinite period at heavy expense and that, too, very much to the annoyance and dissatisfaction of the people of Benares. It was highly imprudent leaving a disgruntled Raja with 15000–20,000 army in a place between English territory and English army in Allahabad. Raja Balwant Singh gave assistance to the English army in taking the possession of Allahabad and Chunar fort, but the English, too, could not escape from the clutches of the immense riches of Benares. Before entering Benares Major Munro had taken Rs. 4 lakh from the merchants on the condition that they would not plunder the city, but still there was plundering in the city that Clive candidly admitted in a letter to Court of Directors. Indubitably, all the powers whether it was *Vizier* or the English had covetous eyes on the alluring riches of the city and looted it either directly or indirectly through ransom and prodigious presents from the Raja.

The English Company could effortlessly get the possession

of the Benares as Emperor had given Benares to the Company in December 1764 as compensation for the battle, but it was restored to the Nawab pursuant to the Treaty of Allahabad in 1765. The assigned reason for repudiation by the Court of Directors was not to follow any expansion policy, but their ulterior motive was to create a buffer state between the English and the Nawab and use the overt hostile relation of Raja Benares to their own advantage. The guarantee of security, which the English gave to the Raja in 1765 Treaty, was used as a ground on which the English interfered in all matters of the Nawab regarding Benares. In 1770, Raja Chait Singh was placed in the *gaddi* through the English interference much against the will of the Nawab. The English staunch support to Raja Chait Singh was not in continuance of their promise to Raja Balwant Singh of security, but to show to other powers of *Hindustan* their influence in the region and their friendship with the *Vizier*, who would not take any measure against their will.

How important it was for the English to place an affable Raja on Benares can only be comprehended when we profoundly study the intricate politics of the time. It was at the same time when the Marathas had immensely increased their influence over Delhi and the English received an intelligence that the Emperor had entered into an alliance with the Marathas and now intended to move to the capital to join the Marathas. They also received information about surreptitious negotiations between the Nawab and the Marathas where former accepted to pay Rs. 80 lakh on the condition that he would get the possession of the country of Rohillas and Kora and Allahabad. Still the Nawab accepted Chait Singh as the Raja with same authority and forces as enjoyed by his father because he did not want any hostility with the English, as Marathas were a grave peril for him unless his negotiations were not productive and if there be any attack English were the lone power from where he could expect military succour according to the terms of 1765 and 1768 treaty. Fundamentally, their policy was guided by the Maratha factor and this Delhi politics had for-reacting impact on the Benares and its Raja.

In 1771, the Court of Directors directed the Bengal Council

to procure Benares from Oudh Nawab in return for Kora and Allahabad. They divulged the motive behind the decision "Our frontiers would be more easily defended, a greater influence would be preserved by us over the neighbouring powers and we might possibly be retrieved from the necessity of keeping up so large and expensive a military establishment as we have at present in Bengal." The question that arises here is what was the reason behind this perceptible change in the policy of the Court of Directors, which had earlier repudiated to follow the policy of extension in 1765. It was a time when Britain was hard pressed by insurmountable problems. Britain had just come out of the seven year War in Europe and Carnatic War in India in 1763. Within a short space of time after the Buxar battle the Company had to confront another battle in Mysore in 1767-1769. The Bengal famine in 1770 had exacerbated the difficulties and Company was in a dire need of finance, but could not expect any aid from Home Government, as Britain was facing boycott of import in the American colonies due to the heavy import duties. Impelled by the boycott of British goods in America, Britain removed the Townsmen duties on all the commodities except tea. These political developments were highly detrimental to the Company's commercial interest. They could realize the tremors in their rule over the American colonies that had started raising the slogan "No taxation without representation." To maintain the rising sun and glory of the Empire, they finally decided to extend their sway in India. Though Hastings failed to cajole the Nawab for the proposal in the Benares Conference of 1773, but he convinced the Nawab to confer on Raja Chait Singh a *Kowlnama* that was extended to posterity. Thus he made it difficult for the Nawab to depose the Raja in future.

In 1775, with the demise of Shuja-ud-daula, the English forced the new Nawab Asaf-ud-daula to enter into a new treaty with them or they would withdraw English troops from Oudh. The Nawab, left with no viable option, entered into a fresh treaty on May 21, 1775, by which Benares was transferred to the East India Company. Thus it was under these circumstances that Benares was transferred from Nawab to the Company and became a gateway through which the English stepped into northern India and moved further to establish a new Empire.

Though the Council resolved that the Raja should exercise free and independent authority in his dominion subject only to the payment of his tribute, yet the Company never abide by those terms in the ensuing years and there were uncountable numbers of encroachments in the just rights of the Raja. In December 1776, the office of Benares Resident was established. How detrimental the office of Resident could be for the Raja was accepted by none other than Hastings himself in 1775, "...it would frustrate the intention of rendering the Rajah Independent if a Resident was appointed to receive the money as it became due at Benares such a Resident would unavoidably acquire an Influence over the Rajah and over his Country which would in effect render him the master of both. This consequence might not perhaps be brought completely to pass without a struggle and many appeals to the Council, which in a government constituted like this, cannot fail to terminate against the Rajah; and by the Construction to which his opposition to the agent would be liable might eventually draw on him severe Restrictions and end in reducing him to the mean and deprived state of a mere Zemindar".

To comprehend the relations of the Raja with the English and the real picture behind all the events, it is obligatory to study the relations which the Councillors were sharing with each other. It was a time when the Council was bifurcated into two groups-first was led by Hastings and Barewell and the second was led by Clavering and his adherents Francis and Monson. With the demise of Monson in September 1776, Hastings came to majority by his (chairman's) casting vote. In 1777, Macleane, Hastings agent at London, informed the Court of Directors about Hastings desire to resign. On receiving the news of resignation, Clavering being the senior most Councillor, assumed the office of Governor-General. Hastings instantly raised the matter in the Court, which on 20th June declared that Macleane's letter was not Governor-General's resignation, but desire of Governor General to resign. The Directors made it clear that the Court resolved to accept the resignation "if it should be made in future." This was highly misinterpreted by the Council, which declared the seat vacant. On the other hand when it became clear that there was no resignation, Hastings, with concurrence of Barewell, declared the seat of senior Councillor and Governor General-in-Council vacant, but without admitting that he had succeeded to the office of Governor General and Barewell was promoted to senior Councillor. The Councillors relations became so intricate and hostile that the matter could be settled only after the interference of the Court, which ordered that each member should be placed in position that they held previously.

Raja Chait Singh on the information that Clavering became the Governor-General sent a Deputation to congratulate him, but with the changing affairs deputation was called back from Murshidabad. It was nothing erroneous on Raja's side to send a deputation to felicitate a newly appointed Governor General, but Hastings was highly nettled by Raja's taking side of his opposing group. It was after this incident that Hastings bent upon to avenge the Raja and he never gave his consideration to any of the appeal or representations of the Raja after this and supported all the enemies of the Raja. The first and foremost was Ausan Singh, who was encouraged by the Governor-General to return to Benares and humiliated the Raja by not only impelling him to give *pargana* of Saidpur yielding a revenue of Rs. 65,000 to Ausan Singh but also to execute a deed of reconciliation with Ausan Singh.

In April 1779, when Sir Eyre Coote joined as new Councillor in place of Clavering, Hastings knew that his (Coote's) support was indispensable for him (Hastings) so he gave him the charge of the military department and many other concessions. Graham had sent many reports expressing his qualms on Raja's probity and expressed that he would be the first to join the enemy He also reported about the fortification of the strategic point and increasing army strength. These were the inviolable rights of the Raja according to the agreement of 1775 and cannot be regarded as infidelity to the government. These reports were used to portray the Raja as a great menace in the eyes of Sir Coote. The adversities of the Raja commenced with the outbreak of the Anglo-French war in 1778, where the Raja was asked to pay Rs. 5 lakhs as his burden of the war for three consecutive years. The point which is to be observed here is, though the Raja paid such a substantial amount within a space of three months still the Council went to an extremity to order march of troops against him and in 1780 it also coerced him to pay a fine of Rs. 1 lakh for delay in payment of the amount demanded. These demands were made in the name of the Anglo-French war, but Francis and Wheeler alluded that the money was being appropriated in general estimate of revenue. The amount was being appropriated even for the Maratha war. On October the Governor General received an information that the Raja had about two crores in his forts. Though Hastings was impelled by the Court orders to appoint Fowke as the Resident of Benares, but in January 1781, he appointed Markham as the Resident with plausible reason that he could not repose confidence in Fowke as he was not his agent and he stands as screen between the Raja and the government, instead of an instrument of control. Since Fowke new appointment was to take effect after three months, he was permitted to draw his salary for the time as the Resident of Benares. Here the significant point to be taken into account is that, at a time when the Company was going through pecuniary stringency, it had taken the burden of the salary of two persons on the same post for three months.

After joining, Resident demanded 1,000 cavalry from the Raja, to which the Raja replied that he could provide 500 horses and 500 *barqandazes*. The annual cost 1,000 horses was more than Rs. five lakhs. After paying Rs. five lakh in October 1780 and a monthly *kist* of tribute, another demand of such a whooping amount within three months was a heavy burden on the Raja. Hastings adroitly evaded giving any response to Raja's reply and planned to move to Lucknow via Benares. He explicitly stated that his ruling motive was to meet the Nawab and Dewagur Pandit, *dewan* of Raja Berar, but his ulterior motive was to take some stringent measures against the Raja. This can be substantiated by his letter to Scott in April 1781, "Something too, will be required at Benares and something more than I shall dare to attempt, for if it were left to my option, I would restore that zamindarry to the Nawab of Oude. Either that ought to be done, or the Raja reduced to the condition of a zemindar." Hastings with astuteness on July 3, 1781, passed a resolution, which invested him with full powers and authority to form an "arrangement" with the Raja. By this resolution now any action or engagement made by the Governor General would be effective as had been passed and sanctioned by the Governor General-in-Council assembled. Hastings had adroitly and with great sagacity choosen this time to pass the resolution, as Wheeler was the lone Councillor. Even if he had objected then also Hastings would have effortlessly passed the resolution using his casting vote. Thus, now there was no impediment in the way to avenge and punish the Raja, on the other hand, the Raja was a novice of 21, encircled by his enemies and frequently hampered by the Resident with no support of the royal family members.

Before departure Hastings made up his mind to impose a heavy fine of Rs. 50 lakhs, but this was nowhere mentioned in the minute. He divulged to Wheeler on the day of departure that the Raja could pay the amount under duress and if he does not comply with the requirement then either he would disinherit or would take the possession of his forts to obtain the treasure deposited. The fact that Hastings was accompanied by Durgbijay Singh, father of Mahip Narain Singh, from Danapur to Benares also raise suspicion. On 15th August, Hastings despatched a letter to Raja Chait Singh charging him for infidility to the government. Hastings charged him for the distress and desertions of Colonel Carnac's army, set to march to Malwa, due to delay in remittance of amount demanded in 1780. He claimed that Raja was very reluctant to meet the demands of 1,000 horsemen and through his agents endeavoured to excite disorders in the Government. He was also charged for maladministration leading to increasing number of robbery and murder cases.

Raja Chait Singh denied all these charges on the same day. He explained that he paid first installment of Rs. 1, 70,000 and requested time for further payment, but after the rejection he made the full payment immediately. Further, remitting of this sum to the army was the onus of the Resident and does not depend on him. Regarding second charge the Raja mentioned that he had 500 horses and 500 *burkandazzes* ready for the service, but he received no response from the Government. For the third charge he stated that except Abdullah Beg and his attendants none of his men had been to Calcutta and his enemies had made false representations to him. Regarding robberies he stated that he had given injunctions and taken penalty bond from the *Ameens*.

In spite of the fact that the answers to all these charges were true, Hastings judged it "unsatisfactory in substance" and "offensive in style". In true sense, these explainations can never be satisfactory for the Governor General, for he had already made up his mind as articulated in his narrative, "I will suppose for a moment that I have erred, that I have acted with an unwarranted and rigorous demand towards Chait Singh, and even with injustice. Let my motive be consulted: I left Calcutta impressed with the belief that extraordinary means were necessary, and those exerted with a strong hand to preserve the Company's interests from sinking under accumulated which oppressed them; I saw political necessity for curbing the overgrown power of a great member of their dominion and for making it contribute to the relief of their pressing exigencies." Next day on 16th August, Hastings took a highly imprudent step to order the arrest of Raja in Shivala fort. The Raja quietly submitted to the arrest and was even ready to give the possession of his forts and treasures. During arrest the Raja sent two *arzees* to the Governor General in a most submissive language. At this time, there were two grenadier companies under the command of Lieutenant Scott, Stalker and Symes and all the servants of the Raja were disarmed. By the time the news of the arrest spread everywhere like a wild fire and multitude of armed men proceeded to the fort to rescue the Raja. This crowd lost its control when Chait Ram, *Chobdar* of Markham, came to deliver a message of Governor General and talked to the Raja in a highly insolent manner.

The question is, if, Hastings' motive was only to extort money from Raja's coffers then why did he kept the Raja under arrest when the Raja was ready to submit all his treasures. There was no reason to arrest the Raja while he was totally submissive to the Governor General during his short meet on 14th August. If Hastings desire was only want of money then he should have captured all the treasures, which, too, was illegal, and release the Raja. Basically, he wanted to disinherit the Raja, but this could be done only under two conditions: either the Raja fail to pay his revenue regularly or he revolts against the Government, on which he was dependent. Hastings knew very well that the first condition would never occur. So by putting the Raja under arrest and making him to go under great humiliation and insolence, he tried to instigate him to stand against the Company. To his surprise, even after that when the Raja submitted to the arrest, Hastings sent Chait Ram, a *Chobdar* of Markham, to deliver his message to the Raja. Chait Ram was specially choosen for this work because he was earlier dismissed by the Raja. Definitely Chait Ram had the support of the English otherwise a mere *Chobdar* would never dare to be so impudent with the Raja in the presence of English officers. Moreover, when Hastings received the intelligence that the crowd assembled in Shivala was armed and the English army was without ammunition. He should have never sent a *Chobdar* unless there be a reinforcement by an army with ammunition.

The incident of Chait Ram excited the people. By the time reinforcement party arrives there was firing, after which Raja's men attacked and every man of the English army was hacked to pieces. In the midst of this confusion Raja fled through a window. Hastings claims that Raja's men first fired, but if they had to rescue the Raja through violence they would have done this when the English army was not in a position to offer resolute resistance and not waited for the arrival of armed reinforcement making situation difficult for them. Hastings instigated the Raja to revolt against the Company by creating such situation and his plans show that it was all premediated but he never thought that so much armed crowd will assemble in such a short space of time in support of the Raja and the situation would become uncontrollable. It was due to this reason that the two companies which were earlier sent to Shivala fort were almost without ammunition except officers and few men. Another fact of great consideration is when the army was sent to Shivala palace for the arrest of the Raja why was it without ammunition and reinforcement with ammunition was ordered only after the requisition from the officers present in the Shivala.

The mind of Hastings before giving the order of the arrest can be clearly read in his letter to Wheeler, "To have left him in full exercise of power which he had notoriously abused and which it was to be apprehended he would employ to the most dangerous purposes was totally inconsistent with the maxims of justice and prudence. To divest him entirely of the zemindary though justifiable on grounds stated above would be attended with an appearance of severity and might have furnished ground for constructions unfavourable to the credit of our government and to my own reputation." This statement makes evident that Hastings created situation to instigate the Raja to stand against the Government in search of that strong reason on the basis of which he could prove himself judicious. He was actuated by his personal resentment against the Raja.

The rising brought the life of Governor General in danger for four days during his stay in Madhodas garden in the Benares city with effete security. Had the Raja been so daring to issue the orders to assassinate the Governor General instantly after the rising in Shivala the history of India and British Empire would have been completely different. The situation was uncontrollable for the English army and Raja's forces were deployed on both banks of the *Ganges* making it hard to receive even a snippet of information. The Raja with his family and effects left to Lateefpur and then to Bijeygurh. Hastings fled to Chunar in night of 21st August and appointed Ausan Singh as *Naib*. He started getting military assistance from different quarters and captured the important forts of Benares, but it took more than a month to restore peace and establish the authority of the government. These forts were impregnable, surrounded by dense forests with single avenue provided for each of them, and were located on exceedingly steep hill rock.

The English army was able to capture the forts of Pateeta, Lateefpur and Bidjeygurh only because they were ushered by some local mens who revealed the secrets of the forts. The people who supported the English against the Raja were mainly *zamindars*, who were ousted from their zamindary during the time of Raja Balwant Singh, and Hastings later restored them to their *zamindary* as a prize for their support to the English. Raja Chait Singh went under the aegis of the Marathas. Mahadaji Sindhia even had plans to attack English from three sides with one army in support of Raja Chait Singh, but with the change of political even and establishment of peace between the Marathas and the English it never happened. Raja was conferred a jageer of Rs. 10 lakhs and died in Gwalior in 1811.

Maheep Narain was made the Raja of Benares and was granted *sunnud* on September 14, 1781 on the condition of payment of Rs. 40 lakhs as annual revenue. Since the Raja was a novice in the field of administration, his father Durgbijay Singh was appointed as *Naib*. In August 1887, Jonathan Duncan was appointed as the Resident of Benares with instructions to form a new settlement for the improvement of administration, with the concurrence of the Raja. The Raja's concurrence was only in name and all the decision were taken by the Resident as he deems conducive, in spite of Raja's objection. On October 27, 1794, an agreement was signed between Raja Benares and the Resident, on behalf of the Company, which introduced Permanent Settlement in Benares, except the Family Domains of the Raja. Thus the Raja's administration was limited to his Family Domains i.e. Gangapur, Bhadohi and Kara Mungroor. By this treaty he was allowed to retain only Rs. 1 lakh out of the annual surplus after paying the revenue. The balance amount was to be used by the Government for defraying the expenses of the administration and other public uses. Thus, the English not only entered into the administration of Benares but also limited the surplus amount, which was the inviolable rights of the Raja, but the Raja was thenceforth so effete as to firmly object to any encroachment of his rights.

In 1826 due to complains made by the inhabitants of Bhadohi against the Raja, Bird was appointed as Special Commissioner to enquire into the matter and suggest measures. Bird submitted the report on May 25, 1826, that the Raja was surrounded by notoriously corrupt and unprincipled agents and recommended that some other intermediate authority may be employed, who would be less exposed to the intrigues of the Raja and more accessible to tenants. Basically, this report was used as a weapon to curb the power of the Raja and a British attempt to enter into the Family Domains of the Raja. Even the Raja complained that the grievances are merely effect of the conspiracy among certain interested and disappointed individuals aided by the authorities of the Mirzapur for the purposes of undermining his rights and interests. Despite Raja's assurances to revise the settlement, Bird recommended that the Raja "being himself indolent, careless and unable to exercise such personal control as necessary to carry his good intentions into effect, those assurances will, I am fully consermative be over linked or disregarded, unless the affairs of the Pergunnah are placed under the sort of Superintendence."

Eventually, Regulation VII of 1828 was declared, by which the English now legally entered the administration of Family Domains, too, by the establishment of superintendent of Family Domains. This hampered the rights and privileges of the Raja whose decisions and actions were then onwards subject to Superintendent's approbation. In this regard, the Raja had raised objections several times, but to no vain. The administration continued in the same manner till 1911, when an Instrument of Transfer was passed, by which Bhadhoi, Kara Mangroor and Fort of Ramnagar was constituted a State of Benares and the Maharaja became the Ruling Chief of the State. It is quiet ironical that when Raja Balwant Singh was having the possession of 96 *pargana* he was regarded only something more than a *zamindar* and now Maharaja Prabhu Narain Singh was given the status of Maharaja only for Bhadohi, Kara Mungroor and Ramnagar fort. During the World Wars the Maharaja supported the Government of India with full military and financial resources. After independence, this State was merged into the Dominion of India by the agreement signed on September 5, 1949, which provided many privileges to the Raja and his family.

APPENDICES

APPENDIX I

आसीद् सुरभूषणो गुणगणाश्लाघ्य रसतामग्रणीः।
श्री मद्वोगतम् वंशजो द्विजवरः श्रीकष्णमिश्रसुधीः।।
ख्याता धर्मधुरीणता कपिलता सांख्ये फणाधीशता।
योगे गोतमता हि तर्क विषये यस्यात्मजिन्मुख्यता ।।1।।

तदन्वये करिधितुल्यताड़गते शौर्य्यादिशाली मनरज्जनोऽजनि।
सर्व्वात्म सम्पादित चारू दर्शनः क्षीरोदधेः पूर्ण हिमांशुमानिव।।2।।

तस्यात्मजः श्री मनसारामोऽभूत् काशिभूपतिः।।
प्रचण्डभुजदण्डाभ्यान्दण्डिताऽरातिमण्डलः।।3।।

तत्सूनुः बरिबण्ड सिंह नष्पतिद्धीरस्सुवीरो महा–
नूर्ज्जत्पक्ष विपक्षकक्षहुत भुग्गाम्भीर्य पाथोनिधिः।
दष्ट्वाकर्मसुदुष्करं सुमनसो लोकोत्तरं तार्किका–
स्वच्छाभन्जमदग्निसुनुमवरं रामं हि यं मेनिरे।।4।।

तदात्मजासूनुरभूत् क्षितीश्वरो महीपनारायणसिंह सत्तमः।
यत्कीर्ति चन्द्रेण विकांशितज्जगदष्ट्वावुधावैध विद्युम्भुधावदन्।।5

श्रीमद्भूपरिशिरोमर्णिगुणिगणाअ्लंकार चूड़ामणि–
र्विद्वतकंजदिवामणिर्विभुयशा उद्योत नारायणः।।
सूनुस्तस्यबभूव यस्य विदितैश्वयर्ये सुराधीशता।
गाम्भीर्य्ये सुपयोधिता मदनता रूपेऽर्थि कल्पद्रुता।।6।।

भ्राता तदीयस्तु बभूवमध्यमः श्री दीपनरायण सिंह सत्तमः।
टौदार्य्यशाली गुणिनाम्महोत्तमः सौन्दर्य गाम्भीर्य गुणैर्महोपमः।।7।।

सहोदरस्तस्य विशुद्धकर्म्मा कनिष्ट आपोष्ट सुसिद्ध धर्म्मा।
विराजते विस्तष्त कीर्तिवर्म्मा प्रसिद्ध नारायण सिंह शर्म्मा।।8।।

विभाति कीर्त्या भुवि शुद्धवेषः स्वतेजसा चारूकृतारिपेषः।
नयेन संलब्ध यशोविशेषः प्रसिद्धनारायण सिंह एषः।।9।।

पितान्वयत्तस्य सुशौर्यशालिनः सुदिप्त तेजोविजितांशु मालिनः।
नीत्याप्रजारक्षण साधुकारिणाः शीलेन लोकस्य मनोपहरिणाः।।10।।

यो विश्रुतो विस्तष्त कीर्तिरीश्वरीप्रसादनारायण सिंह भूपतिः।
भक्त्या समाराधित पार्वतीपतिस्वच्छाभकीर्त्याजितशर्वरीपति।।11।।

गाम्भीर्यादिगुणोदधिः सितिभुजाम्मान्योवदान्यः कर्ष्ती।
प्रोद्यद्वादि करीन्द्रवष्न्द दलन प्रोदभूत पंचाननः।
श्रीमद्गौरव पाद पंकज कष्पा सम्प्राप्त सद्विद्यकः।।
सर्वाशापरिपूरणो सुरतरूर्वव्वति सर्वोपरि।।12।।

पार्थेन सद्बुद्धिमता युधिष्ठिरो यथा सुमित्रातनयेन राघवः।
नराऽऽदिनारायण सिंह शर्म्मणा तथाऽनुकूलेनकनीयसा युतः।।13।।

तेनात्म विल्लोक हितैषिणा सता प्रसिद्ध नारायण सिंह शर्म्मणः।
विस्तीर्ण सच्चित्र विचित्रनान्तरम्पूर्णं सुमेर्वाख्यमिदं सुमन्दिरम्।।14।।

तड़ागमस्युज्ज्वल वारिसंयुतं विधायधारीमपि चारू सत्फलाम्।
संवष्त्वनि प्रानपि वेदपारगाना चार्य मुख्यान् कुशलान् कियावतः।।15।।

युग्मेदुग्रह तारकेश कलिते (1912) श्री वैक्रमेवत्सरे।
राधीये धवले दले हरितिथौ दैवाकरे वासरे।।
कष्त्वाऽऽराम तड़ाग यज्ञमखिलम् वेदोदितैः कर्म्मभिः।
दुर्गा विष्णुशिवैकदन्तरवयो देवाः प्रतिष्ठापिताः।।16।।

श्रीमत्काशी नरेशस्य मुदेभूयाच्चिरायुषः।
कषतिरेषा सुवष्त्ताढ़या मथुरानाथ शर्म्मणः।।17।।

APPENDIX II

का□ीराज–प्र□ास्ति

लिपिरेषा तु सम्प्राप्ता प्राचीनान्पुस्तकालयात्।
वंशपन्जीपूरणार्थं परतः परिलिख्यिते।।

काशीनरेशाद्गुणमण्डनेश्वरीप्रसादनरायणसिंह भूपतेः।
दिगन्त विभ्रान्तयशः सुधाकरान्मक्ष्माश्रयाद्योगपरान्महात्मनः।।2।।

पुरभष्पुर पालकाऽन्वये मनुजेन्द्रो जनतापमोचनः।
अजनिष्टगुणैकसत्स्वनिः प्रभुनारायणसिंह संज्ञक।।3।।

सः श्रीमान्काशीराजः मुरहरनगरे प्राप्यराज्यं पुरस्तात्।
गत्वा देहस्य शुद्धयै मुरहरनगरे सूर्य्यजातीरभूमौ।
घट्टे चौतान् पादेर्वसु युगनवभ(1948) सम्मितैवैक्रमेब्दे।
चक्रे स्वर्णस्य तौलं स्वतनु परिमितं कार्त्तिकै शुक्लपक्षे।।4।।

तुहिनाऽचलतः कुमारिकामथनीलाचलतः प्रभासकम्।
सच भारततीर्थमादरादगमत्काशि पतिः स्वयंप्रभुः।।5।।

काश्मीर–नेपाल,निवार–मराडलेत्रिचीनपल्लीषु मरूस्थलीषु च।
अवन्ति देशेष्वपि तीर्थ कामुको जगाम सामान्य सुहज्जनः प्रभुः।।6।।

वरिवण्ड कुलैकमराडनः प्रभुनारायणसिंह भूपतिः।
अगमत् पितष्कार्य्य सिद्धये मगधे विष्णुपदेपुनःपुनः।।7।।

लेभे स्वराज्यं निजशौर्य्य सूचितं स सार्वभौमेश्वरतो महोदयात्।
गुणैपदीयैः परितुष्ट आसीद् सम्म्राट्स जार्जः सचिवैहि पन्चमम्।।8।।

स्वाधीन काशीश्वर एषनः प्रभुश्चकार राज्ये विविधास्तुसक्रियाः।
रूजार्दितानामथ रोगशान्तये चक्रे चिकित्साशरणं सभेषजम्।।9।।

प्रजाः प्रजाः स्वाइव यस्य राज्ये शिक्षालयादुर्गत लोकगम्या।
विद्वांस आसन्निह वषत्तिभजः क्रियारताविप्रवराश्च सर्वे ।।10।।

लोक प्रसिद्धोऽस्ति स हिन्दु विश्वविद्यालयो योऽत्र पुरारि पुर्याम्।
तत्स्थानमग्रयं प्रददौ समग्रं द्वाविंशतिग्राम गणैरूपेतम्।।11।।

प्राच्य प्रतीच्योभव रूपविद्यानिकेतनार्थं सहि काशिराट् प्रभुः।
प्रापच्छ दिष्टान् बहुभूमि भागान्परोपकाराय सतांहिं भूतयः।।12।।

तस्मान्नरेशात्खलु लब्धजन्मा राजाधिराजो महनीयकर्म्मा।
आदित्य नारायणसिंहशर्म्मा विभातिशुभ्रोज्जवल कीर्तिवर्म्मा।।13।।

वदस्वष्टग्रहतारका पति(1988) मिते श्रीवैक्रमेवत्सरे।
यः प्राप्तातुलसंपदं प्रथमतो राज्ये समस्ताः प्रजाः

कारून्णयाद करोकरादनषणिनीः शिक्षाम् बिना वेतनैः।
सर्वेषां सुलभात्र्यधादनुदिनं काशीधराधीश्वरः।।14।।

सदा सदाचारपरः सतांप्रियः पितष्प्रदिष्टामवलम्ब्य पद्धतिम्।
सशास्तिकाशी सुगष्हीतनामा राजाधिराजोद्विजराजधामा।।15।।

पित्रोॅऋणमथाकर्तुमस कष्त्काशि भूपतिः।
गयां जगाम विधिवत्तीर्थ यात्रा विधानवित् ।।16।।

निजात्मजेन द्विजराजधाम्ना विभूतिनारायणसिंह नाम्ना।
विभिाति पुत्रैण स काशिभूपतिर्यशा जयन्तेन समं शमीपातः।।17।।

— सम्वत्–1993

This stone inscription on white marble is fixed on the gate of Durga temple, Ramnagar. The first is on the left side of the main door and second appendix is on the right side of the door. The inscription shows all the names of Ruling Chiefs of the Dynasty but lapse the name of Raja Chait Singh.

APPENDIX III

Kashirajvanshanuvarnam is a kavya written by Astrologer Sri Vinayak Krishna alias Jadamati that describes about the history of Benares Rajas and Maharajas from the times of Manoranjan Singh to His Highness Maharaja Prabhu Narain Singh and their religious activities. It includes five *sarga*: first includes 20 *shlokas*, second 13 *shlokas*, third 17, fourth 27 and fifth 24 *shlokas*. Its most important feature is details of planets and *lagna chakra* of the rulers during the time of their birth. The original hand written copy is preserved in National Archives of Nepal. Some selected *shlokas* are mentioned below taken from *Vidyamandir Patrika*, Varanasi, 1983.

काशीराजवंशानुवर्णनं काव्यम्

(सर्ग–प्रथम)

स्वस्ति श्रीमनरञजनस्समभवद् गङगापु(र) स्येष्वरस्तद्ग्रामे
समुपागतो द्विजवरः पुत्रः षिवानं(द) जः।।
षाके विक्रमजेंदुबाणमुनिभू 1751 संख्ये मधौ मासके
षुक्लेनंगतिथौ सुगमने पत्न्या सहाकस्मिकं।।2।।

पञचम्यां मिथुनाङगके समभवद् यो वै मयारामकस्
तदभ्राता खलु नागवाणमुनिभू संख्ये मधौ मासके।।
मीनाङगे षनिसंयुते समभ(व)त् प्लक्ष्णो दृढांगषुचिर्मन्साराम
इति प्रथामधिगतो विख्यातकीर्तिः प्रभुः।।8।।

शश्ठ्यां कर्कटलग्नके मृगभके जातो दषारामकः ।
रेजुस्ते किल दाषरथ्य इवे वै सभ्या स राज्ये भष्षम् ।।
काषीषानुगतामतिं दष्ढतरां योज्यंति कार्यागमे ।
मन्साराम मुखोदितं प्रकुरूत स्वाभीश्टहीनास्तथा ।। 10 ।।

चत्वारस्त्वविहिता नष्पेण प्रादुर्भूतष्विवांषो
नष्पगणमहितस्तत्सुतो भीमकर्मा ।।
पूर्वारंभितदुर्गसौधपरिखा रामादिकं पूर्णतां
कष्त्वा राज्यविवर्द्धने दष्ढमतिः संयोजयद्योधिभिः
वाणे भाष्वोषधीषैः विगतसमगणे विक्रमस्यार्कराज्या–
तीतेकाले धनर्तौ नभसि षिवतिथौ कष्णपक्षे
समाजे (स नागे (?) सभागे) ।। 17 ।।

लग्गे वै भषुभे स्वकीयगष्हगो जीवोंवरे संस्थितः
शश्ठस्थः क्षितिजस्स्वतुंगगषनिष्चन्द्रोपि तद्वान् षिखी
रार्जासहगसमं विगुत्वं हि यत्रांगकं
ये जानन्ति बुधाः कुषाग्रमतिना ते वै सुपूज्या भष्षम् ।। 18 ।।

जातो वै वरिवण्डसिंहनष्पतिर्विख्यातकीर्तिमहान्
यष्चाकारि रघोरिवप्रमथनं वीरैस्समं बाहुभिः ।। 19 ।।

राज्यं संप्रकरोदथो कतिपयैर्वर्शैर्दिवं चागमत्
पुत्रो वै वलिवंण्डसिंहनष्पतीराज्येभिशिक्तो जनैः ।। 20 ।।

(सर्ग–द्वितीय)

तत्पुत्रः किल चेतसिंह नष्पती रूद्रेभपष्थ्वीमिते
वर्शे प्रौश्ठपदे सिते हरितिथौ मीनांगके वाक्यपतौ ।
काव्यो वैरिगतो तथा च रविणा युक्तो व्यये भूमिजो–
र्विद्राहू किल द्यूनगौ तु षषभृल्लाभगृहं चाश्रितः ।। 8 ।।

दैवज्ञं ध्वजगं निधाय बहुषो दुर्गाणि रामादिकान्
जित्वा दुर्गविनिर्मितिं समकरोत् वाराणसी दक्षिणे।
गंगापूर्वतटे तरंगललिते व्यासेष्वरस्यालये
निर्मायाऽ खिल सज्जनानुवसतौ पूस्संस्थितिं चाकरोत्।। 9 ।।

तत्पुत्राः किल चेसिंहसमयेप्यध्यक्षतामाश्रिता
राजायत्र पलायनं समकरोत्तेऽपि स्वगेहे गताः।
षाके सप्तयमधृतीमितषके कन्यार्ककाले विभुस्
स्वर्ग्यराज्यमुपाकरोद्बुद्धजनैं पुत्रेऽभिशेक कष्तः ।। 11 ।।

(सर्ग–त▯तीय)

श्रीरंगनाथांगजवालकष्णो व्यधायि सर्वं महिशीहषदिस्थम्।
श्रीचेतसिंहस्य तथाप्यनुज्ञापत्रं महिश्यै स च दत्तवान्स्वयम् ।। 1 ।।

महीपनारायणसिंहषर्मा पुत्रेभिशिक्तो खिल मंत्रिपूगैः।
पूर्वानु (न ?) मात्यान्सकलान्द्विजादीन्संपालयत्सर्वदेव राजा ।। 2 ।।

फणींदुनागेन्दु (?) मिते षकाब्दे भाद्रे सिते वै गणनाथतिथ्याम्।
षनौ झशांगे किल राहुसंयुते मृत्युस्थितार्की रवि वैरिगेहे ।। 3 ।।

भौमस्तु भाग्ये खलु द्यूनसंस्थौ षषींज षुक्रौ षिखिनायुतौ च।
तथाम्बरे देवपुरोहितष्च जातस् क्षितीष्षुभलक्षणान्वितः ।। 4 ।।

श्रुति तष्तीयचरणे तथांगे कायाऽभिधे वाक्पतिसंयुते च।
धनस्थितौ चन्द्रषनी सुतस्थितौ राहु षनी च भाग्ये ।। 6 ।।

सुखेकराज्ये लाभे षिखी यस्य विराजते दष्धा।
ज्येश्ठोति षूरो भुवि सर्वदोदितर्नारायणस्सिंह इवाबभौ कुले।। 7 ।।

षषिबुधौ सौख्यगतौ कवी रवी द्यूने तमोलाभगतष्षनिष्चरः ।
श्रीदीपनारायणासिंहषर्मा मध्योभवत्कांतवपुर्दर्ष्टाढ़ात्मा (. सुखात्मा) ।। 9 ।।

दिवंगते राजनि वै महीपे ज्येश्ठोभिशिक्तोखिलमंत्रिवर्यैः ।
सो वै तदानीं सुषुभे स्वतेजसा किं वा विडौजावरन्भुवस्तले ।। 17 ।।

(सर्ग–पंचम)

प्रथा तदीया भुवनेऽखिलेष्वरीप्रसादनारायणसिंहभूपतिः ।
महामहोत्साह विभुस्सुबुद्धिमान् सच्छास्त्रषस्त्रादिविधौ महापटुः ।। 1 ।।

नारायणीषस्य सुता सुशाव राज्ञसुभ्रात्रोर्महिशी पतिव्रता ।
द्वीपांकचंद्रैर्गजवत्सरेशु मार्गासिते गौरितिथौ महीजे ।। 7 ।।

विप्राःसमूचुः खयमांकभूमिते षके वसंते किलराधषुक्रे (क्ले) ।
कृकृवाक्पति वासरान्विते सर्पस्य तिथ्यां सुखदं व्रतः हिं ।। 12 ।।

ज्येश्ठा सिते वै भषुपंचमीशु श्रीयौवराज्यं हरिलग्नके षुभम् ।।
श्रुत्वा द्विजोक्तिं बहुहर्शसंयुतस् तद्दर्भकाख्यं प्रथमं विधाय ।। 13 ।।

मौंजीबंधः प्रोक्तकाले व्यधायि पष्चात्पुत्रे यौवराज्यं विदत्तम्
दानैर्विप्रास्तोशिता वन्दिवर्गाः भूशावस्त्रैः कार्यकर्तार लोकान् ।। 14 ।।

ततो लौहचापं निशंगाभियुक्तं भष्षुण्डीष्च कालीदमकूपूर्व ख्याता ।
सुतायाददौ रूढसिंहासनाय ततः संदद्राजचिन्हानि राजा ।। 21 ।।

APPENDIX IV

LIST OF RAJAS AND MAHARAJAS OF THE ROYAL DYNASTY OF BENARES

1.	Mansaram	1738-1740
2.	Raja Balwant Singh	1740- Aug 1770
3.	Raja Chait Singh	1770-1781
4.	Raja Maheep Narain Singh Bahadur	Oct 1781- Sep. 1795
5.	Raja Udit Narain Singh Bahadur	1795- April 1835
6.	His Highness Maharaja Ishwari Prasad Narain Singh Bahadur, GCSI	1835-1889
7.	His Highness Maharaja Sir Prabhu Narain Singh Bahadur, G.C.S.I., G.C.I.E, LL.D.	Dec 1889-1931
8.	Capt. His Highness Maharaja Sir Aditya Narain Singh Bahadur, D.Lit, K.C.S.I.	1931- April 1939
9.	His Highness Maharaja Dr. Vibhuti Narain Singh Bahadur	1939 till merger

APPENDIX V

PEDIGREE OF MODERN RAJA OF BENARES

(Source: Benares Duncan Records, Regional Archives, Allahabad)

Roop Sing (Claimant)
↓
Durgbijay Sing (Dead)
↓
Dharmraje Sing——Sernam Sing (Dead) ——Jugerdeo Sing (Dead)

↓ ↓ ↓

Juggut Sing (claimant)—— Sheosant Singà Roop Sing—— Mayaram) (dead)——Shivnarayan Sing (dead)—— Kulender Sing (dead)—— Pratap Sing

↓ ↓ ↓

Luckun Sing (claimant) ← Juggeet Sing (dead) ← Duparam (dead) (dead)—— Munranjan (dead)——Dayaram (dead)——Meherban Sing (dead)——Muniyar Sing—Nunco Sing

↓ ↓ ↓ ↓

Hingun Sing Zalan Sing Mansaram (dead) Shiv Amber Sing (dead) Nygel Sing (dead) ——Ausan Sing

↓

Raja Balwant Sing (dead)

↓

Puddum Thoor (daughter) ← Chet Singh → Sujan Singh(dead)

↓

Maheep Narain Sing (present Raja)

APPENDIX VI

INSTRUMENT OF TRANSFER 1911 COURTESY REGIONAL ARCHIVES, VARANASI

Instrument of Transfer

Whereas it is desirable to remove the [illegible] in the position of His Highness Maharaja Sir Prabhu Narain Singh, G.C.I.E., of which His Highness and his predecessors have consistently complained: And whereas the Governor General of India in Council with the approval of His Majesty's Secretary of State for India has decided that, with this object, Parganas Bhadohi and Kera Mangraur of the Family Domains of the Rajas of Benares at present administered by the British Government, as well as the tract (comprising Fort of Ramnagar and its appurtenances) defined in the Schedule to this Instrument, should be constituted a State under the suzerainty of His Majesty and granted in that condition to the said Rajas of Benares under such restrictions and conditions as may be necessary for safeguarding to the residents of these territories the rights and privileges they have enjoyed under the British administration.

2 - And whereas it is expedient to establish the said Maharaja as a Ruling Chief with full powers in the said territories subject to the suzerainty of His Majesty and the conditions hereinafter set forth: —

It is hereby declared as follows: —

(1) His Highness Maharaja Sir Prabhu Narain [illegible]

Singh, G.C.I.E, shall be as Ruling Chief of Benares from the 1st day of April 1911 entrusted with the administration of the said Parganas of Bhadohi and Kera Mangraur and of the tract (comprising the Fort of Ramnagar and its appurtenances), defined in the Schedule to this Instrument, which Parganas and tract will hereinafter be termed the State of Benares.

(2) His Highness Maharaja Sir Prabhu Narayan Singh G.C.I.E, shall enjoy the same salute and honours as heretofore, and will continue to receive annually a payment of one lakh of rupees from the Lieutenant-Governor of the United Provinces of Agra and Oudh.

(3) The said Maharaja and his successors shall be entitled to administer the State of Benares so long as he and they fulfil the conditions hereinafter prescribed.

(4) The succession to the chiefship of the State of Benares shall devolve on the lineal descendants of the said Maharaja, whether by blood or adoption according to the rules and usages of his family, except in case of disqualification through manifest unfitness to rule.

Provided that no succession shall be valid until it has been recognised by the Governor-General of India in Council.

(5) The said Maharaja and his successors (hereinafter called the Ruling Chief of Benares) shall at all times remain faithful in allegiance and subordination to His Majesty, King of the United Kingdom of Great Britain and Ireland, and of the British Dominions beyond the Seas, Defender of the Faith, Emperor of India, and

and His Heirs and Successors, and perform all duties which, in virtue of such allegiance and subordination, may be demanded of Them.

(6) A sum of Rs. 1,90,000 shall be payable annually by the Ruling Chief of Benares as tribute due from his State to the British Government.

(7) The Ruling Chief of Benares shall not, without the previous sanction of the Lieutenant-Governor of the United Provinces of Agra and Oudh, build any new fortresses or strongholds, or repair the defences of any existing fortresses or strongholds in the State of Benares.

(8) The Ruling Chief of Benares shall not, without the permission of the Lieutenant Governor of the United Provinces of Agra and Oudh, import or permit to be imported into the State of Benares arms, ammunition, or military stores or allow their manufacture.

(9) The military force employed in the State of Benares, for the maintenance of internal order, and the Ruling Chiefs' personal dignity, shall not exceed the strength which the Lieutenant Governor of the United Provinces of Agra and Oudh, under instructions from the Governor General of India in Council, may from time to time fix.

(10) The Ruling Chief of Benares shall abstain from interference in the affairs of any other State or Power and shall have no communication or correspondence with any other State or Power or the Agents or Officers of any other State or Power, except with the previous

previous sanction and through the medium of the Lieutenant-Governor of the United Provinces of Agra and Oudh.

(11) The Ruling Chief of Benares shall not employ in his service any person not a native of India without the previous sanction of the Lieutenant-Governor of the United Provinces of Agra and Oudh, and shall, on being required by the said Lieutenant-Governor, dismiss from his service any person so employed.

(12) The coins of the Government of India shall be the legal tender in the State of Benares, as heretofore, and no separate coinage shall be permitted.

(13) The Ruling Chief of Benares shall grant all land, that may be required by the Lieutenant-Governor of United Provinces of Agra and Oudh for lines of telegraph ~~and~~ or railways or for any other public purposes, and shall receive in respect of such grants such compensation, if any, as may seem to the said Lieutenant-Governor to be proper. Compensation due to under-proprietors and tenants for such appropriations will be paid by the Lieutenant-Governor under the same rules as in British territory

(14) The Postal and Telegraph systems within the State of Benares shall continue under the Government of India, and shall be managed as if the said State had continued to be British territory.

(15) The ~~Ruling~~ Chief of Benares shall cause or permit to be executed in the State of Benares all warrants, summonses, decrees or other processes, civil, criminal or revenue issued by competent authority in British territory as if the said State had continued to be British territ

(16) The Ruling Chief of Benares shall cause to be arrested and surrendered to the proper officers of the British Government any person or persons within the State of Benares accused of having committed an offence in British India for whose arrest and surrender a demand may be made by the Political Agent for the State; and he shall afford every assistance for the trial of such persons by causing the attendance of the witnesses required, and by such other means as may be necessary.

(17) Plenary criminal jurisdiction in the State of Benares over servants of the British Government and over European British subjects shall continue to be vested in the Lieutenant-Governor of the United Provinces of Agra and Oudh and his officers.

(18) The Ruling Chief of Benares shall comply with the wishes of the Lieutenant-Governor of the United Provinces of Agra and Oudh in all questions relating to excise, Opium, intoxicating drugs, salt, and the cultivation of poppy.

(19) The administration of the State of Benares shall, save as otherwise provided by this Instrument, be regulated by the principles and spirit of the laws for the time being in force in the province of Agra, and except with the previous sanction of the Lieutenant-Governor of the United Provinces of Agra and Oudh the Ruling Chief of Benares shall not pass any laws inconsistent therewith.

(20) No material change in the system of administration as established when His Highness Maharaja Sir Prabhu Narain Singh, G.C.I.E. is placed in possession of the State of Benares shall be made without the consent of the Lieutenant-Governor of the United Provinces Agra and Oudh.

(21) All rights acquired under the laws now in force shall be maintained and all settlements of land revenue now current in the State of Benares shall continue until the period for which they have been made has expired and until fresh settlements have been made

(22) Any person who, immediately before the date of this Instrument, being a British subject, was the proprietor of any land or had any kind of right in land or was the owner of, or had any kind of right in, houses or other immoveable property situate in the State of Benares may, within one year from such date but not thereafter, call upon the Ruling Chief of Benares to acquire such land, houses or immoveable property, or such rights therein.

The Ruling Chief of Benares shall thereupon acquire such land, houses or immoveable property or such rights therein, and shall, with all due despatch, pay therefor such compensation as the Lieutenant-Governor of the United Provinces of Agra and Oudh may approve. In determining the amount of compensation to be paid for such land, houses or immoveable property or such rights therein the said Lieutenant-Governor shall, as far as may be, have regard to the corresponding law relating to compensation for the compulsory acquisition of land for the time being in force in British India

(23) The Ruling Chief of Benares shall at all times conform to such advice as the Lieutenant-Governor [illegible] United Provinces of Agra and Oudh, subject [illegible] trol of the Governor-General of India in

in Council, may offer him with a view to the management of his finances, to the settlement and collection of his revenues, the imposition of taxes, the administration of justice, the appointment or dismissal of his principal officers, executive or judicial, and the relations between him and his subjects.

(24). The Commissioner of Benares shall be Political Agent to the Lieutenant-Governor for the State of Benares.

(25) Sentences of death shall be immediately reported to the Political Agent, and shall be subject to confirmation by the Lieutenant-Governor of the United Provinces of Agra and Oudh. The Political Agent shall also exercise general revisionary power in all criminal cases.

(26) The right to repeal or amend in any way and at any time Bengal Regulation VII of 1828 or any other regulation or law in virtue of which the Raja of Benares enjoys any special privileges within the pargana Kaswar Raja which heretofore was included in the Family Domains, but is excluded from the State of Benares constituted by this Instrument, is hereby expressly reserved to the Lieutenant-Governor of the United Provinces of Agra and Oudh.

Within the other estates now in possession of His Highness Sir Prabhu Narayan Singh, G.C.I.E. which are outside the State of Benares, he shall continue to have the status and responsibilities of a landholder under the ordinary law and within the pargana of Kaswar Raja he shall assume that status and those responsibilities,

(27) In the event of the breach or non-observance by the Ruling Chief of Benares of any of the foregoing conditions, the Lieutenant-Governor of the United Provinces of Agra and Oudh, under the instructions of the Governor General of India in Council, may resume possession of the State of Benares and assume the direct administration thereof, or make such other arrangements as may be thought necessary to provide adequately for the good Government of the people concerned, or for the security of British rights and interests.

(28) Should any question arise as to whether any of the above conditions have been faithfully performed, or as to whether any person is entitled to succeed or is fit to succeed, to the administration of the State of Benares, the decision thereon by the Governor General of India in Council shall be final.

Fort William
The 1st April 1911.

Hardinge of Penshurst.
Viceroy and Governor-General of India.

Schedule.

1 (a) Bhadohi Pargana :- area 391.6 square miles
(b) Kera Mangraur Pargana :- area 473.9 square miles.
(c) Ramnagar Fort and its appurtenances as specified in the two specifications, following :- area 23.3 acres.

I- The specification of Fort Ramnagar and its immediate appurtenances as shown on the map No. I attached.

The boundary begins on the north west corner, where the moat or ditch surrounding a good deal of the fort joins the River Ganges. It goes along in an almost easterly direction following the outward boundary of the ditch, skirting the huts called Gualbahia Tola + beyond that Ram nafas khana. The line makes a turn much more to the south just in front of the big tamarind tree and passes in front of the Bhunja's shop following the watercourse into the front of the north-eastern bastion of the fort, where it takes an almost southerly course just in front of the lane going northward to Tamoli Tola. After going almost southward up to the front of the temple it takes a sharp turn towards east, skirting pucca shops and passing beyond Diwan's quarters up to a point just opposite the north-eastern corner of the saluting enclosure and on the western extremity of another lane going to Tehana. Here it crosses the main metalled road and passes due eastward touching the eastern masonry boundary of the saluting ~~enclosure of the~~ enclosure. It turns again on the south eastern corner of the enclosure following its southern boundary due west and deflects due north from the southwest corner of the enclosure up the southern end of the western gate of the enclosure, where it goes straight westward touching the southernmost wall of the Tahsil building, crossing the workshop (Karkhana) in a straight westerly direction ~~eastern~~ behind the lines, till it emerges into the ditch near a nim tree just in the front of the eastern bastion of the fort. From here it turns southwards, following the course of the ditch, skirting the waste called the Nowcanti up to the south eastern bastion, where it takes a westerly direction till the ditch joins the riverbed. Here the line takes a south westerly direction to include a temple and the priest's house and deflects again westward till it joins the river. The len boundary line passes six feet in front of the shops. The ~~rivers~~ river boundary shown in the map is from the low watermarks.

The area of this fort and appurtenances is 20.7 acres.

II — Specification of the further appurtenance as shown in the map No. II attached.

The boundary line of the additional appurtenance of the Fort of Ramnagar (Benares). begins just at the foot of a banyan tree (practically opposite the big well with the Hanuman got temple) at a point where a Kachcha road branches off due west from the pucca public road, from Ramnagar town towards the Dufferin Bridge at Benares, skirting the garden belonging to the Ausanganj estate. The boundary leaves this Kachcha road on its left hand passing by its northern extremity skirting the huts of the Ahirs belonging to His Highness's cow stall.. After going in a straight westerly direction up to the point where there is a plum-tree it takes an almost southern turn following the bend of the Kachcha road enclosing the Maharaja's elephant stables and almost parallel to the enclosure of the Ausangunj garden to a point where there is a pucca well. From this point it turns straight westward leaving a narrow Kachcha road on its south to a point where there is a nim tree & cross road. From here the line takes a due northerly direction following the course of the public Kachcha road to Kathesar village leaving the road on its western side flanking the garden and some fields till a point where there is junction of three roads from here it takes due easterly direction following another Kachcha road leading to the public main road (pucca) from Ramnagar town to the Dufferin Bridge. After cutting this public road it goes straight to the enclosure wall of the Kumar's s[illegible] -house often named the guest-house and [illegible] belonging to it. After touching the enclosure ~~northwards~~ of.

of this house the line follows almost touching
the enclosure the northwards behind the district
board avenues of trees, leaving the latter on its
western side till a point where there is a small
bridge and where the enclosure ends in its
northernmost extremity. From this point the
boundary line runs straight eastwards enclosing
a private road flanking some fields and enclosing
the parade ground of the Maharaja's troops and
the mango-groves known as Bharat Bag up to
the north eastern extremity of the latter named garden
to a point where a channel for the discharge of the
surplus water of the tank is met. From here the
boundary line takes an almost south easterly
direction following the bend of the Kachcha
private road and enclosing it till it
meets the pucca private road encircling the
big pucca tank opposite the north-western
minaret adorning the tank. From this point the
line takes a due easterly direction enclosing the
pucca private road and touching the fencing
of a field and parallel to the northern side of the big
tank till it reaches the wall of a garden named
Durga Bag containing a masonry well and a
reservoir for a fountain almost opposite the
north eastern minaret adorning the temple. ~~following~~
Following the southern wall of this garden and
running parallel to the channel for the inflow
of the water to the big tank the line takes a due
eastern direction to a point where there is a mango
tree off 50 feet north - from here it turns due
south enclosing the temple garden and ~~the~~ temple
of the family gods of His Highness parallel

to the western side of a garden named Khalwa-
Ka-baré to a point 69 feet from the south-
eastern corner of the pucca Temple enclosure. From
here the line turns due west parallel to the walls
of the Temple till it joins the pacca private
road encircling the tank and then turns south-
ward parallel to the road enclosing it till a
point opposite to a mound of earth belonging
to the Kachcha tank of Ausanganj estate, 24 feet
west of a mango tree. From here the line turns
straight west parallel to the walls of the garden
named Ram Bag, the Maharaja's summer residence
and leaving the Kachcha tank on the suthern
side till it reaches another mound of earth of
the same tank and passing it touches the masonry
enclosure wall of another garden called Gulab Bag,
leaving the basti Kutloopur on the south side.
From here it takes a due southern course touching
the masonry walls of this garden and leaving the
village on its eastern side and then turning to west
at a point where the eastern garden wall ends. From
here it goes straight westwards touching the boundary
of this garden till it touches the enclosure of another
mango garden called Gorja Bag. From here it turns
southward again till it joins a private Kachcha
road leading from the public pucca road and
then turns due west taking in the private Kachha
road touching some orchards and parallel to the
Kachcha enclosure of Gorja Bag till it again
touches the main pucca public road from
Ramnagar to Benares and then cutting it
joins the eastern walls of the Maharaja's cow
stables and then almost touching it turns south-
ward till it touches the banyan tree again
app[illegible] [illegible]re it began. The area of this additional
[illegible] is 212.3 acres.

TRUE COPY
[signature]
Superintendent,
Benares Agency Office.

Whereas the State of Benares was constituted by the Instrument of Transfer dated the 1st April 1911;

And whereas it has been brought to the notice of Government that paragraph 2(2) of the said Instrument may be interpreted as meaning that the annual payment by the British Government of a lakh of rupees to the Benares State is personal to His Highness Maharaja Sir Prabhu Narain Singh Bahadur, G.C.I.E.;

And whereas the said Instrument of Transfer is silent regarding the undermentioned annual payments made to the Maharaja:—

(a) Rs 14,856 (Rupees fourteen thousand eight hundred and fifty six), for the Mulki treasuries.

(b) Rs 4,562/8/- (Rupees four thousand five hundred and sixty two and annas eight) compensation for the abolition of the Kamachha abkari; and

(c) Rs 1,000 (rupees one thousand) for surrendering to Government his right as hereditary revenue collector of Karanadandi.

It is, with the approval of Government of India, hereby declared as follows:—

(1) That the various payments described above will be continued to His Highness Maharaja Sir Prabhu Narayan Singh Bahadur G.C.I.E. of Benares, and his successors in perpetuity.

(2) That it was not the intention of the Instrument of Transfer dated the 1st April 1911 to limit the payment of one lakh of rupees to the life-time of the present Maharaja.

(3)— That the omission to mention the other payments was not intentional and does not affect them.

Dated, Nainital
9th July 1913.

Sd. J. S. Meston
Lieutenant Governor of the
United Provinces of Agra
and Oudh.

TRUE COPY
Superintendent,
Benares Agency Office.

APPENDIX VII

Agreement of Merger of Benares State dated Sep 5, 1949
Courtesy UP State

No. 7-172-P/49

GOVERNMENT OF INDIA

MINISTRY OF STATES

From:
THE DEPUTY SECRETARY TO GOVT. OF INDIA.

To:
THE CHIEF SECRETARY TO GOVT. OF UNITED PROVINCES, LUCKNOW.

New Delhi, the 7th September 1949.

Dear Sir,

Subject: Merger of Banaras State.

I am directed to enclose copies of the marginally cited correspondence regarding

1. Agreement dated 5.9.1949 signed by His Highness the Maharaja of Banaras.
2. Collateral Letter issued to His Highness the Maharaja of Banaras dated 5.9.1949.
3. List of private properties of His Highness the Maharaja of Banaras.

the merger of Banaras State and to state that it has been decided that Banaras should be taken over on 15th October 1949, and to request that the Government of United Provinces may now proceed with preliminary action in the matter. An advance copy of the notification which will be published on the 15th October 1949 is also enclosed for your information.

Yours faithfully,

(S. Narayanaswamy)
DEPUTY SECRETARY.

Enclo:

AGREEMENT MADE THIS 5th day of September 1949 between the Governor General of India and His Highness the Maharaja of Benares.

WHEREAS in the immediate interests of the State and its people, His Highness the Maharaja of Benares is desirous that the administration of the State should be integrated as early as possible with that of the United Provinces in such manner as the Government of the Dominion of India may think fit;

It is hereby agreed as follows :-

ARTICLE I

The Maharaja of Benares hereby cedes to the Dominion Government full and exclusive authority jurisdiction and powers for and in relation to the governance of the State and agrees to transfer the administration of the State to the Dominion Government on the 15th day of October 1949, (hereinafter referred to as " the said day ").

As from the said day, the Dominion Government will be competent to exercise the said powers, authority and jurisdiction in such manner and through such agency as it may think fit.

ARTICLE 2

The Maharaja, his heirs and successors, shall with effect from the said day be entitled to receive from the revenues of the State annually for his privy purse the sum of Rupees 2,80,000/- free of taxes. This amount is intended to cover all the expenses of

+ 2 +

the Ruler and his family, including expenses on account of his personal staff, maintenance of his residences, marriages and other ceremonies, etc. and will neither be increased nor reduced for any reason whatsoever.

The said sum may be drawn by the Maharaja in four equal instalments in advance at the beginning of each quarter by presenting bills at the State Treasury or at such other Treasury as may be specified by the Dominion Government.

ARTICLE 3.

The Maharaja shall be entitled to the full ownership, use and enjoyment of all private properties (as distinct from State properties) belonging to him on the date of this agreement.

The Maharaja will furnish to the Dominion Government before the 5th September, 1949, an inventory of all the immovable property, securities and cash balance held by him as such private property.

If any dispute arises as to whether any item of property is the private property of the Maharaja or State property, it shall be referred to such officer with judicial experience as the Dominion Government may nominate and the decision of that officer shall be final and binding on both parties.

ARTICLE 4.

The Maharaja and his family shall be entitled to all personal privileges enjoyed by them whether within or outside the territories of the State, immediately before the 15th day of August, 1947.

+ 3 +

ARTICLE 5.

The Dominion Government guarantees the succession, according to law and customs, to the gaddi of the State and to the Maharaja's personal rights, privileges, dignities and titles.

ARTICLE 6.

No enquiry shall be made by or under the authority of the Government of India and no proceedings shall lie in any court against the Maharaja whether in a personal capacity or otherwise in respect of anything done or omitted to be done by him or under authority during the period of his administration of that State.

ARTICLE 7

(1) The Government of India hereby guarantees either the continuance in service of the permanent members of the public services of Benares on conditions which will be not less advantageous than those on which they were serving on the first day of August 1949 or the payment of reasonable compensation.

(2) The Government of India further guarantees the continuance of pensions and leave salaries sanctioned by the Maharaja to members of the public services of the State and of the Benares State Forces who have retired or proceeded on leave preparatory to retirement and also guarantees grant of pensions, gratuities and leave earned by and due to the members of the aforesaid public services of the State and of the Benares State Forces.

+ 4 +

ARTICLE 8

Except with the previous sanction of the Government of India no proceedings, civil or criminal, shall be instituted against any person in respect of any act done or purporting to be done in the execution of his duties as a servant of the State before the said day.

In confirmation whereof Mr. Vapal Pangunni Menon, Adviser to the Government of India in the Ministry of States, has appended his signature on behalf and with the authority of the Governor-General of India and His Highness Maharaja Vibhuti Narain Singh, Maharaja of Benares has appended his signature on behalf of himself, his heirs and successors.

Sd/- VIBHUTI NARAIN SINGH
MAHARAJA OF BENARES

Sd/- V.P. MENON

ADVISER TO THE GOVERNMENT OF INDIA, MINISTRY OF STATES.

Dear Maharaja Saheb,

Arising out of the Agreement entered into between His Excellency the Governor General of India and Your Highness whereby Your Highness ceded to the Dominion Government the full and exclusive authority and jurisdiction and powers for the governance of the Banaras State, I convey the following assurances in this Collateral letter on behalf of the Government of India :-

(1) If and when Banaras is renamed Kashi, Your Highness' title will be changed from "Maharaja of Banaras" to "Maharaja of Kashi".

(2) Your Highness will be accorded the same precedence in and outside the State as you are enjoying at present as the Maharaja of Banaras. There is no question of the Commissioner, Banaras Division or any other officer of the District taking precedence over Your Highness in Banaras District at official functions.

(3) The Gaddi of the Maharaja shall continue at Fort Ramnagar and the Fort and its appurtenances and Your Highness' private palace known as Nandesur Palace in Banaras shall not be liable to attachment or sale and shall descend to the successors of Your Highness. This will continue as hitherto to be exempt from all property or other municipal taxation.

(4) Adequate police arrangements will be made during Your Highness' visit to Banaras for Darshan and in connection with the Ramlila held at Ramnagar. The United Provinces Government will issue instructions to the Commissioner, Banaras Division to maintain Your Highness' dignities on these occasions.

(5) Your Highness has expressed your desire to set apart a sum of Rs.5.00.000/- from the balances of the State for

+ 2 +

creating a Trust (known as All India Kashi Rajya Trust) for the promotion of Hindu culture and Sanskrit learning. Your Highness' idea of the objects and the composition of Trust are contained in Appendix A to this letter. While the details of this Trust will have to be worked out by Your Highness, Government of India agree to the creation of the Trust for the purposes mentioned in Appendix A, and assure Your Highness of their support to make the Trust a useful institution for the good of the people. Government of India further hope that the Provincial Government particularly the Government of United Provinces will give such aid and encouragement as they might deem essential and proper.

(6) The United Provinces Government have a proposal to start a Sanskrit University at Banaras. If and when the proposal matures, it is the intention of the United Provinces Government to associate Your Highness with the University in a manner befitting Your Highness' position and dignity.

(7) Your Highness will have the privilege of entertaining Government guests visiting Banaras and we hope that Your Highness will extend the same hospitality to important persons visiting Banaras as heretofore. Instructions will in future be issued by the Government of India to Your Highness direct whenever important persons visit India so that Your Highness may have sufficient notice to make adequate arrangements.

(8) The existing position regarding prohibition of shooting and fishing in the river Ganges in front of the Ramnagar Fort will be maintained and Your Highness' exclusive shooting rights in the forest blocks in the attached list are recognised.

(9) The United Provinces Government have every intention of maintaining the municipal arrangements and supply of electric energy for Ramnagar.

+ 3 +

(10) The United Provinces Government will as far as possible consult Your Highness regarding all appointments of officers to be posted to Ramnagar, and will instruct their officers to maintain fully the dignity and prestige of Your Highness.

(11) Your Highness desired that you would like the water works situated in the Fort to be removed in about a year's time to some other place. The Premier of United Provinces has assured us that after obtaining technical advice every effort will be made to meet Your Highness' wishes in this matter.

(12) It is the intention of the United Provinces Government to utilise the balances and the investments of the State as far as possible for completion of the schemes of development undertaken by Your Highness.

(13) The Government will pay annually to Your Highness a lakh of rupees for expenditure in connection with the Ramlila, the management of the temples within the State and other charitable institutions hitherto maintained by the State.

(14) The allowances sanctioned to relations and Sardars by Your Highness as in the list enclosed to this letter will be continued for their lifetime.

(15) Pensions and other charitable payments hitherto met from Your Highness' Civil List will be continued for the lifetime of the recipients. A list of such payments and the names of the beneficiaries is attached to this letter.

(16) The annual payment of Rs.1,00,000/- which is made to Your Highness under the Agreement of 1794 on account of the surplus revenue of the 4 Sircars taken over by Government shall be paid to Your Highness and your successors in perpetuity in addition to the privy purse amount fixed under the Agreement.

+ 4 +

(17) No land or building being Your Highness' private property shall be requisitioned or acquired without Your Highness' consent and without payment of full compensation.

(18) The facilities at present enjoyed by Your Highness in respect of attachment of your saloon to trains will be continued.

(19) In regard to the State buildings which have been handed over by Your Highness to Government, Your Highness will have the right of first refusal in case any of these buildings are not required by Government.

(20) Your Highness has expressed a desire to be associated with organisations set up by the Government of United Provinces in Banaras to look after the welfare of pilgrims and general public. Government of India will issue suitable instructions to the Provincial Government to meet Your Highness' wishes in this respect whenever a suitable opportunity arises in the futume.

2. The Ministry of States will shortly be issuing a Memorandum on Privileges and Dignities which has been finalised in consultation with the Rajpramukhs of Unions and Rulers of other States. Your Highness will find that the Memorandum adequately deals with the various suggestions made by Rulers from time to time.

This Collateral Letter shall be read and construed as forming part of the Agreement signed by Your Highness.

Yours sincerely,

(V.P.Menon)
Adviser

His Highness Maharaja Vibhuti Narain Singh,
Maharaja of Banaras,
BANARAS STATE (U.P.

APPENDIX A.

A trust may be created by the Government of India with His Highness of Benares and his successors as Chairman, with members nominated by His Highness, the Government of India and the United Provinces Government. The members who are appointed Trustees should be men well-versed in ancient learning and culture.

(1) A sum of Rs.5000,000/- may be set apart from the State Funds as the corpus for the Trust.

(2) The United Provinces Government should make a grant of Rs.200,000/- per year to this Trust.

(3) The Central Government should give a substantial grant for furthering the educational activities of the Trust.

(4) Trust Properties: Temples, Dharamshalas and other institutions now conducted by His Highness should be transferred to the Trust.

(5) Objets: Objects inter alia would be:

(a) promotion of Sanskrit learning and Indian culture generally,

(b) the maintenance of temples,

(c) holding of annual All-India conference of scholars connected with Sanskrit learning,

(d) management of other charitable institutions that may be taken over by the Trust,

(e) translation and publication of literature of ancient Indian culture into other languages and books of culture of other languages in Indian languages,

(f) repairs of ghats and other properties in Khasi, and

(g) to arrange for and look after the pilgrims and visitors to Khasi.

List of forest blocks in which His Highness would have exlusive shooting rights.

Shikarganj. .... 1. Bairanth.

2. Bhaurha.

3. Kothilwa.

4. Nadahwa.

Musakhand. 1. Keora Khand.

2. Jiria No. 1.

3. Jiria No. 2.

4. Saiya Garah.

5. Mowarakhpur.

6. Modhwa.

7. Kharbhar.

8. Majhwa.

9. Ghaghrà.

10. Kawchiya No. 1.

11. Kawachya No. 2.

12. Aundhwa.

Baraul. ....l........ 1. Jamsoti.

2. Matihani.

3. Bhalui.

4. Deo.

5. Danava.

6. Buran.

7. Jaimohni.

8. Gahla.

Naugarh. .... 1. Ghari Muhan.

2. Baira.

3. Jangal on the southern side of Kothi Naugarh.

4. Ghorha Bir.

5. Khaiwa Khonch.

LIST OF PRIVATE PROPERTIES OF HIS HIGHNESS THE MAHARAJA OF BENARES AS ACCEPTED BY THE GOVERNMENT OF INDIA.

......

DISTRICT RAMNAGAR

1. Fort at Ramnagar including its appurtenances, fittings etc. (plan attached).
2. Four Pakkies with rooms rented to shopkeepers including houses occupied by Maharaja's librarian H.Jafar Ali.
3. Parsidhodyan.
4. Gulab Bagh garden.
5. Rambagh garden.
6. Ratan Bagh with tank.
7. Bhauji Sahiba's garden.
8. Ambarkhana.
9. Ayurvedic Bhawan.
10. House occupied by Accountant General.
11. Scattered small houses in possession of His Highness' servant.
12. House of Maharaja's ancestor near Janakpur together with compound including Club and Chief Guest rooms etc. located within the buildings.
13. Peely Kothi.
14. Three bungalows attached to Parade grounds. (His Highness has agreed that if these buildings are required by the United Provinces Government, His Highness should hand them over to that Government.)
15. Old Hospital Building. (His Highness has agreed that if these buildings are required by the United Provinces Government, His Highness should hand them over to that Government.)
16. Bodyguard barracks.
17. Motor Garage.
18. Chankla.
19. Cook's family quarter and Farrash Khana.
20. Stables, Feelkhana, Garikhana.
21. The parade ground on both sides of road and the grass farm at Ramnagar.
22. State Press at Ramnagar.
23. State Brick Kiln.
24. Permanent lease regarding ferry service between Ramnagar Ghats and Benares held in the name of His Highness the Maharaja subject to the terms of the lease.

DISTRICT CHAKIA

1. Dilkhusha Bagh with building.
2. Khurshed Bagh with buildings.
3. Farrash Khana.
4. Shikarganj Kothi – two.
5. Mushakhand Kothi.
6. Naugarh Kothi.
7. Bhaisaura.
8. Latif Shah Building.
9. 1000 bighas waste land and jungle land in Shikarganj (Chakia) subject to assessment.

DISTRICT BHADOHI

Khurshed Manzil with garden compound and three small buildings.

LANDS

1. The Sir lands recorded in the name of His Highness.

Location	Area Bighas	Bis.	Dhurs.
Bhadohi	2148	- 13	- 5
Chakia	219	- 19	- 6
Ramnagar	316	- 6	- 17
	2684	-19	- 8

CASH AND INVESTMENTS

Serial No.	Particulars	Investment amount	Remarks
1.	Shares of Vibhuti Glass Works Ltd.	Rs. 11,500/-	
2.	3% U.P. Loan 1952.	Rs. 1,00,170/-	
3.	3% loan 1951-54.	Rs. 2,00,000/-	
4.	3% Govt. of India Defence Loan 1953-55.	Rs. 7,00,000/-	
5.	3% Victory Loan 1957.	Rs. 3,00,000/-	
6.	3% Victory Loan 1959-61	Rs. 1,00,000/-	
7.	2½ Loan 1961	Rs. 1,59,700/-	
8.	3% 1st. Development Loan 1970-75.	Rs. 2,11,212/8/-	
9.	12 years National Savings Certificates.	Rs. 2,00,000/-	
10.	Shares of the Benares State Bank Ltd.	Rs. 1,00,000/-	
11.	Fixed Deposit.	Rs. 62,524/7/1	
12.	Pionner Ltd. Lucknow.	Rs. 5,000/-	
13.	India Cold storage & Ice Co. Ltd. Lucknow.	Rs. 10,000/-	
14.	Federal Standard Ltd. Bombay	Rs. 10,000/-	

ZAMINDARI

All properties outside the State standing in the name of His Highness the Maharaja of Benares in his capacity as zamindar will continue to be His Highness' private property.

....

MOTOR CARS.

Model.	Number.
Buick.	One.
Olds Mobile.	Two.
Studebaker.	One.
Kaisar.	One.
Hindustan 10.	One.
Jeep Car.	One.
Transport Lorries.	Two.
Trucks.	Two.
Cadillac.	One (Old car about 35 years).

LIVESTOCK.

Elephants.	Seven.

MINISTRY OF STATES.

New Delhi,
the ~~7th September~~ [illegible] 1949.

Notification.

WHEREAS the Central Government has full exclusive extra-provincial jurisdiction for, and in relation to, the governance of the State of Banaras;

Now, therefore, in exercise of the powers conferred by sub-section (2) of section 3 of the Extra-Provincial Jurisdiction Act, 1947, (XLVII of 1947), and of all other powers enabling it in this behalf, the Central Government is pleased to delegate to the Provincial Government of the United Provinces, the extra-provincial jurisdiction aforesaid, including the power conferred by section 4 of the said Act to make orders for the exercise of that jurisdiction:

Provided that: -

(i) the exercise of the jurisdiction here delegated shall be subject to the control of the Central Government; and

(ii) the delegation shall not preclude the Central Government from exercising the jurisdiction hereby delegated.

(A. B. CHATTERJI)
JT. SECRETARY TO THE GOVERNMENT OF INDIA.

APPENDIX VIII

PRIVILEGES GIVEN TO MERGED STATES RULERS COURTESY UPSALUCKNOW

MEMORANDUM

Article 4 of the Agreement signed by the Rulers of Orissa and Chhattisgarh States provided that the Rulers as also the members of his family would be entitled to all personal privileges which they enjoyed immediately before the 15th day of August 1947. During the discussion prior to the signing of the Agreement the Rulers sought clarification of the privileges which would be guaranteed. Many of the Rulers have also since submitted long lists of privileges enjoyed by them.

The privileges, dignities, etc., enjoyed by the Rulers are a matter of practice and are nowhere detailed or defined. The Rulers have accordingly been advised that it would neither be possible nor desirable to draw up a complete list of privileges. At the same time it is considered desirable that the Provincial Governments should be made aware of the more important of these privileges and the Government of India's views on them.

This memorandum is an attempt in this direction. Part A of the memorandum sets out the personal privileges claimed by the Rulers: Part B certain privileges affecting the States.

The memorandum will apply *mutatis mutandis* to all other Rulers whose States have merged into Provinces, or formed Unions.

PART A

1. *The Civil List Reserve Fund should be made private property of the Rulers.*—The Government of India agree that the amount standing at the credit of the Civil List Reserve Fund should be held by the Rulers as a sort of trust for meeting all obligations for which it was created, but no addition made to the Fund during December 1947 will ordinarily be taken into consideration.

2. *The residences of the Rulers both inside and outside the State should be treated as the private property of the Rulers.*—The Government of India consider that a reasonable number should be treated as private property. The rest should be available to the State either for its own use or as a regular source of income on rent or hire. No personal residence should be saleable or available for being hired out to others.

3. *The vehicles, livestock, jewellery and other Rajki - Saman and paraphernalia to be treated as the private property of the Ruler.*—The vehicles, livestock, jewellery and other articles required for State functions, etc., should be considered as State property, but in the custody and management of the Ruler who would be accountable for them subject to periodic inspection by the Ministry. The maintenance cost of the property referred to is to be met by the Ruler.

4. *No changes should be made in the Civil List Budget for 1947-48.*—The Government of India see no objection to the Civil List budgeted for 1947-48 being allowed to stand and the new arrangements regarding privy purse coming into force from 1st April 1948 subject to the condition that the allotment for Civil List in the budget does not exceed that fixed by the Political Department.

2

5. *Free medical attendance and supply of medicines to the Rulers and their staff and members of the Ruling family and also cost of expert medical advice etc.*—The Ruler and his family should be entitled to free medical attendance and to such treatment as may be available in the Government hospitals. Personal staff of the Ruler will not be entitled to this privilege.

6. *Prerogative of mercy and grant of titles.*—The Rulers have surrendered all jurisdiction and powers. In the circumstances it is considered that it would not be appropriate for them to exercise the prerogative of mercy or to grant titles to any person inside the State.

7. *Palace Guards.*—The Rulers have claimed that palace guards should be maintained for them at Government expense. The Government of India consider that reasonable guards should be provided at the expense of Government at the official residence of the Ruler. The adequacy, etc., of the guards will be a matter for the Provincial or Union Government to decide in the circumstances of each case but the scale to be fixed should be liberal because this would be the symbol of authority which the Rulers would enjoy.

8. *Escort for the Ruler and his family when travelling abroad.*—It is not possible to provide for guards for the Rulers when they travel outside the State.

9. *That the Civil List Reserve Fund should be continued and that Government should make annual contributions as hitherto.*—The Government of India have already decided that the Civil List Reserve Fund should be treated as the private property of the Ruler. There is therefore no question of either continuing the Fund or making any annual contribution to it.

10. *The right of the Rulers to fly their own flags and declare a holiday on their birthday.*—There is no objection to the Ruler flying his flag on his residence but not on public places, where only the flag of the Indian Dominion will be flown. It is not possible to declare a holiday on the birthday of the Ruler since this would not be possible where the States have been formed into districts or have been tagged on to existing districts. The request of the Rulers is therefore not practical.

11. *Exemption from Arms Act.*—Existing exemptions from the Indian Arms Act, 1878, and the Rules thereunder in favour of the Rulers will be continued.

12. *Exemption from the operation of the Indian Income-Tax Act and the Rules made thereunder.*—A general exemption from the operation of the Indian Income-Tax Act and the rules made thereunder is not practicable. The Rulers are doubtless aware that their privy purse would be completely exempt from both income-tax and super-tax and would also be excluded from the computation of total income and world income. Any other exemption admissible under the Income Tax Act to "Ruling Chiefs and Princes in India" will continue to be admissible to the Rulers of the States who are parties to the merger Agreement.

13. *Exemption from Motor Vehicles Act, etc.*—The Government of India agree that the Rulers may be permitted to have their cars registered and to take out driving licenses without any payment. But in all other respects they should conform to ordinary rules and regulations under the Act.

14. *Exemption from local taxation.*—This is primarily the concern of the Provincial Governments and the Government of India hope that as far as possible practice which prevailed in this respect before 15th August 1947 will be continued.

3

15. *Privy purse should be made impartible and the law of primogeniture should apply to it.*—The Government of India are advised that the privy purse payable to the Rulers under the Agreement is not liable to attachment by any court in a Province of India or by any court set up in the States under the authority of the Central or Provincial Government. Succession to the *gaddi* is regulated by the law of primogeniture in all these States and accordingly the eldest son who succeeds to the *gaddi* will be the only person entitled to the privy purse amount.

16. *Continuance of grants of villages for services rendered and for performing religious ceremonies of Rajbatti.*—This is a matter which is mainly for the Provincial Governments to decide in the light of local circumstances.

17. *Jagir and personal property of the Rulers and members of the family should be free from all taxes and outside the land revenue jurisdiction of Provincial Governments, etc.*—This is also a matter for the Provincial Governments to decide but Government of India feel that ordinary land revenue law should apply.

18. *Existing right of precedence enjoyed by the Rulers in India should be continued.*—This is a part of the personal privileges and dignities of the Rulers and the Government of India are pleased to agree that the existing precedence of the Rulers should be continued.

19. *Use of red number plates by the Rulers of States on their cars.*—Government of India have no objection and the practice may be continued, but in addition the Provincial registration number should also be fixed to the car.

20. *Marriage expenses of the brothers and sisters of the Rulers to be borne by the State.*—Government of India consider that the expenses on this account should be met out of the Civil List Reserve Fund, and where no such fund exists, out of the privy purse of the Ruler.

21. *Right of the Ruler to import free of customs or any other duties goods intended for his personal use or use of the members of his family.*—The privilege of importing articles intended for the personal use of the Ruler or the members of his family free of customs or any other duties has been extended only to Rulers with a permanent salute of nineteen guns and over, and the Rulers neither in the Orissa States nor in the Chhattisgarh have enjoyed that right. It is not proposed to extend the privilege to the Rulers of the States who were not in the enjoyment of this privilege prior to 15th August 1947.

22. *Right of exemption from customs or any other duties on the personal luggage or belonging of the Ruler while returning from any place within India or abroad.*—Government of India cannot extend this privilege which is enjoyed only by the Rulers of salute States of ten guns and over.

23. *Immunity from the process of Courts of Law.*—It would be for the Courts to decide whether a Ruler is immune from Civil and criminal process and if so to what extent and under what circumstances. The Government of India have no doubt that such immunity as the Rulers enjoyed before the 15th of August 1947 in British Indian Courts would be regarded as a personal privilege of the Rulers and in view of the express provision in Article 4 of the Agreement it will continue to be granted to them by all courts in India. The Government of India do not consider that any statutory provision is necessary.

PART B

24. *That the accumulated balances of the States should be spent in the States concerned.*—Government of India agree that these amounts should be

4

utilised, as far as possible, in the respective areas and should not be available for general purposes.

25. *Continuance of the customary religious ceremonies in the traditional manner.*—The Government of India consider that the customary ceremonies should be observed consistently with the dignity of the Rulers. Such ceremonies as are purely personal should be paid for by the Rulers themselves.

26. *No State servant should be punished or harassed for his past views or loyalties.*—The Government of India agree that there should be no victimization and it is hoped the Provincial Governments will give effect to the wishes of the Rulers in this respect.

27. *Continuance of service of the State servants.*—The existing staff of the Eastern States Union should be taken over by the Government. The Government of India have already given an assurance that the staff would be taken over as circumstances may permit on their existing terms and absorbed in the Provincial services as far as possible.

28. *Previous commitments of the Rulers should be honoured.*—While as a general principle there would be no objection to recognition of the previous commitments of the Rulers, it has come to the notice of the Government of India that the Rulers have entered into many transactions which cannot stand scrutiny, especially after the 15th December 1947. The Government of India are therefore of the opinion that the Provincial Governments which are taking over the administration of the States and assuming their liabilities should not be saddled with all these commitments. The Provincial Governments will, therefore, make enquiries and confirm such of them as are reasonable and *bona fide*.

APPENDIX IX

INSTRUMENT OF TRANSFER 1911 COURTESY REGIONAL ARCHIVES, VARANASI

MESSAGE OF THE HON'BLE SARDAR VALLABHBHAI PATEL ON THE OCCASION OF THE MERGER OF THE BANARAS STATE WITH THE U.P. ON 15TH OCTOBER 1949.

The merger of the Banaras State in the United Provinces completes, with one exception, the administrative and territorial integration of SANYUKTA PRANT. I need hardly commend to the people of Banaras State their new Government or the new administrative system in which they are merging. As neighbours they must be familiar with them. I am sure they realise that their future is safe in the hands of both. I pray that, under the new dispensation, the people of Banaras State will take their due share in moulding the destinies of the Province as a whole.

Today may mark the end of a State, but it can never obliterate the existence of an institution, the roots of which go back to the remote past. Kashi Raj is our ancient heritage; the holy city of Kashi receives the homage and devotion of millions throughout the country. The name of Kshi will live as long as humanity takes pride in its heritage, its religion and the very essence of culture and civilisation. I can assure the Ruler and the people of Banaras State that the sanctity and name of Kashi will be preserved by us in the best manner possible.

I know how much affection and devotion His Highness the Maharaja has for his people. Though young, he has striven his utmost to safeguard the interest of his people under the new set-up and I can assure him that both the Government of India and the Government of the United Provinces will give him no cause for regret.

May the people of the State be happy, contented and prosperous as part of the larger entity in which

- 2 -

they are merging today.

(VALLABHBHAI PATEL)

RAJA CHAIT SINGH 1770-1781

RAJA UDIT NARAIN SINGH *BAHADUR* 1795- APRIL 1835

MAHARAJA ISHWARI PRASAD NARAIN SINGH, AUGUST 1835-1889

MAHARAJAS OF BENARES

...ER CLIPPINGS
Port Richmond, NY
NEW YORK, N. Y.

CLIPPING FROM

NAME OF PAPER New York Times
New York City
April 17 1932
ADDRESS
DATE

A NEW INDIAN POTENTATE ON HIS THRONE: THE MAHARAJAH OF BENARES, Photographed in His Coronation Robes After His Investiture at a Durbar in Benares.
(© Alice Benson's Studios.)

MAHARAJA ADITYA NARAIN SINGH *BAHADUR*,
FEBRUARY 1932-APRIL 1939

MAHARAJA VIBHUTI NARAIN SINGH *BAHADUR*,
DECEMBER 1939-1949

MAPS OF BENARES

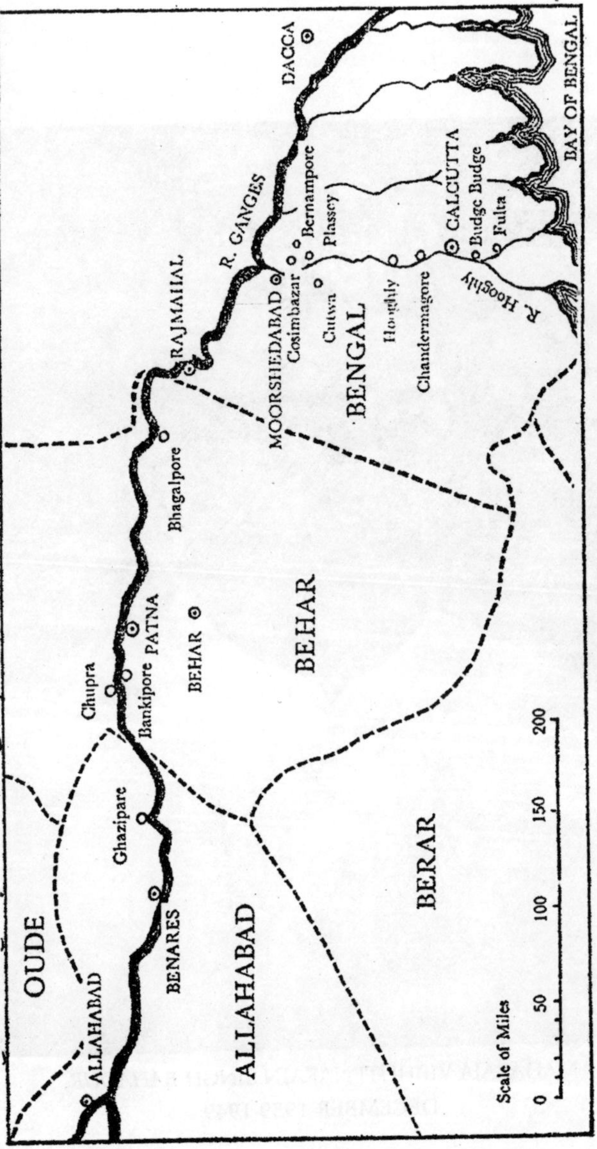

Bengal and Oude

BENGAL AND OUDE (COURTESY E.W. SHEPPARD'S BOOK A *LIFE OF LT. GENERAL SIR EYRE COOTE*), 1956, LONDON

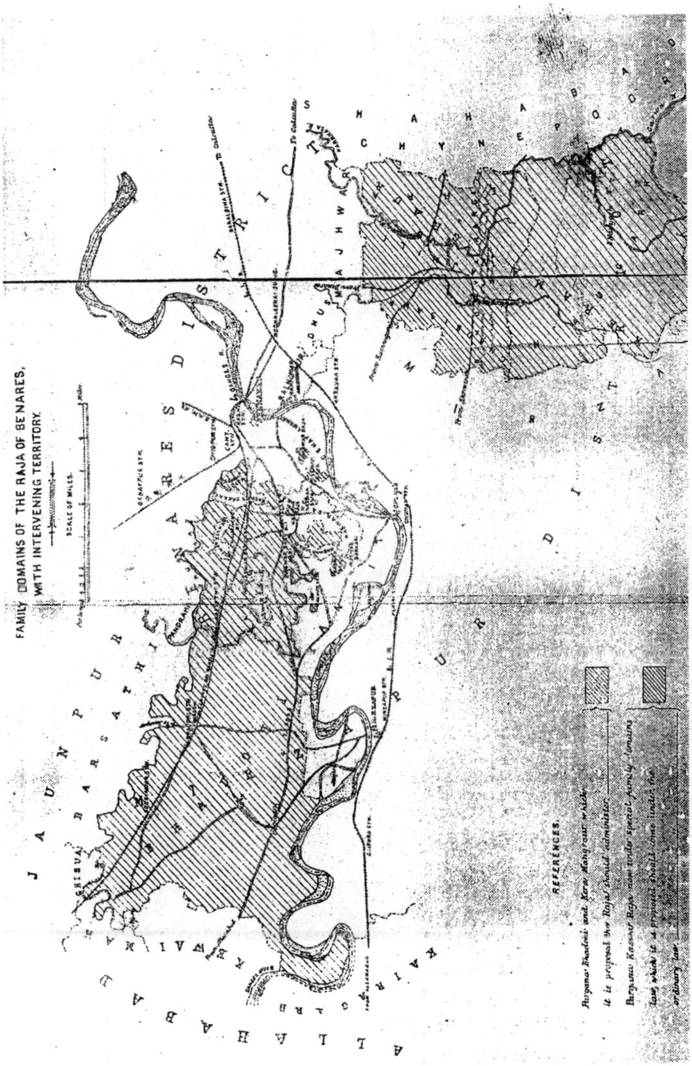

MAP OF FAMILY DOMAINS OF MAHARAJA BENARES COURTESY REGIONAL ARCHIVES, VARANASI

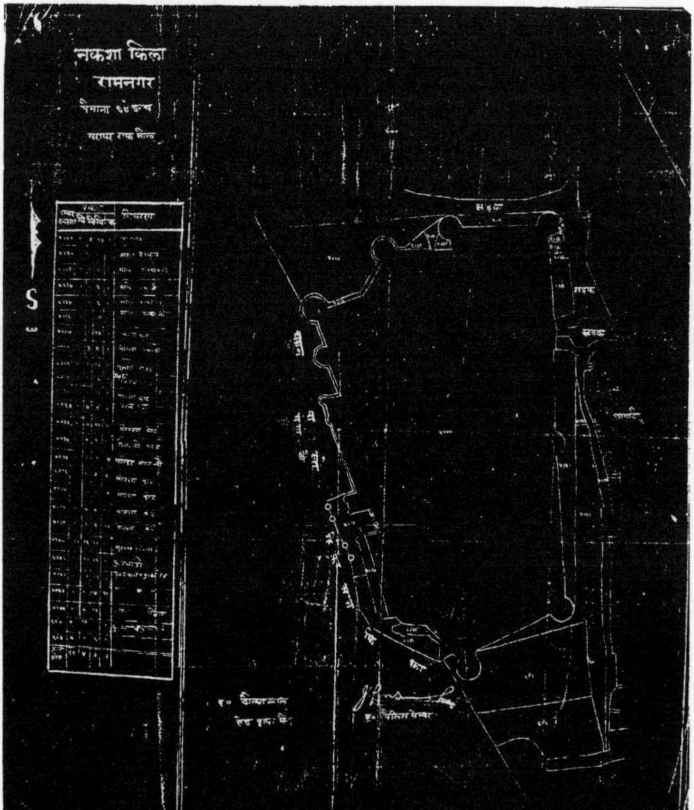

LAYOUT OF RAMNAGAR FORT, VARANASI.
COURTESY U.P. STATE ARCHIVES, LUCKNOW

THE EMBLEM OF THE STATE OF BENARES

RAMNAGAR FORT, VARANASI (BACK VIEW)

DURGA TEMPLE, RAMNAGAR

Bibliography

PRIMARY SOURCES

National Archives of India, New Delhi

Proceedings of Foreign and Political Department

1. Secret Proceedings, January-July, 1764, Vol. 3.
2. Secret Proceedings, 8 December 1763-2 July 1764, Vol. 2.
3. Secret Proceedings, 24 July-December 1764, vol 4.
4. Select Committee, 1756-1759, vol 4.
5. Select Committee, 4 January 1758-19 December 1758, Vol. 8.
6. Select Committee, 15 January 1759- 2 November 1759, Vol. 10.
7. Secret Proceedings, 3 January 1765-29 April 1765, Vol. 6.
8. Secret Proceedings, 17 May 1765-27 December 1765, Vol. 18.
9. Select Committee, 7 May 1765-27 December 1765, Vol. 17.
10. Select Committee, 5 January 1761-28 December 1761, Vol. 14. (This Proceeding is not in a readable condition.)
11. Secret Proceedings, 31 May 1773 -30 December 1773, Vol. 18.
12. Secret Proceedings, 30 May 1776-27 June 1776, Vol. 41.

13. Secret Proceedings, 11 November 1776-30 December 1776, Vol. 45.
14. Secret Proceedings, 3 July 1779-23 December 1779, Vol. 57.
15. Secret Proceedings, 4-19 January 1781, Vol. 62.
16. Secret Proceedings, 11 June 1781-6 August 1781, Vol. 67.
17. Secret Proceedings, 4 September 1781-22 October 1781, Vol. 68.
18. Secret Proceedings, 2 January 1782-18 February 1782, Vol. 70.
19. Secret Proceedings, 29 April 1782-24 June 1782, Vol. 73.
20. Secret Proceedings, 5 August 1782-12 September 1782, Vol. 75.
21. Secret Proceedings, 23 September 1782-24 October 1782, Vol. 76.
22. Secret Proceedings, 11 November 1782-31 December 1782, Vol. 77.
23. Secret Proceedings, 12-30 June 1783, Vol. 83.
24. Secret Proceedings, 16-31 December 1783, Vol. 92.
25. Secret Index, 1780-1782, No. 3
26. Secret Consultations, 1775-1783

Microfilms (From British Museum, London held at Private Paper Section of National Archives of India, New Delhi.)

1. Addl. Mss. No. 29198-29199, Acc.No. 270, Roll. No. Minutes of members of the Council and Governor General on the subject of new defensive treaty with Oudh Nawab, and their policy towards Benares, March 3, 1775.
2. Addl. Mss. No. 29205, Acc-273, Roll No. 273. Details of the military force and forts of Raja Chait Singh, his agreement with EIC relative to duties in 1773
3. Addl. Mss. No. 29212, Acc-276, Roll No. 276. Diary of Transactions and Occurrences in Voyage to Benares, 24 June-4 October 1773, Diary of his visit to Benares and Lucknow, 17 February-19 May 1784.
4. Addl. Mss. No. 29132, Acc-230, Roll No. 231. General Correspondence of Warren Hastings.
5. Addl. Mss. No. 29210, Acc-275, Roll No. 275. Account of several powers bordering British and Vizier's Dominion.

6. Addl. Mss. No. 29200-29202, Acc-271, Roll No. 271. Definition of nature of the office of zamindar used by Mr. Pitt in June 1786.
7. Addl. Mss. No. 29206, Acc-274, Roll No. 274. Matter related to administration of Benares after 1781
8. Addl. Mss. No. 17066-17082, Acc-1046, Roll No. 145. Minutes of portions of proceedings on trial of Hastings between 13 February 1788- 24 May 1793.
9. Addl. Mss. No. 29148-29150, Acc-242, Roll No. 242. General Correspondence of Warren Hastings from Benares and Chunar in April 1781-September 1781.
10. Addl. Mss. No. 39875, Acc-139, Roll No. 337. Warren Hastings Papers, letters from Governor General in Council to Court of Director's, 20 July 1776- 29 December 1781.
11. Addl. Mss. No. 29197, Acc-269, Roll No. 269. Letters from Warren Hastings to his wife, 19 August- 17 December 1780.
12. Addl. Mss. No. 29150-29152, Acc-243, Roll No. 243 General Correspondence of Warren Hastings, September 1781-December 1781.

Regional Archives, Varanasi

1. Varanasi Division Records, Different Departments, 1901-1929.
2. Varanasi Collectorate Records, Miscellaneous Files, 1881-1923
3. Varanasi Collectorate Records, 1880-1923.
4. Varanasi Collectorate Records, 1893-1925
5. Varanasi Collectorate Records, 1909-1925.
6. Varanasi Collectorate Records, 1913-1923
7. Varanasi Collectorate Records, Miscellaneous files, 1913-1928
8. Varanasi Collectorate Records, Benares State, 1945-1950
9. Correspondence of Commissioner Office, Benares Division with Deputy Superintendent Benares, 1875.
10. Correspondence of Commissioner Office, Benares Division

with Deputy Superintendent, Family Domains, 1871 (137).

11. Correspondence of Commissioner Office, Benares Division with Board of Revenue, 1870 (146).
12. Board's Correspondence 1879 (143).
13. Board's Correspondence 1880.

Documents Related to Family Domains of Maharaja Benares

1. Status of Maharaja Benares, 1901-1929.
2. File regarding Family Domains His Highness Maharaja Benares, Department XII, 1881.
3. Administration of Family Domains Maharaja Benares, Department II, 1881-1923.
4. Settlement of pargana Bhadohi in Family Domains of Maharaja Benares, Department I, 1881-1923.
5. Expenses consulted with Settlement Operation in Family Domains of Maharaja Benares, Department X, 1881-1823.
6. Draft Rules for Regulating Administration of Family Domains of Maharaja Benares, Department II, 1881-1823.
7. Draft Rules of Family Domains of Maharaja Benares, Department II, 1888.
8. Contingent Grant of Deputy Superintendent of Family Domains of Maharaja Benares, Department XII, 1887.
9. Maharaja Benares and Secretary of State for India, 1893-96, Department VI.
10. Exemptions under Arms Acts, 1896-1901, Department, XVIII.

Documents related to Benares State, 1911-1950

1. Instrument required for New Benares State, 1913-1917, Department XVI.
2. Permission to Maharaja Benares of his sardars to cut freely with armed retainers into British territory, 1910-1911.
3. Exemptions from Arms Act, 1913-17, Department, XVIII.
4. Transfer of Ramnagar, 1917-1919, Department, XVI.
5. Representation by His Highness Maharaja Benares on the Modification introduced by UP Act VI of 1915, 1917-19121, Department, XVI.

6. Decision His Highness regarding Personal or State Property, 1940-41, Department I, dominion/Indian Arms Licenses extended upto Benares State, 1948-49.
7. Hiss Highness Crest and Coat of Arms, 1945-1946, Department IV.
8. List of Act enforce in Benares State, 1917-1921, Department XV.
9. Gaddi shine of Maharaja Vibhuti Narain Singh Bahadur to Benares State Imloth in Ramnagar Fort April 5, 1939.
10. The Return of Insignia possessed by His Highness Maharaja Benares, 1938-39, Department IV.
11. Arrangement in connection with the Investiture Darbar of His Highness Vibhuti Narain Singh Bahadur at Fort Ramnagar in 11 July 1947.

Regional Archives, Allahabad

Benares Commissioners Office, Duncan Records

1. Volume 2, December 1776, Basta 1.
2. Volume 3, Basta 1, 1777-1780
3. Volume 4, Basta 1, 1782-1788
4. Volume 6, Basta 2, August 1785
5. Volume 9, Basta 2, January 1788
6. Volume 10, Basta 2, June 1788, Resident's Proceedings
7. Volume 12, Basta 2, 1788
8. Volume 85, Basta 40, October 1794, Resident's Correspondence and Proceedings
9. Volume 85A, Basta 40, November 1794, Resident's Correspondence and Proceedings
10. Volume 75, Basta 38, January 1794
11. Volume 84, Basta 40, September 1794
12. Volume 83, Basta 40, August 1794.
13. Volume 77, Basta 38, April 1794.
14. Volume 87, Basta 41, January 1795.
15. Volume 88, Basta 41, February 1794.
16. Volume 90, Basta 41, April 1794.

Letter issued by the Agent to Governor General, Benares

1. Basta 15, volume 69, 1828
2. Basta 16, volume 72, 1831

Family Domain of Maharaja Benares

1. Volume 190(ii), letters received, February 1832-October 1848
2. Volume 190(iii), letter received, October 1848-1863
3. Volume 190(iv), letter issued, November 1826-January 1832
4. Volume 190(v), letter issued, 8 October 1831-March 28, 1833
5. Volume 190(vi), letter issued, 1833-1835
6. Volume 190(viii), letter issued, 1839- 1842
7. Volume 190(ix), letter issued, 1842- 1850
8. Volume 190(x), letter issued, 1851- 1853
9. Volume 190(xi), letter issued, 1853- 1856
10. Volume 190(xii), letter issued, 1856- 1859

Uttar Pradesh State Archives, Lucknow

Documents Related to Family Domains of Maharaja Benares

1. Darbar List of Benares State, GAD, 1888-1942.
2. Proceedings of Government GAD, 1903, Index of Collection of Government Orders from 1879-1957.
3. Old Personal Records of His Highness The Maharaja of Banaras, GAD, 11950-51.
4. Extension of Act XIV of 1859 to the Family Domains Raja of Benares and other district, Board of Revenue, Part I, No. 19.
5. Erection of an Office at Benares for the Deputy Superintendent of Family Domains of Raja Benares, Board of Revenue, Part II, No. 19.
6. Office and Salary of Deputy Superintendent Family Domains of Maharaja Benares, Board of Revenue, Part II, No. 19.
7. History of Family Domains and Revision of Settlement of pargana Bhadohi, Board of Revenue, Part II, No. 19.
8. Position of Maharaja of Benares in Quarterly Civil List, 1899, Political Department.

9. Table of Salutes to Native Chiefs, 1846, Political Department.

Documents Related to Merger of Banaras State

1. File related to Merger of Benares State, GAD, 1946-51.
2. Integration of Benares State consequent on Merger, GAD, 1946-51.
3. Integration of Benares State in U.P. Proposal, GAD, 1946-51
4. Application of law to Merged States of Rampur, Tehri and Benares GAD, 1946-51.
5. State Forces of Merged Sates (Non ISF)- general questions regarding Absorption of Personal and Mustering out Concessions, GAD, 1936-58.
6. Disposals of Buildings etc. of Benares State Forces, GAD, 1936-58.
7. Old Personal Records of His Highness The Maharaja of Banaras, GAD, 1950-51.
8. Question of Compensation to the Employees of the Department of the Merged Banaras State, GAD, 1950-51.
9. Entertainment of Important Persons Visiting Banaras by His Highness The Maharaja of Banaras, GAD, 1950-51.
10. Increases of Pay and Allowances to the Gazetted and Non-Gazetted employees of the Former Banaras State after 1 August 1749.
11. General Orders regarding Absorption of Tehri Garhwal, Banaras and Rampur, GAD, 1950-54.
12. Medical Facilities to the Rulers of Merged and Integrated States, GAD, 1941-58
13. Privy Purses of Rulers of Merged States- Payments to be made by Union Government, GAD, 1941-58.
14. Immovable Property given to the Maharaja of Benares in Chakia Tehsil at the time of Merger of Banaras State, GAD, 1950-51.
15. Memorandum on the Personal Privileges of the Rulers of the Merged States, GAD, 1950-51.
16. Payments to His Highness the Maharaja of Banaras, GAD, 1950-51.

17. Compensatory Payment of Rs 1 lakh annually to Maharaja of Banaras, GAD (E), 1946-50.
18. Disposal of Customs Staff in Merged States, GAD (E), 1946-50.

Other Published Primary Sources

1. Hastings, Warren, *A Narrative of The Late Transactions At Benares*, London, 1782.
2. Aitchison, C.U., *A Collection of Treaties, Engagements and Sanads relating to India and Neighbouring Countries,* Vol. II, *Mittal Publications*, Delhi, 1983.
3. Calendar of Persian Correspondence, 9 Vols., Central Publication Branch, Government of India, 1925.
4. Fort William-India House Correspondence and other Contemporary Papers Relating Thereto, Public Series, 9 Vols., National Archives of India, Government of India, Delhi, 1981.
5. Firminger, W.K., *Affairs of the East India Company,* Being 5th report from the select Committee of House of Commons 28 July 1812, Vol. II, B.R. Publishing Corporation, 2001.
6. Gleig, G.R., *Memoirs of Life of Warren Hastings*, 3 Vols., London, 1841.
7. Grier, C., *Letters of Warren Hastings To His Wife*, London, MCMV.
8. Oldham, Wilton, *Historical and Statistical Memoirs of the Ghazipore District*, 2 Vols., Allahabad, 1870.
9. Forrest G.W., *Selections From Letters, Despatches and other State Papers preserved in the Foreign Department of Government of India*, 1772-1785, 3 Vols., Calcutta, 1890.
10. Forrest, G.W., *Selections from State Papers of the Governor Generals of India, Warren Hastings*, 2 vols, Oxford, 1910.
11. Dodwell, H.H., *Letters of Warren Hastings to Sir John Macpherson*, 1927.
12. Saletore, G.N., *Banaras Affairs*, 2 Vols., Central Record Office, Allahabad, 1959.
13. Shakespeare, *Selection from Duncan Records*, 2 Vols., 1873.
14. Khan, Seid Gholem Hussain, *The Seir Mutaqherin*, translated

by Mustapha, 4 Vols., Calcutta, 1902.

15. Hodges, William, Travels in India During the Years 1780-1783, London, 1793.

Some Important Articles

1. Cohn. B.S., *Political System in Eighteenth Century India: The Banaras Region*, Journal of the American Oriental Society, Vol. lxxxii, July-September, 1962.
2. Qunungo, K.R., *Some Sidelights on the History of Benares*, Proceedings of the Indian Historical Records Commission, Vol. XIV, 1937
3. Srivastava, A.L., *The Benares Conference*, Indian Historical Records Commission, 1944.
4. Irwine, William, *The Bangash Nawabs of Farukhabad*, A Chronicle (1713-1857), Journal of Asiatic Society of Bengal, Part II, Vol. xlviii, 1878.
5. Altekar, A.S., *History of Benares*, Journal of the Benares Hindu University, Vol. I, 1937.
6. Roberts, P. E., *Hastings and His Accusers*, Journal of Indian History, III, Madras.
7. S. Nurul Hasan, *Warren Hastings and Zamindari Rights*, Proceedings of Indian History Congress, Vol. 32, 1970.
8. S. Chandra, *The Role of the Banaras Bankers in the Economy of Eighteenth Century Upper India*, Proceedings of Indian History Congress, 1973.
9. Articles from Souvenir titled *Introducing Varanasi*, xxxi session of Indian History Congress and VI session of Indian Congress of American History, Bharat Kala Bhavan, BHU.

Gazetteers

1. Fisher and Hewett, *Statistical, Descriptive and Historical Account of North Western Provinces of India*, Vol. , XIV, Part I, Benares, North Western Provinces and Oudh Government Press, Allahabad, 1884.
2. Nevill, H.R., Benares: A Gazetteer, Vol. XXVI, 1909.
3. Imperial Gazetteer of India, Vol. VII, Published under authority of His Majesty's Secretary of State for India in Council, Oxford, 1908.

4. Uttar Pradesh District Gazetteers, Ballia, Government of Uttar Pradesh, 1988.
5. Uttar Pradesh District Gazetteers, Jaunpur, Government of Uttar Pradesh, 1986.
6. Uttar Pradesh District Gazetteers, Ghazipur, Government of Uttar Pradesh, 1982.
7. Uttar Pradesh District Gazetteers, Mirzapur, Government of Uttar Pradesh, 1988.
8. Uttar Pradesh State Gazetteers, Vol. I, Government of Uttar Pradesh, 2001.
9. Uttar Pradesh State Gazetteers, Vol. IV, Government of Uttar Pradesh, 1997.

Secondary Sources

1. Alam, Muzaffar, *The Crisis of Empire in Mughal North India* (Awadh and Punjab) 1707-1748, Oxford University Press, New Delhi, 1986.
2. Altekar, A.S., *History of Benares*, Cultural Publications, Benares, 1937.
3. Ali Subhan, *History of Benares*, Benares, 1852.
4. Babar, *Babarnama*, 2 vols, Translated by Beveridge, H., Low Price Publication, 1921.
5. Badaoni, Muntrkhab-ut-Tawarikh, 3 Vols, Translated by Wolseley Heig, Asiatic Society, Calcutta, 1925.
6. Barnett, B., Richard, *North India Between Empires- Awadh, The Mughals and the British (1720-1801)*, University of Calfornia Press, London.
7. Basu, Major B.D., *The Rise of the Christian Power in India*, 2 Vols., Calcutta, 1892.
8. Beal, S., *Buddhist Records of the Western World*, translated from Chinese of Hiuen Tsang A.D. 629, first published in 1884, Munshiram Manoharlal Publishers Pvt. Ltd, New Delhi, 1983.
9. Begam, Badshal, *Tarikh Badshah Begum*, Translated by Mohammad Taqi Ahmad, Indian Press, Allahabad, 1938.
10. Begum, Gulbadan, *Humayunama*, Translated by A.S., Beveridge, London, 1902.

11. Beveridge, H., *A Comprehensive History of India*, vol II, London.
12. Bolts, *William. Considerations on Indian Affairs (1772-1775)*, Vol. 3
13. Broome, *History of the Rise and Progress of Bengal Army*, London, 1850.
14. Cowell, E.B.(ed.), *The Jataka or the Stories of the Buddha's Former Births*, Vol. II, Low Price Publications, Delhi, 1997.
15. Davies, C.C., *Warren Hastings and Oudh*, London, 1939.
16. Davis, W.F., *Vizier Ali Khan or The Massacre at Benares*, London, 1844; reprint, Benares, 1881
17. Deane, A., *A Tour Through the Upper Provinces of Hindustan*, London, 1823.
18. Dodwell, H.H., *Cambridge History of India*, Vol. V, New Delhi, 1968.
19. Dodwell, H.H., *Dupleix and Clive: The Beginning of Empire*, Methuen and Co. Ltd, London.
20. Dutt, Romesh, *Economic History of India and Early British Rule*, London, 1908.
21. Elliot and Dowson, *The History of India as told by its own Historians*, Vol. II, first published in 1867, Low Price Publication, New Delhi, 2001.
22. Fazl Abul, *Aini-I-Akbari*, Translated by Blochman and Jarett, 3 Vols., Oriental Books Reprint Corporation, New Delhi.
23. Feiling, Keith, *Warren Hastings*, London, 1954.
24. Firminger, Walter Kelly, *The Fifth Report from the Select Committee of the House of Commons on the Affairs of the East India Company*, July 28, 1812, Calcutta, 1917.
25. Forrest G.W., *Selections From Letters, Despatches and other State Papers preserved in the Foreign Department of Government of India*, 1772-1785, 3 Vols., Calcutta, 1890.
26. Forrest, G.W., *Selections from State Papers of the Governor Generals of India, Warren Hastings*, 2 vols, Oxford, 1910.
27. Forrest, G.W., *Historical Documents of British India, Warren Hastings*, Vol. I, Delhi.
28. Forrest, G., *Life of Lord Clive*, London, Casell, 1918.
29. Forrest, G., *Selections from the State Papers of Governor General of India- Lord Cornwallis*, 2 Vols., Oxford, Blackwell, 1926.

30. Forrest, G.W., *India Under Hastings*, London, 1892.
31. Forrest G.W., *The Administration of Warren Hastings* (1772-1775), Calcutta, 1892.
32. Forrest, G.W., *Cities of India*, New Delhi, 1977.
33. Fuhrer, A., *The Monumental Antiquities and Inscriptions of North Western Province and Oudh*, Vol. II, Government Press, North Western Province and Oudh, Allahabad, 1891.
34. Gleig, Rev. G.R., Memoirs of the Life of the Right Hon'ble Warren Hastings, 3 Vols., London, 1841.
35. Grier, Sydney C., *The Letters of Hastings to His Wife*, Edinburgh, 1905.
36. Hand, J. Reginald, *Early English Administration of Bihar* (1781-1785), Bengal Secretariat Press, Calcutta, 1894.
37. Hastings, W., *Memoirs Relative to the State of India*, Oxford University Press, New Delhi, 1973.
38. Havell, E.B., *Benares: The Sacred City*, Thacker, London, 1905.
39. Herber, R., Bishop, *Narrative of a Journey Through the Upper Provinces of India*, Calcutta, 1828.
40. *History of the Province of Benares*, Carruther and Sons, Inverness, Medical Hall Press, 1882, Benares.
41. Husain Gulam, *Riyaz-us-Sultani*, Translated by Abdus Salam, Idarah-I-Adabiyat-I-Dilli, Delhi, 1975.
42. Ibnbatuta, *Travels in Asia and Africa* (1325-1354), Translated by H.A.R. Gibb, Oriental Books Reprint Corporation, New Delhi, 1929.
43. Irwine, Williams, *Later Mughals*, 2 vols, Oriental Books Reprint Cooperation, Reprint January 1971, New Delhi.
44. Irwin, H.C., *The Gardens of India or Chapters on Oudh History and Affairs*, Asian Educational Services, New Delhi, 2001.
45. Jayaswal, K.P., *History of India 150 A.D. to 350 A.D.*, first published in 1933, Low Price Publication, New Delhi, 1990.
46. Kane, P.V., *History of Dharmasastra*, Vol. IV, Bhandarkar Oriental Research Institute, Poona, 1953.
47. Khan, Seid Gholem Hussain, *Seir Mutaqherin*, translated by Mustapha, 4 Vols., Calcutta, 1902.
48. Lyall, Sir Alfred, *The Rise and Expansion of the British Dominion in India*, London, 1913.

49. Majumdar, R.C., *History and Culture of Indian People*, 10 vols, Bhartiya Vidya Bhavan Series, 1996.
50. Malik, Zahir-uddin, *The Reign of Mohammad Shah* (1719-1748), Asia Publishing House, Bombay, 1977.
51. Malleson, Col. G.B., *Life of Warren Hastings*, London, 1894.
52. Malleson, G.B., *The Decisive Battles of India*, 1746-1849, Jaipur, 1986.
53. Mcpherson, W.C., *Soldiering in India, 1764-1787 (Extracts from Journals and letters left by Lt. Col. Allah Mcpherson and Lt. Col. John Mcpherson of the East India Company's Service)*, London, 1828.
54. Mill, James, *History of British India,* volume 2, Associated Publishing House, New Delhi, 2nd reprint, 1978.
55. Mishra, Kamala Prasad, *Benares In Transition* (1738-1795), Munshiram Manoharlal Publishers Pvt. Ltd., New Delhi, 1975.
56. Mohammad Nooruddin Jahangir, *Tuzuk-I-Jahangiri*, 2 Vols., Translated by H., Beveridge, Low Price Publication, 1909-1914, New Delhi.
57. Moon, Pederal, *Warren Hastings and British India*, London, 1947.
58. Prinsep, H.T., *Views and Illustrations of Benares*, Calcutta, 1825.
59. Prinsep, W.T., *Indian Antiquities*, Calcutta, 1858.
60. Roberts, P.E., *The History of British India Under the Company and the Crown*, Oxford University Press, London, first ed. 1921, 1st Indian ed. 1976.)
61. Sachau, Edward, C., *Alberuni's India*, Vol. II, Atlantic Publishers, New Delhi, 1989.
62. *Sacred Books of East*, Motilal Banarasidas, Varanasi, first published in 1881 by Oxford University Press.
63. Sardesai, *New History of the Marathas*, 3 vols, Bombay Phoneix Publication, Bombay.
64. Sarkar, J.N., *Fall of Mughal Empire*, Vol. I, 2nd ed., M.C. Sarkar and Sons Ltd., Calcutta, 1949.
65. Sarkar, J.N., *Fall of Mughal Empire*, 3 Vol., Orient Longman, New Delhi.
66. Sarkar, J.N., *Massir-I-Alamgir* (1658-1707), Asiatic Society of Bengal, Calcutta, 1947.

67. Sarawani Abbas Khan, *Tarikh-I-Shershahi*, Translated by B.P. Awbashthy, K.P. Jaiswal Research Institute, Patna, 1974.
68. Sarawani Abbas Khan, *Tarikh-I-Shershahi*, Translated by S.M. Imam-al-din, 2 Vols., University of Dacca, Dacca, 1962
69. Sherring, M.A., *Benares: The Sacred City of Hindus in Ancient and Modern Times*, B.R. Publishing Corporate, New Delhi, 1975.
70. Shamas Siraj, Afif, *Tarikh-I-Firozshahi*, Translated by R.C. Jawahari, Sandeep Prakashan, 2001.
71. Sherring, M.A., *Benares and its Antiquities*, Benares, 1863.
72. Shakespere, H., *Selections From the Duncan Records*, Benares, 1873.
73. Smith, V.A., *The Oxford History of India*, Oxford, 1923.
74. Srivastava, A.L., *Akbar The Great, Political History* (1542-1605), Vol. I, Shiva Lal Agarwal and Co., Agra, 1972.
75. Srivastava, A.L., *The First Two Nawabs of Awadh*, Agra, 1954.
76. Srivastava, A.L., *Shuja-ud-daula*, 2 vols, Agra, 1961, Lahore 1945
77. Talib, Abu, *History of Asaf-ud-daulah*, Translated by W. Hoey, Pustak Kendra, Lucknow, 1971.
78. Thornton, Edward, *History of the British Empire in India*, Vol. III and VI, London, 1842.
79. Trotter, L.J., *Rulers of India: Warren Hastings*, New Delhi, 1961.
80. Watters, T., *On Yuan Chwang's Travels in India*, (A.D. 629-645), Vol. II, originally published in the *Journal of Royal Asiatic Society*, 1904-1905, Munshi Ram Manohar Lal Publishers Pvt. Ld., 1973.
81. Wheeler, J. Talboys, *Early Records of British India*, Calcutta, 1878.

Index